Hermeneutics

Northwestern University
STUDIES IN *Phenomenology &*
Existential Philosophy

Richard E. Palmer

Hermeneutics

Interpretation Theory in Schleiermacher, Dilthey, Heidegger, and Gadamer

NORTHWESTERN UNIVERSITY PRESS

1969   EVANSTON

To Hans-Georg Gadamer,
WITH RESPECT AND APPRECIATION

Contents

[ix]

x / CONTENTS

Preface

THIS BOOK could have been called *What Is Hermeneutics?* or *The Meaning of Hermeneutics*, for it is, among other things, a record of its author's own quest for an understanding of a term at once unfamiliar to most educated people and at the same time potentially significant to a number of disciplines concerned with interpretation, especially text interpretation.

This study arose out of a more specific project concerning the significance of Bultmannian theory of biblical interpretation for literary theory, during which the need for some fundamental clarification of the development, meaning, and scope of hermeneutics itself became evident. Such clarification, in fact, became a prerequisite for the original project. As I went about this preliminary work, the richly suggestive possibilities of general, nontheological hermeneutics (which actually is the basis for Bultmannian theory and that of the "new hermeneutic") led me to focus solely on the pretheological form of hermeneutics as it relates to theory of literary interpretation.

Because the primary sources in this relatively little-known field are largely in German, I have been obliged to give considerable exposition of them. And because the very definition of the term *hermeneutics* has become the subject of vehement controversy, it has been necessary to go into the definitional problem at some length before discussing the four major theorists. And finally, a detailed examination of the implications of hermeneutics for literary interpretation, which was the purpose for having undertaken the project in the first place, has been reserved for a second volume, although the first and last two chapters of the present work will give the interested reader a hint of what is to come.

Perhaps it is well to add a technical note explaining my choice of "hermeneutics" rather than "hermeneutic" to designate the field of hermeneutics. James M. Robinson in *The New Hermeneutic* has suggested that there is no philological justification for an *s* at the end of this word; neither "arithmetic" nor "rhetoric" requires an *s*, and both designate a general field. Furthermore, "hermeneutics" is feminine singular in other modern languages—German, *Hermeneutik;* French, *herméneutique*—and comes from the Latin *hermeneutica.* Robinson has suggested that the dropping of the *s* might also suggest the new turn in hermeneutical theory, which has come to be called the New Hermeneutic.

I do not question the philological cogency of the argument advanced by this leading American theologian, nor should my retention of the *s* on "hermeneutics" be taken as a rejection of the hermeneutical position represented by the New Hermeneutic. On the contrary, the contributions of Heidegger and Gadamer to hermeneutics are the foundation of the New Hermeneutic, and I propose to move away from a narrowly philological approach to hermenuetics and to suggest the fruitfulness of their more phenomenological view of the hermeneutical problem. I have decided, however, to leave "hermeneutics" in its state of philological sin on strictly practical grounds: the word is strange and unfamiliar enough without this added difficulty.

Also, there are some advantages in flexibility of usage to be had in retaining the *s*. One can, for instance, then refer to the field of hermeneutics generically, and to the specific theory by Bultmann as Bultmann's hermeneutic. There is in addition the factor that the adjective form may be "hermeneutic" or "hermeneutical"—as in hermeneutic theory or hermeneutic theology. Since "hermeneutic" tends to sound like an adjective unless accompanied by "the" or some other modifier, and since the *s* suggests "rules" and "theory," I have continued the standard usage.

I wish to thank the American Council of Learned Societies for a Post-Doctoral Study Fellowship which enabled me to spend the academic year 1964-65 at the Institut für Hermeneutik at the University of Zurich and at the University of Heidelberg. Special thanks are tendered to Professor Gerhard Ebeling, then director of the Institut, and his executive assistant, Friedrich Hertel, for enabling me to study and type there at all hours, not to mention their unfailing courtesies and helpfulness. At Heidelberg, Professor Gadamer kindly allowed me to attend his *Hegelkreis,* and to present a paper, "Die Tragweite von Gadamers *Wahrheit und Methode* für die Literaturauslegung"; the criticisms and personal reflections by Professor Gadamer on that occasion were most helpful. I would also like to thank him for introducing me to Heidegger, and to thank Professor Heidegger for his generally favorable reaction to the idea of using his theory of understanding as the basis for a phenomenological approach to literary interpretation.

Thanks are also due to the trustees of MacMurray College for a supplementary grant to the ACLS fellowship, which enabled me to take my family with me to Europe, and also for more recent aid in expenses of typing the final manuscript. The following colleagues were kind enough to read and criticize portions of the manuscript: Lewis S. Ford (Raymond College), Severyn Bruyn (Boston College), William E. Umbach and William W. Main (University of Redlands), John F. Smolko (Catholic University of America), Gordon E. Michalson (School of Theology, Claremont), Karl Wright, J. Weldon Smith, Gisela Hess, Philip Decker, and Ruth O. Rose (all of MacMurray College), and James M. Edie (Northwestern University). Special thanks are tendered to the following colleagues who at one stage or another read the entire manuscript: Calvin Schrag (Purdue University), Theodore Kisiel (Canisius College), Ruth Kovacs (MacMurray College), and most especially Roger Wells (emeritus from Bryn Mawr, now at MacMurray), whose editorial suggestions were greatly appreciated. The author wishes to thank Miss Victoria Hargrave and Mrs. Glenna Kerstein of the MacMurray Library for their unfailing helpfulness. For typing and suggestions, the author thanks the following students at MacMurray College: Jackie Menefee, Ann Baxter, Shamim Lalji, Sally Shaw, Peter Brown, and Ron Heiniger.

Finally, my wife and children have foregone without complaint many hours of my time, and my wife has proofread the entire manuscript. I appreciate also the careful reading of my manuscript by Edward Surovell for the Northwestern University Press.

R. E. P.

MacMurray College
January, 1968

List of Abbreviations

BOOKS

AAMG   Betti, *Allgemeine Auslegungslehre als Methodik der Geisteswissenschaften*

D   Bollnow, *Dilthey: Eine Einführung in seine Philosophie*

DI   Ricoeur, *De l'interprétation*

DT   Heidegger, *Discourse on Thinking*

EB   Heidegger, *Existence and Being*

EHD   Heidegger, *Erläuterungen zu Hölderlins Dichtung*

F H   Fuchs, *Hermeneutik*

G   Heidegger, *Gelassenheit*

G&V   Bultmann, *Glauben und Verstehen*

GGHK   Ast, *Grundlinien der Grammatik, Hermeneutik und Kritik*

GS   Dilthey, *Gesammelte Schriften*

H   Schleiermacher, *Hermeneutik*, ed. Heinz Kimmerle

H&K   Schleiermacher, *Hermeneutik und Kritik*, ed. Friedrich Lücke

HAMG   Betti, *Die Hermeneutik als allgemeine Methodik der Geisteswissenschaften*

HE   Bultmann, *History and Eschatology*

HH   *History and Hermeneutic*, ed. Robert W. Funk and Gerhard Ebeling

Ho   Heidegger, *Holzwege*

HPT   Fuchs, *Zum hermeneutischen Problem in der Theologie*

IINT   Ernesti, *Institutio Interpretis Novi Testamenti*

IM   Heidegger, *An Introduction to Metaphysics*
KPM   Heidegger, *Kant und das Problem der Metaphysik*
L   Bollnow, *Die Lebensphilosophie*
NH   *The New Hermeneutic*, ed. James M. Robinson
            and John B. Cobb, Jr.
PhWD   Hodges, *The Philosophy of Wilhelm Dilthey*
PL-BH   Heidegger, *Platons Lehre von der Wahrheit: Mit
            einem Brief über den "Humanismus"*
SZ   Heidegger, *Sein und Zeit*
TGI   Betti, *Teoria generale della interpretazione*
TPhT   Richardson, *Heidegger: Through Phenomenology
            to Thought*
UK   Heidegger, *Der Ursprung des Kunstwerkes*,
            ed. H.-G. Gadamer
US   Heidegger, *Unterwegs zur Sprache*
V   Wach, *Das Verstehen*
VA   Heidegger, *Vorträge und Aufsätze*
VEA   Wolf, *Vorlesung über die Enzyklopädie der
            Altertumswissenschaft*
VII   Hirsch, *Validity in Interpretation*
WF   Ebeling, *Word and Faith*
WM   Gadamer, *Wahrheit und Methode*, 1st ed. unless
            otherwise indicated

PERIODICALS, DICTIONARIES, AND ENCYCLOPEDIAS

ERE   *Encyclopedia of Religion and Ethics*
GEL   *Greek-English Lexikon*, ed. Liddell and Scott
ISN   *Illinois Speech News*
JAAR   *Journal of the American Academy of Religion*
M&W   *Man and World*
MLR   *Modern Language Review*
OED   *Oxford English Dictionary*
OL   *Orbis Litterarum*
PhR   *Philosophische Rundschau*
RGG   *Die Religion in Geschichte und Gegenwart*, 3d ed.
RM   *Review of Metaphysics*
RPTK   *Realenzyklopädie für protestantische Theologie
            und Kirche*, 3d ed.
TDNT   *Theological Dictionary of the New Testament*,
            ed. G. Kittel
YFS   *Yale French Studies*
ZThK   *Zeitschrift für Theologie und Kirche*

PART I

On the Definition, Scope,
And Significance of Hermeneutics

1 / Introduction

HERMENEUTICS is a word heard increasingly in theological, philosophical, and even literary circles. The New Hermeneutic has emerged as a dominant movement in European Protestant theology, asserting that hermeneutics is the "focal point" of today's theological issues.[1] Three international "Consultations on Hermeneutics" have been held at Drew University,[2] and several recent books in English are available on hermeneutics in the theological context.[3] Martin Heidegger, in a recently published group of essays, discusses the persistently hermeneutical character of his own thinking, both early and late.[4] Philosophy itself, Heidegger asserts, is (or should be) "hermeneutical." And in 1967 the splendid isolation of American literary criticism from hermeneutics was shattered by E. D. Hirsch's book *Validity in Interpretation*. A full-dress essay in hermeneutics, Hirsch's treatise offers

1. See the statement by Gerhard Ebeling that hermeneutics is the *Brennpunkt* (focal point) of the theological problems of today. "The Significance of the Critical-Historical Method for Church and Theology in Protestantism," *WF* 27; this article was originally published as a programmatic essay in *ZThK*, XLVII (1950), 1–46.

2. In 1962, 1964, and 1966. Papers from the 1962 Consultation were published in *NH*, and from the 1966 meetings as *Interpretation: The Poetry of Meaning*, ed. Stanley R. Hopper and David L. Miller. Closely associated with the Consultations is *The Later Heidegger and Theology*, ed. James M. Robinson and John B. Cobb, Jr.

3. In addition to *NH*, and more recently Robert W. Funk, *Language, Hermeneutic, and Word of God*, see the Journal of Theology and the Church series of books edited by Robert W. Funk and Gerhard Ebeling, especially *The Bultmann School of Biblical Interpretation: New Directions?* and *History and Hermeneutic*.

4. "Aus einem Gespräch von der Sprache," *US*, esp. 95–99, 120–32, 136, 150–55.

[3]

major challenges to widely held ideas in prevailing criticism. According to Hirsch, hermeneutics can and should serve as a foundational and preliminary discipline for all literary interpretation.

With these contemporary claims for the central importance of hermeneutics in three humanistic disciplines—theology, philosophy, and literary interpretation—it is becoming ever more clear that this field will figure importantly on the frontiers of American thinking in the next few years. But the term is not a household word in either philosophy or literary criticism; and even in theology its usage often appears in a restricted sense that contrasts with the broad usage in the contemporary theological "new hermeneutic." Hence the question is often asked: What is hermeneutics? *Webster's Third New International Dictionary* says: "the study of the methodological principles of interpretation and explanation; *specif*: the study of the general principles of biblical interpretation." Such a definition may satisfy those who merely wish a working understanding of the word itself; those who hope to gain an idea of the field of hermeneutics will demand much more. Unfortunately, there is as yet in English no full-length expository treatment of hermeneutics as a general discipline, although there are some very good introductions to "hermeneutic" (without the *s*) in the context of theology. But even these sources do not claim to furnish an adequate foundation for comprehending the nature and significance of hermeneutics as a general, nontheological discipline.

There is a pressing need, therefore, for an introductory treatment of hermeneutics in a nontheological context which will be directed at clarifying the meaning and scope of the term. The present study attempts to meet this need. It will give the reader some idea of the fluidity of hermeneutics and the complex problems involved in defining it, and it will discuss the basic issues which have concerned four of the most important thinkers on the subject. It will also furnish the basic bibliographical references for further exploration.

For its author, however, this book stands in the context of another project—that of moving toward a more adequate approach to literary interpretation. In German hermeneutical theory can be found the philosophical foundations for a radically more comprehensive understanding of the problems in literary interpretation. Thus, the aim of exploring hermeneutics has in this book been conformed to another purpose: to delineate the matrix of considerations within which American literary theorists can meaningfully reopen the question of interpretation on a philosophical level prior to all considerations of application in techniques of literary analysis. Put programmatically, this book's purpose is to call upon American literary interpretation to reexplore in a phenomenological context the question: What is interpretation? This study ultimately suggests a specific orientation to the question—the phenomenological approach. It sees in phenomenological hermeneutics, as over against other forms, the most adequate context for exploring the question.

In light of the programmatic purpose of this study in relation to literary interpretation, the following two sections present some preliminary remarks on the condition of American literary criticism and the need in American literary thinking for a philosophical reappraisal.

Some Consequences of Common-sense Objectivity in American Literary Criticism

Literary interpretation in England and America operates, philosophically speaking, largely in the framework of realism.[5] It tends to presuppose, for instance, that the literary work is simply "out there" in the world, essentially independent of its perceivers. One's perception of the work is considered to be separate from the work itself, and the task of literary interpretation is to speak about the "work itself." The author's intentions, too, are held rigidly separate from the work; the work is a "being" in itself, a being with its own powers and dynamics. A typical modern interpreter generally defends the "autonomy of being" of the literary work, and sees his task as that of penetrating this being through textual analysis. The preliminary separation of subject and object, so axiomatic in realism, becomes the philosophical foundation and framework for literary interpretation.

The tremendous fruitfulness of such a framework shows itself in the highly developed art of recent textual analysis. In its technical power and subtlety, this art cannot be compared

5. See Neal Oxenhandler, "Ontological Criticism in America and France," *MLR*, LV (1960), 17-18.

to anything in the history of Western literary interpretation. Yet the time has come to question the foundation of presuppositions upon which it rests. This is best done not from within the realistic perspective itself but by going outside it and holding it up for inspection. One movement in European thinking which has submitted a radical critique of realistic conceptions of perceiving and interpretation is phenomenology. By furnishing the key to a reevaluation of the presuppositions upon which English and American literary interpretation is based, phenomenology could provide the impetus for the next decisive advance in American theory and practice of interpretation.

A study of phenomenology makes especially apparent the essential kinship between realism and the "scientific" perspective, and the extent to which literary interpretation has fallen into the scientist's ways of thinking: his down-to-business objectivity, his static conceptualizing, his lack of an historical sense, his love of analysis. For, with all its humanistic pretensions and flamboyant defenses of poetry in an "age of technology," modern literary criticism has itself become increasingly technological. More and more, it has imitated the approach of the scientist. The text of a literary work (despite its autonomous "being") tends to be regarded as an object—an "aesthetic object." The text is analyzed in strict separation from any perceiving subject, and "analysis" is thought of as virtually synonymous with "interpretation."

Even the recent rapprochement with social criticism in some sort of enlightened formalism only broadens the definition of the object to include its social context in the analysis.[6] Literary interpretation, by and large, is still generally seen as an exercise in the conceptual "dissection" (a biological image!) of the literary object (or "being"). Of course, since this being or object is an "aesthetic" object, dissecting it is somehow thought to be vastly more "humanizing" than dissecting a frog in a laboratory; yet the image of a scientist taking an object apart to see how it is made has become the prevailing model of the art of interpretation. Students in literature classes are sometimes even told that their personal experience of a work is some kind of fallacy irrelevant to the analysis of the work.[7] And professors, gathered in huge conventions, ritually

6. See the valuable final chapter, "Criticism as a Social Act," in Walter Sutton, *Modern American Criticism*, pp. 268-90.

7. I am thinking of the well-known "affective fallacy" as presented, for example, in William K. Wimsatt, Jr., *The Verbal Icon*.

bewail the fact that their students find literature "irrelevant"; but their technological conception of interpretation, with its undergirding metaphysics of realism, actually promotes the very irrelevance they ineffectually lament.

"Science manipulates things and gives up living in them," the late French phenomenologist Maurice Merleau-Ponty tells us.[8] This, in one sentence, is what has happened to American literary interpretation. We have forgotten that the literary work is not a manipulatable object completely at our disposal; it is a human voice out of the past, a voice which must somehow be brought to life. Dialogue, not dissection, opens up the world of a literary work. Disinterested objectivity is not appropriate to the understanding of a literary work. The modern critic, of course, pleads for passion—even surrender to the "autonomous being" of the work—yet all the while he is treating the work as an object of analysis. Literary works are best regarded, however, not primarily as objects of analysis but as humanly created texts which speak. One must risk his personal "world" if he is to enter the life-world of a great lyric poem, novel, or drama. What is needed for this is not some scientific method in disguise, or an "anatomy of criticism" with the most brilliant and subtle typologies and classifications,[9] but a humanistic understanding of what interpretation of a work involves.

LITERARY INTERPRETATION, HERMENEUTICS, AND THE INTERPRETATION OF WORKS

THE TASK OF INTERPRETATION and the meaning of understanding are different—more elusive, more historical— in relation to a work than in relation to an "object." A "work" is always stamped with the human touch; the word itself suggests this, for a work is always a work of man (or of God). An "object," on the other hand, can be a work or it can be a natural object. To use the word "object" in reference to a work blurs an important distinction, for one needs to see the work not as object but *as* work. Literary criticism needs to seek a "method" or "theory" specifically appropriate to deciphering the human imprint on a work, its "meaning." This "deciphering" process, this "understanding" the meaning of a work, is the focus of

8. "Eye and Mind," trans. Carleton Dallery, in Merleau-Ponty, *The Primacy of Perception and Other Essays*, ed. James M. Edie, p. 159.
9. Preeminently, Northrop Frye's *Anatomy of Criticism*.

hermeneutics. Hermeneutics is the study of understanding, especially the task of understanding texts. Natural science has methods of understanding natural objects; "works" require a hermeneutic, a "science" of understanding appropriate to works as works. Certainly the methods of "scientific analysis" can and should be applied to works, but in doing so the works are treated as silent, natural objects. Insofar as they are objects, they are amenable to scientific methods of interpretation; as works, they call for more subtle and comprehensive modes of understanding. The field of hermeneutics grew up as an effort to describe these latter, more specifically "historical" and "humanistic" modes of understanding.

As will be seen in succeeding chapters, hermeneutics achieves its most authentic dimensions when it moves away from being a conglomeration of devices and techniques for text explication and attempts to see the hermeneutical problem within the horizon of a general account of interpretation itself. Thus it involves two different and interacting focuses of attention: (1) the event of understanding a text, and (2) the more encompassing question of what understanding and interpretation, as such, are.

One of the essential elements for an adequate hermeneutical theory, and by extension an adequate theory of literary interpretation, is a sufficiently broad conception of interpretation itself.[10] Consider for a moment the ubiquity of interpretation, and the generality of the usage of the word: The scientist calls his analysis of data "interpretation"; the literary critic calls his examination of a work "interpretation." The translator of a language is called an "interpreter"; a news commentator "interprets" the news. You interpret—or misinterpret—the remark of a friend, a letter from home, or a sign on the street. In fact, from the time you wake in the morning until you sink into sleep, you are "interpreting." On waking you glance at the bedside clock and interpret its meaning: you recall what day it is, and in grasping the meaning of the day you are already primordially recalling to yourself the way you are placed in the world and your plans for the future; you rise and must interpret the words and gestures of those you meet on the daily round. Interpretation is, then, perhaps the most basic act of

10. See my article, "Toward a Broader Concept of Interpretation," *ISN* (November 1967), 3–14, and my review of *VII*, in *JAAR*, XXXVI (September 1968), 243–46.

human thinking; indeed, existing itself may be said to be a constant process of interpretation.

Interpretation is more encompassing than the linguistic world in which man lives, for even animals exist by interpreting. They sense the way they are placed in the world. A piece of food sitting before a chimpanzee, a dog, or a cat will be interpreted by the animal in terms of his own needs and experience. Birds know the signs that tell them to fly south.

Of course constant interpretation on many nonlinguistic levels is woven into the fabric of all human living together. Human existence is conceivable without language, observes Joachim Wach, but not without mutual comprehension of one man by another—i.e., not without interpretation.[11] Yet human existence as we know it does in fact always involve language, and thus any theory of human interpreting must deal with the phenomenon of language. And of all the variegated symbolic media of expression used by man, none exceeds language in communicative flexibility and power, or in general importance.[12] Language shapes man's seeing and his thought—both his conception of himself and his world (the two are not so separate as they may seem). His very vision of reality is shaped by language.[13] Far more than man realizes, he channels through language the various facets of his living—his worshiping, loving, social behavior, abstract thought; even the shape of his feelings is conformed to language. If the matter is considered deeply, it becomes apparent that language is the "medium" in which we live, and move, and have our being.[14]

Interpretation, then, is a complex and pervasive phenomenon. Yet how complexly, how deeply, does the literary critic conceive it in his understanding? We need to ask whether critics do not tend to equate analysis with interpretation. We need to ask whether the realistic metaphysics and assumptions underlying modern criticism in most of its forms do not present an oversimplified and even distorted view of interpretation. A work of literature is not an object we understand by conceptualizing or analyzing it; it is a voice we must hear, and through "hearing" (rather than seeing) understand. As the

11. VI, 1.
12. See Ernst Cassirer, *Philosophy of Symbolic Forms*, and the chapter on language in his book *An Essay on Man*.
13. See Benjamin Whorf, *Language, Thought, and Reality*.
14. See the chapters on Heidegger and Gadamer, below.

coming chapters will suggest, understanding is both an epistemological and an ontological phenomenon. Understanding of literature must be rooted in the more primal and encompassing modes of understanding that have to do with our very being-in-the-world. Understanding a literary work, therefore, is not a scientific kind of knowing which flees away from existence into a world of concepts; it is an historical encounter which calls forth personal experience of being here in the world.

Hermeneutics is the study of this latter kind of understanding. It tries to hold together two areas of understanding theory: the question of what is involved in the event of understanding a text, and the question of what understanding itself is, in its most foundational and "existential" sense. As a German current of thought, hermeneutics came to be profoundly influenced by German phenomenology and existential philosophy. And of course its significance for American literary interpretation is enhanced by the application of such thinking to the issues of text interpretation.

The constant effort to deal with the phenomenon of understanding as it goes beyond mere textual interpretation gives to hermeneutics a potentially broad significance for all those disciplines customarily called the humanities. Hermeneutics, when defined as the study of the understanding of the works of man, transcends linguistic forms of interpretation. Its principles apply not only to works in written form but to any work of art. Since this is so, hermeneutics is fundamental to all the humanities—all those disciplines occupied with the interpretation of the *works* of man. It is more than merely interdisciplinary, for its principles comprise a theoretical foundation for the humanities;[15] its principles should be a required fundamental study for all the humanistic disciplines.

The contrast made above between scientific and what we may call historical, or hermeneutical, understanding brings to greater clarity the distinctive character of the interpretive task in the humanities. And by contrast, it also clarifies the character of interpretation in the sciences. Through a study of hermeneutical theory, the humanities can achieve a fuller measure of self-knowledge and a better understanding of the character of their task.

The present study attempts, however, to lay the philosophical foundation for exploring the significance of hermeneutics

15. See *HAMG* and *AAMG*.

for literary interpretation. This foundation must be an adequate understanding of hermeneutics itself. In quest of that understanding, this book begins with the Greek roots of the modern word "hermeneutics," then traces the development of certain conceptions of hermeneutical theory (insofar as it has called itself hermeneutics) in modern times, and finally explores in some detail the issues that have concerned four principal thinkers on the subject. The quest is by no means exhaustive, but preliminary; it does not enter into the use of hermeneutics in contemporary theology,[16] nor does it attempt to discuss developments now taking place in France.[17] The closing chapters do give some indications of the significance of phenomenological hermeneutics for literary interpretation, but the present study is intended principally as a philosophical introduction to hermeneutics which can at the same time serve as the foundation for a second volume discussing hermeneutics in relation to literary theory.

16. Note 3 above lists references in this area.
17. With the minor exception of the discussion in Chap. 5 of Ricoeur's *DI;* see also his "Existence et herméneutique," *Dialogue,* IV (1965-66), 1-25, and his "La Structure, le mot, l'événement," *M&W,* I (1968), 10-30.

2 / *Hermēneuein* and *Hermēneia:* The Modern Significance of Their Ancient Usage

THE ROOTS FOR THE WORD HERMENEUTICS lie in the Greek verb *hermēneuein,* generally translated "to interpret," and the noun *hermēneia,* "interpretation." An exploration of the origin of these two words and of the three basic directions of meaning they carried in ancient usage sheds surprising light on the nature of interpretation in theology and literature, and will serve in the present context as a valuable prelude to understanding modern hermeneutics.

Hermēneuein and *hermēneia* in their various forms occur in a considerable number of the texts which have survived from ancient times. Aristotle found the subject worthy of a major treatise in the *Organon,* the famous *Peri hermēneias,* "On Interpretation." [1] The word occurs in the noun form in *Oedipus at Colonus,* and several times in Plato. Indeed, various forms are found in most of the more familiar ancient writers, such as Xenophon, Plutarch, Euripides, Epicurus, Lucretius, and Longinus. [2] A study could be fruitfully devoted to the context of every occurrence to determine the nuances of meaning in each case; the present chapter, however, will simply note the association of the words with the god Hermes, point out three basic directions of their meaning, and suggest something of their modern significance, especially for literary and biblical interpretation.

1. Aristotle, *The Basic Works,* pp. 40–61. Of interest is a recent translation of the treatise: Aristotle, *On Interpretation,* with commentary by St. Thomas Aquinas and Cajetan, trans. with an introduction by Jean T. Oesterle.

2. *Hermēneia* and *hermēneuein, GEL.* See also Johannes Behm, *Ermēneuo, ermēneia,* in *TDNT* II, 661–66.

THE ORIGINS AND THREE DIRECTIONS OF THE
MEANING OF *Hermēneuein-Hermēneia*

THE GREEK WORD *hermeios* referred to the priest at the Delphic oracle. This word and the more common verb *hermēneuein* and noun *hermēneia* point back to the wing-footed messenger-god Hermes, from whose name the words are apparently derived (or vice versa?). Significantly, Hermes is associated with the function of transmuting what is beyond human understanding into a form that human intelligence can grasp. The various forms of the word suggest the process of bringing a thing or situation from unintelligibility to understanding. The Greeks credited Hermes with the discovery of language and writing—the tools which human understanding employs to grasp meaning and to convey it to others.

Martin Heidegger, who sees philosophy itself as "interpretation," explicitly connects philosophy-as-hermeneutics with Hermes. Hermes "brings the message of destiny; *hermēneuein* is that laying-open of something which brings a message, insofar as what is being exposed can become message. Such 'laying-open' becomes a 'laying-out' explaining of that which was already said through the poets, who themselves according to Socrates in Plato's dialogue the *Ion* (534e) are 'messengers [*Botschafter*] of the gods,' *hermēnēs eisin tōn theōn*."[3] Thus, traced back to their earliest known root words in Greek, the origins of the modern words "hermeneutics" and "hermeneutical" suggest the process of "bringing to understanding," especially as this process involves language, since language is the medium par excellence in the process.

This mediating and message-bringing process of "coming to understand" associated with Hermes is implicit in all of the three basic directions of meaning of *hermēneuein* and *hermēneia* in ancient usage. These three directions, using the verb form (*hermēneuein*) for purposes of example, are (1) *to express* aloud in words, that is, "to say"; (2) *to explain,* as in explaining a situation; and (3) *to translate,* as in the translation of a foreign tongue.[4] All three meanings may be expressed by the English verb "to interpret," yet each constitutes an

3. *US* 121-22.
4. Regarding these three directions of meaning, see the valuable article by Gerhard Ebeling, "Hermeneutik," *RGG* III, 242.

independent and significant meaning of interpretation. Interpretation, then, can refer to three rather different matters: an oral recitation, a reasonable explanation, and a translation from another language—both in Greek and in English usage. Yet one may note that the foundational "Hermes process" is at work: in all three cases, something foreign, strange, separated in time, space, or experience is made familiar, present, comprehensible; something requiring representation, explanation, or translation is somehow "brought to understanding"—is "interpreted."

Literary interpretation, it may be noted at the outset, involves two of these processes and often a third. Literature makes a representation of something which must "come to be understood." The text may be separated in its subject from us by time, space, language, and other barriers to understanding. This applies also to the understanding of a scriptural text. The task of interpretation must be to make something that is unfamiliar, distant, and obscure in meaning into something real. near, and intelligible. The various aspects of this interpretation process are vital and integral to literature and theology. Let us examine each of them as to its significance for literary and theological interpretation. (It is of interest to note how ignorant most literary critics are of the approaches to the task of interpretation which can be found in contemporary Christian theology.)

Hermēneuein as "to Say"

THE FIRST BASIC DIRECTION of the meaning of *hermēneuein* is "to express," "to assert," or "to say." This is related to the "announcing" function of Hermes.

Of theological significance is a disputed etymology which notes that the form of the initial *hermē* is close to the Latin *sermo,* "to say," and to the Latin *verbum,* "word." [5] This suggests that the minister, in bringing the Word, is "announcing" and "asserting" something; his function is not merely to explain but to proclaim. The minister, like Hermes, and like the priest at Delphi, brings fateful tidings from the divine. In his "say-

5. *Ibid.* James M. Robinson notes, *NH* 2-3, that *hermēneia* was also used in ancient times to designate a work on logical formulation or artistic elocution, what today is called "oral interpretation."

ing" or proclamation, he is, like Hermes, a "go-between" from God to man. Even simply saying, asserting, or proclaiming is an important act of "interpretation."

Within this same first direction of meaning is a slightly different shade suggested by the phrase "to express," which still carries the meaning of "saying" but is a saying which is itself an interpretation. For this reason, one is directed to the way a thing is expressed—the "style" of a performance. We use this nuance of the word "interpretation" when we refer to an artist's interpretation of a song or a conductor's interpretation of a symphony. In this sense interpretation is a form of saying. Likewise, oral saying or singing is an interpretation. In Greek times, *hermēneia* could refer to an oral recitation, of Homer, for instance. In the *Ion* of Plato, the young interpreter recites Homer and through his intonations "interprets" him, expressing and even subtly explaining him, conveying more than he realizes or understands. He thus becomes, like Hermes, a vehicle for Homer's message.

Of course, Homer himself was a go-between from the gods to man, an "interpreter" who, in Milton's words, "justified the ways of God to man." So Homer was an interpreter in a more primary sense, in that before him the words were not yet said. (Obviously, the legends existed before; hence, one could say he only "interpreted" and enunciated the legends.) Homer himself was said to be inspired by the gods; in his "saying," he was their interpreter.

Saying and oral recitation as "interpretation" remind literary people of a level too many of them tend to discount or even to forget. Yet literature derives much of its dynamism from the power of the spoken word. From time immemorial the great works in language have been meant to be spoken aloud and heard. The powers of spoken language should remind us of an important phenomenon: the weaknesses of written language. Written language lacks the primordial "expressiveness" of the spoken word. Admittedly, the writing down of language fixes and preserves it, gives it durability, and is the foundation of history (and literature), but at the same time it weakens it. Plato emphasizes the weakness and helplessness of written language in his *Seventh Letter* and also in the *Phaedrus*. All written language calls for retransformation into its spoken form; it calls for its lost power. Writing language down is an "alienation of language" from its living power—a *Selbstentfremdung der Sprache*,[6] a self-estrangement from speaking. (The German word for language, *Sprache*, is itself suggestive of the primordial form of language as that which is spoken.)

Oral words seem to have an almost magical power, but in becoming visual images they lose much of this power. Literature uses words so as to maximize their effectiveness, yet much of their power is drained out when hearing becomes the visual process of reading. Naturally we cannot today go back to oral transmission of literature (and there are advantages to written transmission), but we should not forget that language in its original form is heard rather than seen, and that there are good reasons why oral language is "understood" more easily than written language.

Consider the act of reading aloud. Oral interpretation is not a passive response to the signs on the paper like a phonograph playing a record; it is a creative matter, a performance, like that of a pianist interpreting a piece of music. Any pianist can tell you that a musical score itself is a mere shell; the "meaning" of the phrases must be grasped to interpret the music. It is the same with reading written language. An oral interpreter has the mere husk of the original—"outlines" of the sounds without indications of pitch, emphasis, and attitude, and yet he must "reproduce" them in living sound. Again, the reproducer must grasp the meaning of the words in order to express even one sentence. How does this mysterious grasping of meaning take place? The process is a puzzling paradox: in order to read, it is necessary to understand in advance what will be said, and yet this understanding must come from the reading. What begins to emerge here is the complex dialectical process involved in all understanding as it grasps the meaning of a sentence, and somehow in a reverse direction supplies the attitude and emphasis which alone can make the written word meaningful. Oral interpretation thus has two sides: it is necessary to understand something in order to express it, yet understanding itself comes from an interpretive reading—expression.

What does the fact of spoken language as itself an interpretive phenomenon mean to those engaged professionally in "literary interpretation," particularly to teachers of literature? Basically it suggests the need to reexamine the role of

6. See *WM* 370–71.

oral interpretation in all teaching of literature. Is not the reading of literature (by the student) a "performance" analogous to interpreting music? How much literature, we need to ask, was written primarily to be read silently? Novels are, clearly, and some recent poems do rely occasionally on visual effects; yet even here do we not often (and rightly) imagine the sound as we read?

For instance, in reading a novel of Dostoevsky, is not the dialogue heard with the "inner ear"? Is not meaning, therefore, inseparable from the aural intonations which are supplied in conformity with the "circle of contextual meaning" that has been built up in the process of reading the work? (This is actually, as we shall see, the "hermeneutical circle.") Here is that reverse direction in the dialectic again: the reader supplies the "expression" in accordance with his "understanding" of the text. Clearly, the task of oral interpretation is not a purely technical one of expressing a fully transcribed meaning; it is philosophical and analytical, and can never be divorced from the problem of understanding itself. More specifically, the "understanding problem," especially the understanding of language, is one that is intrinsic to all "literary interpretation." It is this problem that is the subject of hermeneutics.

Let this be stated as a principle: Every silent reading of a literary text is a disguised form of oral interpretation. And the principles of understanding at work in good oral interpretation also apply to literary interpretation as a whole. A literary criticism which aspires to be an "enabling act" is in part an effort to make up for the weakness and helplessness of the written word; it tries to put back in the work the dimensions of speech. Consider the question: Would not a literary critic give a different interpretive performance in confronting an oral recitation of a sonnet than in confronting it in writing? Were it oral, would he not in actuality be offering a competing interpretation, actually a comparison with his own imagined performance? Were it written, would he not be searching for other written words (and therefore likewise emasculated, retaining their basic conceptual, visual, nonaural content) to replace what was lost with the sound of the words? Would he not be supplying, in a sense, what a good oral interpretation supplies in the medium of pure sound?

Especially in the New Criticism, it is customary to imagine the text speaking by itself without the help of biographical,

historical, or psychological background data. The text itself
has its own "being" in the words themselves, in their arrangement, in their intentions, and in the intentions of the work
as a being of a special kind. If so, does not the critic, who ideally
does not master but surrenders to the being of the work (and
this is as it should be), help to restore the loss implicit in written words? When the critic brings outside conceptual elements
(his tools) into consideration (whether they be formal or material), is he not building a context of meaning (a "hermeneutical circle") out of which a more adequate oral performance
will proceed, even if in the guise of a more deeply interpretive
silent reading? This is still fulfilling the intention of the New
Critic to preserve the integrity of being of the work itself from
the "heresy of paraphrase," for he is working to enable the text
itself to speak. In light of this, the New Critic would undoubtedly
agree that a truly "enabling" criticism is one that is aimed at a
more adequate oral reading of the text itself, so that the text
can again exist as a meaningful oral happening in time, a being
whose true nature and integrity can shine forth.

Literary criticism is helped by oral interpretation to recall
to itself its own inner intention when it takes (in a more conscious way) the definition of the "being" of a work not as a
static, conceptual thing, not an atemporal "essence" that has
become a thing as word-expressed concept, but rather as a being
that realizes its power of being as oral happening in time. The
word must cease being word (i.e., visual and conceptual) and
become "event"; the being of a literary work is a "word event"
that happens as oral performance.[7] *An adequate literary
criticism moves toward the oral interpretation of the work
on which it is focused.* There is nothing in the "autonomy of
being" of the literary work that contradicts this principle; on
the contrary, autonomy of being harmonizes with it.[8]

The power of the oral word is also significant in that text-
centered religion, Christianity. Both St. Paul and Luther are
famous for saying that salvation comes through the ears. The
Pauline Letters were composed to be read aloud, not silently.
We need to remind ourselves that rapid, silent reading is a

7. I have intentionally used the familiar vocabulary of "speech-event"
theology here; see WF 295n, 313, 318-19, and *passim*.

8. Certain modern theories of oral interpretation move in the direction of
centering on a word event; see Don Geiger, *The Sound, Sense, and Performance of Literature.*

modern phenomenon brought on by printing. Our speed-oriented age has even made a virtue of "speed reading"; we take pains to stamp out the semivocalization of words in the child learning to read, yet this was quite normal in earlier ages. St. Augustine states that this was the manner in which he read. Christian theology must remember that a "theology of the Word" is not a theology of the written Word but of the spoken Word, the Word that confronts one in the "language event" of spoken words. The Scriptures (especially in Bultmannian theology) are *kerygma,* a message to be proclaimed. Certainly the task of theology is to explain the Word in the language and context of each age, but it also must express and proclaim the Word in the vocabulary of the age. The effort at wide dissemination of the printed Bible will be self-defeating if the Bible is seen primarily as a contract, as a legal document, or as a conceptual explanation of the world. The Bible's language operates in a totally different medium from a direction manual for building something or an information sheet. "Information" is a significant word; it points to a use of language different from that found in the Bible. It appeals to the rational faculty and not to the whole personality; we do not have to call upon our personal experience or risk ourselves in order to understand information—and information does not suffer much from silent reading. But the Bible is not information; it is a message, a "proclamation," and is meant to be read aloud, and meant to be heard. It is not a set of scientific principles; it is a reality of a different order from that of scientific truth. It is a reality which is to be understood as an historical story, a happening to be heard. A principle is scientific; a happening is historical. The rationality of a principle is not that of an event. In this deeper sense of the word "historical," literature and theology are as disciplines more strictly "historical" than "scientific."[9] The interpretational processes appropriate to science are different from the interpretational processes appropriate to historical happenings, or to the happenings theology or literature tries to understand.

The present consideration of the first direction of meaning in the ancient usage of *hermēneuein*—interpretation as "saying" and as "expressing"—has led to the assertion of some fundamental principles of interpretation, both literary and

9. See Carl Michalson, *The Rationality of Faith.*

theological. It has led us back to the primordial form and function of language as living sound filled with the power of meaningful utterance. Language, as it emerges from nonbeing, is not signs but sound. It loses some of its expressive power (and therefore its meaning) when it is reduced to visual images — the silent world of space. Therefore theology and literary interpretation must retransform writing into speech. The principles of understanding which enable this transformation constitute a major concern of modern hermeneutical theory.

Hermēneuein as "to Explain"

THE SECOND DIRECTION of meaning in *hermēneuein* is "to explain." Interpretation as explanation emphasizes the discursive aspect of understanding; it points to the explanatory rather than expressive dimensions of interpretation. Words, after all, do not merely *say* something (though they also do this, and this is a primary movement of interpretation); they explain something, rationalize it, make it clear. One may express a situation without explaining it; expressing it is an interpretation, but explaining it is also a form of "interpretation." Let us consider some of the dimensions of this second and more obvious form of interpretation, and their modern significance.

The cryptic messages from the oracle at Delphi did not interpret a preexistent text; they were "interpretations" of a situation. (The messages themselves required interpretation.) They brought something to expression (the first and more primordial direction of meaning), but what they brought was at the same time an explanation of something — something formerly unexplained. They brought into a verbal formulation the "meaning" of a situation; they explained it, sometimes in words that concealed as much as they revealed. They said something about the situation, about reality, in words. The meaning was not hidden in the style or manner of saying; this was not a central consideration. Rather it was explanation in the sense of saying something about something else. Thus while in one sense the oracles simply said or enunciated, as explanation they moved toward a second moment of interpretation — to explain or account for something.

Aristotle's treatise *Peri hermēneias* defines interpretation as "enunciation." Such a definition suggests the first direction of meaning, "to say" or "to announce." Yet if the text is gone into more deeply, as English-speaking readers may now do thanks to a recent translation of the text with St. Thomas' extensive commentary,[10] the second direction may also apply.

Aristotle defines *hermēneia* as referring to the operation of the mind in making statements which have to do with the truth or falsity of a thing. "Interpretation" in this sense is the primary operation of the intellect in formulating a true judgment about a thing. A prayer, a command, a question, or a deprecative sentence is not a statement, according to Aristotle, but is derived from a statement; it is a secondary form of sentence which applies to some situation which the intellect originally perceived in the form of a statement. (For Aristotle, typically, the intellect perceives meaning as statement.) The original statement or interpretation, "The tree is brown," precedes any statement expressing a wish or use of it. "Interpretations" are therefore not statements aiming toward a use—as is a prayer or a command—but rather statements of something that is true or false. Aristotle defines them as "speech in which there is truth and falsity" (17a2). A consequence of this definition of interpretation is that both rhetoric and poetics are outside the scope of the treatise on interpretation, since they are aimed at moving the hearer (17a5).

Enunciation (interpretation) is not, according to Aristotle, to be confused with logic, for logic proceeds from comparing enunciated statements. Enunciation is the formulation of the statements themselves, not the process of reasoning from known to unknown things. In general, Aristotle divides the basic operations of the intellect into (1) the understanding of simple objects, (2) the operations of composing and dividing, (3) the operation of reasoning from known to unknown things. Enunciation, as discussed in *On Interpretation,* deals only with the second: the constructive and divisive operation of making statements in which there is truth or falsity. Enunciation, then, is neither logic, nor rhetoric, nor poetics, but is more fundamental; it is the enunciation of the truth (or falsity) of a thing as statement.

What is to be made of this restricted yet fruitfully specific definition of interpretation? First, it is significant that enunciation is not the "understanding of simple objects" but deals with the processes involved in constructing a true statement.

10. See note 1 above.

It operates on the level of language, but is not yet logic; enunciation reaches into the truth of a thing and embodies it as statement. The *telos* of the process is not to move the emotions (poetics) or to bring about political action (rhetoric) but to bring understanding to statement.

Enunciation, in seeking to express the truth of a thing as propositional statement, belongs to the higher and purer operations of the mind, the theoretical rather than the practical; it is concerned with truth and falsity rather than utility. Is this not the first rather than the second direction of meaning? That is, is this not to express or say, rather than to explain? Perhaps so; but one should note that the expressing had to do with style, and the saying was almost a divine operation: it announced the divine rather than enunciating the rational. Enunciation, for Aristotle, is not a message from the divine but an operation of the rational intellect. As such, it imperceptibly begins to shade into explanation. Already one is composing and dividing to find the truth of a statement; already, as saying is thought of as statement, the rational element is asserting itself and truth is becoming static and informational; it is a statement about a thing, that corresponds to its essence. Already truth is "correspondence" and saying is "statement"; imperceptibly, the truth of "happening" has shaded into the static truth of principles and statements.

Yet Aristotle was right to situate the moment of interpretation earlier than the processes of logical analysis. This calls attention to an error in modern thinking, which tends too quickly to fix interpretation automatically at the moment of logical analysis. Logical processes are also interpretation, but the prior and more foundational "interpretation" must be remembered. For instance, a scientist will call interpretation his analysis of given data; it would be correct *also* to call his seeing of the data interpretation. Even in the moment that the data becomes statement, interpretation has occurred. Likewise, the literary critic calls his analysis of a work interpretation; it would be correct also to call his way of seeing the work itself interpretation.

But the "understanding" that serves as the foundation for interpretation is itself already shaping and conditioning interpretation—it is a preliminary interpretation, but one that can make all the difference because it sets the stage for subsequent interpretation. Even when a literary interpreter turns toward the poem and, in effect, says, "This is a poem; I shall understand it by doing thus and thus"—he has already interpreted his task and by extension shaped his seeing of the poem.[11] And he has already, with his method, shaped the meaning of the object. Indeed, method and object cannot be separated: method has already delimited *what* we shall see. It has told us what the object is *as* object. For this reason, all method is already interpretation; it is, however, only one interpretation, and the object seen with a different method will be a different object.

Explanation, then, must be seen within the context of a more basic explanation or interpretation, the interpretation that occurs even in the way one turns toward an object. Explanation will certainly rely on the tools of objective analysis, but the selection of the relevant tools is already an interpretation of the task of understanding. Analysis is interpretation; feeling the need for analysis is also an interpretation. Thus analysis is really not the primary interpretation but a derivative form; it has preliminarily set the stage with an essential and primary interpretation before it ever begins to work with the data. This is unfortunately as true as of the "news analysis" that interprets the events of the day as it is of scientific analysis in the laboratory or literary analysis in the classroom. The derivative character of logic as it depends on the propositions is clear enough; the characteristically derivative character of explanation or analysis is not so obvious, but no less real.

An interesting use of the word *hermēneuein* occurs in the New Testament, Luke 24:25–27. Jesus, now resurrected, appears:

And he said to them, "O foolish men, and slow of heart to believe all that the prophets have spoken! Was it not necessary that the Christ should suffer these things and enter into his glory?" And beginning with Moses and all the prophets, he interpreted [*diermēneusen*] to them in all the scriptures the things concerning himself.

Note that the Christ appeals to their rational faculties: "Was it not necessary . . . ?" Then he opens up the meaning of the texts by placing them in the context of his redemptive suffering

11. This is a weakness inherent in genre criticism, for example on tragedy. For brilliant strictures on such criticism as applied to Aeschylus, see H. D. F. Kitto, *Form and Meaning in Drama,* and more recently his *Poiesis.*

and by placing that suffering in the context of prophecies of the Old Testament. Although the New Testament use of the Old Testament is of great interest in itself, let us leave the theological problem aside and ask what the example suggests about interpretation as explanation. The quotation is clearly an example of explanation, for Jesus was doing more than merely repeating or reasserting the older texts; he *explained* them, and himself in terms of them. Here interpretation involves the bringing of an *outside* factor, the Christ, to point up the "meaning" of the older texts. Only in the presence of this factor do the texts become meaningful. On the other hand, the Christ is equally concerned to show that only in the light of the texts does his atonement become meaningful as the historical fulfillment of the prophesied Messiah.

What does this suggest hermeneutically? It suggests that meaning is a matter of context; the explanatory procedure provides the arena for understanding. Only within a specific context is an event meaningful. Furthermore, the Christ, in relating his death to the hopes for a Messiah, is relating this historical event to the personal hopes and intentions of the listeners. His significance then becomes that of a personal and historical Redeemer. Significance is a relationship to the listener's own projects and intentions; it is not something possessed by Jesus in himself outside of history and outside of a relationship to his hearers. We may say that an object does not have significance outside of a relationship to someone, and that the relationship determines the significance. To speak of an object apart from a perceiving subject is a conceptual error caused by an inadequate realistic concept of perception and the world; but even granting this concept, does it make sense to speak of meaning and significance apart from perceiving subjects? Theologians are fond of emphasizing the *pro nobis* (for us) aspect of the Christ; but one may assert that in principle all explanation is "for us," all explanatory interpretation assumes intentions in those to whom the explanation is directed.

Another way of saying this is to state: Explanatory interpretation makes us aware that explanation is contextual, is "horizonal." It must be made within a horizon of already granted meanings and intentions. In hermeneutics, this area of assumed understanding is called preunderstanding. One may fruitfully ask what preunderstanding is necessary in order to understand the (given) text. Jesus supplied his listeners with the element necessary to understand the prophetic texts; this was part of the necessary explanation. Even so, he had to assume a pre-understanding of what prophecy was and what it could mean to them before he could explain himself to his listeners. It might be asked what horizon of interpretation a great literary text inhabits, and then how the horizon of an individual's own world of intentions, hopes, and preinterpretations is related to it. This merging of two horizons must be considered a basic element in all explanatory interpretation.

A form of literary interpretation which, as has been suggested, takes as its goal the fullest possible oral interpretation will still not neglect the explanatory dimensions of interpretation. Far from it, the framing of the horizon within which understanding arises is the foundation of a truly communicative oral interpretation. (Oral interpretation, it should be remembered, is what we all do when in reading a text we try to supply the nuances of its meaning; it need not be public or even out loud.) For the interpreter to "perform" the text, he must "understand" it: he must preunderstand the subject and the situation before he can enter the horizon of its meaning. Only when he can step into the magic circle of its horizon can the interpreter understand its meaning. This is that mysterious "hermeneutical circle" without which the meaning of the text cannot emerge. But there is a contradiction here. How can a text be understood, when the condition for its understanding is already to have understood what it is about? The answer is that somehow, by a dialectical process, a partial understanding is used to understand still further, like using pieces of a puzzle to figure out what is missing. A literary work furnishes a context for its own understanding; a fundamental problem in hermeneutics is that of how an individual's horizon can be accommodated to that of the work. A certain preunderstanding of the subject is necessary or no communication will happen, yet that understanding must be altered in the act of understanding. The function of explanatory interpretation in literary interpretation may be seen, in this context, as an effort to lay the foundations in "preunderstanding" for an understanding of the text.

As the first two directions of interpretation (saying and explanation) are considered, the complexity of the interpretive process and the way in which it is grounded in understanding begins to emerge. Interpretation as saying is reminiscent of the performatory nature of reading; yet even for the perform- ance of reading a literary text, the performer must already "understand" it. This implies explanation; yet here again explanation is grounded in preunderstanding, so that prior to any meaningful explanation, he must enter the horizon of the subject and situation. He must in his own understanding grasp and be grasped by the text. His stance in this encounter, the preunderstanding of the material and situation which he must bring to it, the whole problem, in other words, of the merging of his horizon of understanding with the horizon of understanding which comes to meet him in the text—this is the dynamic complexity of interpretation. It is the "hermeneu- tical problem."

To consider the above elements of the interpretative problem is not, as some might think, to fall back into "psychologism." For the perspective within which the charge of "psycholo- gism" and the attitude of antipsychologism (presupposed in the charge) have any meaning assumes at the outset the separation and isolation of the object and then looks pejoratively at the "subjective" reaction as in the intangible realm of "feel- ings." The discussion presented here, however, has not dealt with feelings but with the structure and dynamics of under- standing, the conditions under which meaning can arise in the interaction of reader with the text, the way in which all analysis presupposes an already shaped definition of the situation. Within the framework of such considerations the truth of Georges Gurvitch's observation is seen—that object and method can never be separated.[12] Of course, this is a truth foreign to the realistic way of seeing.

Hermēneuein as "to Translate"

THE IMPLICATIONS OF THE THIRD DIMENSION of the meaning of hermēneuein are almost as suggestive to herme- neutics and theory of literary interpretation as the first two. In this dimension, "to interpret" means "to translate." When a text is in the reader's own language, the clash between the

12. Georges Gurvitch, *Dialectique et sociologie*.

world of the text and that of its reader may escape notice. When the text is in a foreign language, however, the contrast in perspectives and horizons can no longer be ignored. Yet, as we shall see, the problems of the interpreter of languages are not structurally different from those of the literary critic working in his own language. They do enable us, however, to see more clearly the situation present in any interpretation of a text.

Translation is a special form of the basic interpretive process of "bringing to understanding." In this case, one brings what is foreign, strange, or unintelligible into the medium of one's own language. Like the god Hermes, the translator mediates between one world and another. The act of translation is not a simple mechanical matter of synonym-finding, as the ludicrous products of translation machines make only too clear, for the translator is mediating between two different worlds. Translation makes us aware of the fact that language itself contains an overarching interpretation of the world, to which the translator must be sensitive even as he translates individual expressions. Translation only makes us more fully aware of the way that words actually shape our view of the world, even our perceptions. Language is clearly a repository of cultural experience; we exist in and through this medium; we see through its eyes.

The translation of the Bible may serve as an illustration of the problems of translation in general.[13] The Bible comes to us from a world distant in time, space, and language, a strange world which we must interrogate (and which interrogates us). Somehow the horizon of our world of understanding must meet and merge with the horizon of understanding in the text. Mediated not only through language but through history (a time gap of two thousand years), the New Testament must come to speak in the words that are of our world, our medium of seeing what is. How shall we hope to understand happenings within a radically different context from that of the modern secular city, mass communication, world conflict, gas, napalm, atomic weapons, and germ warfare? Should we try to preserve the literal action of the New Testament, or present what would be its equivalent in modern times? For instance, Eugene Nida in his book on the science of translation cites the example of Paul's familiar phrase, "Greet one another with a holy kiss."

13. Eugene A. Nida, *Toward a Science of Translating: With Special Reference to Principles and Procedures Involved in Bible Translating.*

While the kiss was the customary form of greeting in New Testament times, it is not today. Should a twentieth-century version read "Greet one another with a hearty handshake all around"?

This example poses a minor problem, however, compared to the deeper question of the way the whole world view of the New Testament times clashes with the modern "scientific" or post-deistic world view. This issue is exactly the one which the German theologian Rudolf Bultmann tried to confront with his controversial project of demythologizing. Bultmann notes that the biblical message is set in the context of a cosmological conception of the heavens above, the earth in the middle, and the underworld below—the three-level universe. His response to this situation is to assert that the message of the New Testament is not dependent on its cosmology, which is only the context of a message about personal obedience and transformation into a "new man." Demythologizing is an attempt to separate the essential message from the cosmological "mythology" which no modern man can believe.

Whatever the theological merits of demythologizing as a solution to this interpretive dilemma, the project itself points to a profound problem: How are we to "understand" the New Testament? What is it we are trying to understand? How fully does the historical world of thought and experience of the New Testament have to be entered into before it can be interpreted? Is it at all possible to find equivalents for "understanding" the New Testament? Can it be that our world will be so changed within a century that the New Testament will be unintelligible? Already today it is harder for young people in urban settings to understand Homer because the simple components of Homeric life—boats, horses, plows, spears, axes, wineskins—are often items they have seen only in books or museums. This is not to suggest that Homer will soon be out of date but that the effort to understand him becomes more difficult as we mechanize our way of life.

Demythologizing is not a purely theological problem; it occurs with lesser, but still significant, urgency in trying to understand any great ancient work. The "God is dead" theology of today is really another form of demythologizing, but it makes the problem of modern understanding of ancient Greek drama a little more clear: How can we feel any meaning for ourselves in a Sophoclean play, for instance, if the old metaphysical God is dead and the living God of interhuman relationships is not yet born? Is the Greek play a monument to a dead God or set of gods? Is it, perhaps, as the critic Raleigh said of *Paradise Lost,* a "monument to dead ideas"? How should a Greek play be translated into modern language? Or how should the ancient terms be understood? How can ancient works be kept from seeming mere comedies of errors? What many professors of classics have been doing, I suggest, is really demythologizing when they plead for the relevance of a work on the basis of its perennial human significance.

Even so, this "human significance" has to be interpreted to modern ears (the explanatory phase of interpretation), and to do so we must be clearer on how a thing *is* significant. An approach in literary interpretation that concentrates on counting images of one sort or another, or that focuses on the "form" of a work, or that does thematic analysis within a work or between works, actually passes over the issue of "significance." An approach to literature which sees the work as an object apart from perceiving subjects easily and automatically avoids the question of what really constitutes the human significance of a work. American literary criticism may awake one morning, however, to discover that since it has cut itself off from the question of how a great work is to be made humanly relevant through interpretation, its elaborate exercises in imagistic, formal, or thematic analysis have become a pointless pastime for English teachers. Their dissections lose their point if, like God, "literature is dead," dead because its interpreters are more interested in knowing its structure and autonomous function than in keeping it alive and humanly significant. Literature too can die, starved through lack of perceived relationship to the reader. Theological and literary interpretation are either humanly significant for today or worthless.

Teachers of literature need to become experts in "translation" more than "analysis"; their task is to bring what is strange, unfamiliar, and obscure in its meaning into something meaningful that "speaks our language." This does not mean "souping up" the classics and dressing Chaucer in twentieth-century English; it means recognizing the problem of a conflict of horizons and taking steps to deal with it, rather than sweeping it under the rug and concentrating on analytical games. The world view implicit in a poem, or presupposed by it and therefore integral to its understanding, should not be treated as some sort of fallacy of long-gone historical criticism.

For instance, a fundamental prerequisite for understanding *The Odyssey* is the recognition from the first that natural things are alive and intentional, that the universe is a matter of land and water as far as one can see, that every natural process is the result of the will of a supernatural being, and that the gods are superhuman overlords with all the foibles of human beings yet beings who are operating on an elevated version of the honor-centered code of the Greek hero. Only as we move into this world which is no longer real for us do we focus on the man of endless stratagems, that hero who ventures forth dauntless into the jaws of death, that yarn-spinner who could tell a tale likely to deceive (almost) his patroness Athena, that insatiable quester for adventurous knowledge, Odysseus. The genius of Erich Auerbach's textual analyses (dealing with "Odysseus' scar," for instance) lies not only in his loyalty and responsiveness to the way the story is told but also in his realization that *the underlying sense of reality* is a key to understanding.[14] Thus the sense of reality and the way of being-in-the-world represented in the work must be the focus of an "enabling" literary interpretation, the foundation for a reading of the work that can grasp (and be grasped by) the human significance of its action. The metaphysics (definition of reality) and ontology (character of being-in-the-world) in a work are foundational to an interpretation which makes a meaningful understanding possible.

Translation, then, makes us conscious of the clash of our own world of understanding and that in which the work is operating. While the language barrier renders these two worlds of understanding more noticeable, they are present in any interpretation of a written work in our own language, and indeed in any genuine "dialogue," especially between partners separated by geographical difference. In English literature, even a gap of a hundred years works some transformation in language, so that the problems of interpreting Wordsworth, Pope, Milton, Shakespeare, or Chaucer involve the meeting of two contrasting historical and linguistic worlds, and for Americans who have never visited England there is a further separation.

14. "Odysseus' Scar," *Mimesis*, pp. 1-20.

An effort of historical imagination and "translation" is required just to envisage the world of Wordsworth's England, on the edge of industrialization but still essentially rural. To see Dante's Italy and to move into that world in understanding the *Divine Comedy* is not merely a matter of linguistic translation (although the language tells us much); it is a matter of historical translation. Even with the finest imaginable English translation, the understanding problem involved in the encounter with another distinct horizon of understanding human existence is still present. Demythologizing is a recognition of this problem in terms of biblical interpretation; but in principle, as has been noted, demythologizing must take place with any reading of historical documents or literary texts, even if the demythologizing does not seek to rob the original of its dramatic immediacy. In short, an explication of the world view implicit in the language itself, and then in the use of the language in a literary work, is a fundamental challenge for literary interpretation.

Modern hermeneutics finds in translation and translation theory a great reservoir for exploring the "hermeneutical problem." Indeed, hermeneutics in its early historical stages always involved linguistic translation, either as classical philological hermeneutics or as biblical hermeneutics. The phenomenon of translation is the very heart of hermeneutics: in it one confronts the basic hermeneutical situation of having to piece together the meaning of a text, working with grammatical, historical, and other tools to decipher an ancient text. Yet these tools are, as we have said, only explicit formalizations of factors which are involved in any confrontation of a linguistic text, even in our own language. There are always two worlds, the world of the text and that of the reader, and consequently there is the need for Hermes to "translate" from one to the other.

This discussion of the origin of *hermēneuein* and *hermēneia* and the three directions of their meaning in ancient usage was undertaken in the context of the hermeneutical problem in general. Because of this, it serves as an introduction to some of the basic issues and concepts in hermeneutics to be encountered in the coming chapters. The modern definitions of hermeneutics will emphasize now one, now another direction of the rich reservoir of meaning resident in the Greek roots from which the term "hermeneutics" was derived. The field of hermeneutics does well to return ever and again to the significance of the three directions of meaning in interpretation as saying, explaining, and translating.

3 / Six Modern Definitions
of Hermeneutics

As IT HAS EVOLVED in modern times, the field of hermeneutics has been defined in at least six fairly distinct ways. From the beginning the word has denoted the science of interpretation, especially the principles of proper textual exegesis, but the field of hermeneutics has been interpreted (in roughly chronological order) as: (1) the theory of biblical exegesis; (2) general philological methodology; (3) the science of all linguistic understanding; (4) the methodological foundation of *Geisteswissenschaften;* (5) phenomenology of existence and of existential understanding; and (6) the systems of interpretation, both recollective and iconoclastic, used by man to reach the meaning behind myths and symbols.

Each of these definitions is more than an historical stage; each points to an important "moment" or approach to the problems of interpretation. They might be called the biblical, philological, scientific, *geisteswissenschaftliche,* existential, and cultural emphases.[1] Each represents essentially a standpoint

1. All of these characterizing adjectives are somewhat inadequate and unsatisfactory; I use them very tentatively and provisionally simply to indicate the diversity among the six different approaches. "Biblical" hermeneutics has many different directions; in the eighteenth century alone it included grammatical, historical, pietistic, and other schools, and it continues to be many-sided to the present time. "Philological" hermeneutics also enjoyed a complex development in the eighteenth century. "Scientific" is somewhat misleading in reference to Schleiermacher and is simply meant to suggest his effort to put hermeneutics on a universal, systematic foundation. *Geisteswissenschaftliche* refers to Dilthey's project, but it is hardly sufficient to suggest the emphasis on the historical in Dilthey. "Existential" is stretched to designate both Heidegger's and Gadamer's conceptions of hermeneutics. Finally, "cultural" can hardly suggest the richness of Ricoeur's application of hermeneutics to the quest for a more adequate philosophy centered on the interpretation of symbols. Juridical hermeneutics is omitted altogether.

from which hermeneutics is viewed; each brings to light different but legitimate sides of the act of interpretation, especially text interpretation. The very content of hermeneutics itself tends to be reshaped with these changes of standpoint. An outline of these six moments will illustrate this point and serve as a brief historical introduction to the definition of hermeneutics.

HERMENEUTICS AS THEORY OF BIBLICAL EXEGESIS

THE OLDEST and probably still the most widespread understanding of the word "hermeneutics" refers to the principles of biblical interpretation. There is historical justification for this definition, since the word came into modern use precisely as the need arose for books setting forth the rules for proper exegesis of Scripture. Probably the earliest recorded occurrence of the word as a book title is J. C. Dannhauer's *Hermeneutica sacra sive methodus exponendarum sacrarum litterarum,* published in 1654.[2] Even from the title of the book, one gathers that hermeneutics is distinguished from exegesis as the methodology of interpretation. The distinction between actual commentary (exegesis) and the rules, methods, or theory governing it (hermeneutics) dates from this earliest usage and remains basic to the definition of hermeneutics both in theology and, when the definition is later broadened, in reference to nonbiblical literature.

After the appearance of Dannhauer's book, the term appears to have occurred with increasing frequency, especially in Germany. Protestant circles there strongly felt the need for interpretive manuals to assist ministers in the exegesis of Scripture, since the minister was cut off from recourse to the authority of the Church to decide questions of interpretation. Thus there was a strong impetus to develop viable, independent standards for interpreting the Bible; between 1720 and 1820, hardly a year passed without the appearance of some new hermeneutical manual to aid Protestant ministers.[3]

In England and later in America, the usage of the word "hermeneutics" followed the general tendency to refer to

2. Ebeling, "Hermeneutik," *RGG* III, 243.
3. See *ibid,* 242; Heinrici, "Hermeneutik," *RPTK* VII, 719; and E. Dobschütz, "Interpretation," *ERE* VII, 390-95.

specifically biblical exegesis. The first use recorded by the *Oxford English Dictionary* dates back to 1737: "Taking such liberties with sacred writ, as are by no means allowable upon any known rules of just and sober hermeneutics."[4] Longfellow, about a century later, has Brother Bernardus in *Hyperion* speak of "my papers and my great work on Biblical Hermeneutics."[5]

When the usage of the word is broadened in English to refer to nonbiblical texts, it is notable that the texts are obscure, so as to require special methods to extract a hidden meaning. For instance, the reference to an "apprenticeship to the hermeneutic muse" in one case (W. Taylor, 1807)[6] suggests such an interpretation, as does "the hermeneutic method of the profound and hidden meaning" (D. Hunter, in translating Reuss's *Historical Canon*, 1884).[7] Likewise, the assertion by Edward Burnett Tylor in *Primitive Culture* (1871): "No legend, no allegory, no nursery rhyme, is safe from the hermeneutics of a thoroughgoing mythologic theorist."[8] In English usage, then, the word may refer to nonbiblical interpretation, but in these cases the text is generally obscure or symbolic, requiring a special type of interpretation to get at its hidden meaning. The more general definition in English has remained that of the theory of scriptural exegesis.

While the term "hermeneutics" itself dates only from the seventeenth century, the operations of textual exegesis and theories of interpretation—religious, literary, legal—date back to antiquity. Thus, once the word is accepted as designating theory of exegesis, the field it covers is generally extended (retroactively, one might say) in biblical exegesis back to Old Testament times, when there were canons for properly interpreting the Torah.[9] An important hermeneutical relationship exists between the New and Old Testaments as Jesus interprets himself to the Jews in terms of scriptural prophecy. Scholars

4. V, 243.
5. Henry Wadsworth Longfellow, *Prose Works*, II, 309. *Hyperion* is a prose romance, one of only two prose fiction works Longfellow wished preserved.
6. *OED* V, 243.
7. *Ibid.*
8. *Primitive Culture*, I, 319.
9. Ebeling's definitive article cited above divides the development of biblical hermeneutics into seven historical periods: Pre-Christian, Primitive Christian, Patristic, Medieval, Reformation and Orthodox, Modern, and Contemporary. He also offers abundant bibliographical references for each period.

of the New Testament can detect in the Gospels (especially John)[10] and in the Pauline Letters the operations of "interpreting" Jesus to their audiences according to a certain system of understanding. Already, "theology" is at work; in a certain sense, theology itself as the historical interpreter of the biblical message is hermeneutics. The history of biblical hermeneutics could be traced through the primitive Church; the patriarchs; medieval fourfold interpretation of the Bible; Luther's struggle against mystical, dogmatic, humanistic, and other systems of interpretation; the rise of the critical-historical method in the eighteenth century and the complex forces at work in this period to reshape the interpretation of Scripture; Schleiermacher's contribution; the history-of-religions school in relation to interpretation; the rise of dialectical theology in the 1920's; and the New Hermeneutic of contemporary theology. Such a detailed history cannot be presented here; rather, two points will simply be noted, one about the nature of hermeneutics as indicated by the example of biblical hermeneutics, and the other a question of the scope of hermeneutics.

Without going into details, it is interesting to note the general tendency of biblical hermeneutics to rely on a "system" of interpretation out of which individual passages can be interpreted. Even in Protestant hermeneutics, there is the search for a "hermeneutical principle" which will serve as a referential guide.[11] The text is not interpreted in terms of itself; indeed, this may be an impossible ideal. The scriptural text in the Enlightenment, for instance, is the vessel of great moral truths; yet those truths were found there because an interpretive principle was shaped to find them. In this sense hermeneutics is the interpreter's system for finding the "hidden" meaning of the text.

The other question involves the scope of hermeneutics. Even if one grants the legitimacy of retroactively encompassing in biblical hermeneutics all theory of exegesis from Old Testament times to the present, there is still the question as to whether hermeneutics includes both explicit theorizing — actually expressed rules of exegesis — and unstated, implicit theory of exegesis as revealed through practice. For instance,

10. See Frederick W. Herzog, "Historico-Ontological Hermeneutic in the Fourth Gospel," *Understanding God,* pp. 65–88.
11. See "Das hermeneutische Prinzip der theologischen Exegese," *F H* 111–18.

theologian Gerhard Ebeling has done a study of "Luther's hermeneutic." [12] Is one concerned here only with Luther's statements on the subject of biblical interpretation, or also with his practice of exegesis as revealed by an analysis of his sermons and other writings? Ebeling's study includes both. This vastly broadens the scope of biblical hermeneutics, and in an instant the task of writing, for example, a history of biblical hermeneutics is expanded from a consideration of relatively manageable sources which discuss the hermeneutical problem to an examination of the systems of interpretation implicit in all major commentary on the Bible from ancient times to the present.[13] In essence, such a history becomes a history of theology.[14]

Carrying the implications of this broader scope of hermeneutics (as systems of interpretation both implicit and explicit) into a definition of hermeneutics applying to both biblical and nonbiblical literature, the perimeter of nonbiblical hermeneutics becomes so historically vast as to be unmanageable. Who could think, for instance, of writing a history of hermeneutics, so defined? The implicit interpretive system in every commentary on a text (legal, literary, religious) in Western thought— indeed, why not include Oriental systems, too?—would have to be included. In his two-volume masterwork,[15] Emilio Betti has made an important contribution toward presenting a cross-section of various interpretive disciplines as they understand interpretation today, yet this voluminous effort is only a fraction of what such a "history of hermeneutics" would involve.

It can be asked, furthermore, whether either a full history of hermeneutics or an inclusive synthesis of the many different disciplinary theories of interpretation (assuming that either

12. *Evangelische Evangelienauslegung: Eine Untersuchung zu Luthers Hermeneutik.*
13. Several good treatments of biblical hermeneutics which give historical detail are: E. C. Blackman, *Biblical Interpretation;* Frederic W. Farrar, *History of Interpretation;* Robert M. Grant, *A Short History of the Interpretation of the Bible;* Stephen Neill, *The Interpretation of the New Testament:* 1861–1961; B. Smalley, *The Study of the Bible in the Middle Ages;* and James D. Wood, *The Interpretation of the Bible.* In German, Lothar Steiger's recent *Die Hermeneutik als dogmatisches Problem* is to be recommended for its treatment of theological hermeneutics since Schleiermacher.
14. See Gerhard Ebeling, *Kirchengeschichte als Geschichte der Auslegung der Heiligen Schrift.*
15. *TGI,* translated by its author into German and abridged by one-third as *AAMG.* See also Joachim Wach's contribution to this project, *V,* a three-volume history of hermeneutics in the nineteenth century.

were possible) would really constitute an adequate response to the hermeneutical problem today. Both projects look to what has already been actualized, in the past or in the present, and as such represent an effort to conserve and to consolidate. But to innovate and put forward perspectives not yet in existence, more than history or a scientific synthesis is needed. What is needed as much as either of these (and no one denies their value) is a deeper understanding of the phenomenon of interpretation itself, an understanding that is philosophically adequate both epistemologically and ontologically. Histories of interpretation theory in specific disciplines are certainly vital to the continuing quest for a deeper understanding of interpretation, as are syntheses of several disciplinary approaches; but they are not in themselves sufficient.

HERMENEUTICS AS PHILOLOGICAL METHODOLOGY

THE DEVELOPMENT OF RATIONALISM and, concomitantly with it, the advent of classical philology in the eighteenth century had a profound effect on biblical hermeneutics. There arose the historical-critical method in theology;[16] both the "grammatical" and "historical" schools of biblical interpretation affirmed that the interpretive methods applying to the Bible were precisely those for other books. For instance, in his hermeneutical manual of 1761, Ernesti asserted that "the verbal sense of Scripture must be determined in the same way in which we ascertain that of other books."[17] With the rise of rationalism, interpreters felt duty-bound to try to overcome advance judgments. "The norm of biblical exegesis," according to Spinoza, "can only be the light of reason common to all."[18] "The accidental truths of history can never become proofs of the necessary truths of reason," said Lessing;[19] thus, the chal-

16. See Hans-Joachim Kraus, *Geschichte der historisch-kritischen Erforschung der Alten Testaments von der Reformation bis zur Gegenwart*, esp. Chap. 3, pp. 70-102.
17. F. W. Farrar, *History of Interpretation*, p. 402, citing Johann August Ernesti, *IINT*. Two English translations of the treatise were made in the early nineteenth century (see Bibliography).
18. Chap. 7 of *Tractatus theologico-politicus* (1670); cited in Ebeling, "Hermeneutik," *RGG* III, 245.
19. *Über den Beweis des Geistes und der Kraft* (1777): "Zufällige Geschichtswahrheiten können der Beweis von nothwendigen Vernunftswahr-

lenge for interpretation is to make the Bible relevant to the enlightened rational man.

This challenge, as Kurt Frör in his book on biblical hermeneutics has observed, led to the "intellectualizing of biblical assertions." [20] Since the accidental truths of history were viewed as inferior to the "truths of reason," biblical interpreters held that scriptural truth was above time and above history; the Bible does not tell man anything true which he would not eventually have recognized through using his reason. It was simply rational, moral truth revealed before its time. The task of exegesis, then, was to go deeply into the text, using the tools of natural reason, and to find those great moral truths intended by the New Testament writers but hidden within different historical terms. What was needed, they argued, was a developed historical understanding which could grasp the spirit (*Geist*) behind the work and translate it into terms acceptable to enlightened reason. One might call this an Enlightenment form of "demythologizing," although the term in the twentieth century means to interpret, not simply to purge, the mythical elements in the New Testament.

Despite the Enlightenment faith in "moral truths," which led to what now seems a distortion of the biblical message, the effect on hermeneutics and on biblical research in general was salutary. Biblical interpretation developed techniques of grammatical analysis to great refinement,[21] and interpreters were more than ever before committed to full knowledge of the historical context of the biblical accounts. J. S. Semler, for instance, contended that the interpreter "must be capable of speaking about these subjects [in the Bible] now in such a way as changing times and different circumstances of men other than ourselves require." [22] The true task of the interpreter became an historical one.

---

heiten nie werden," cited in Kurt Frör, *Biblische Hermeneutik: Zur Schriftauslegung in Predigt und Unterricht*, p. 26. See "On the Proof of the Spirit and of Power," in *Lessing's Theological Writings*, ed. Henry Chadwick, pp. 51–56.

20. *Ibid.*

21. Ernesti, *IINT*, is the preeminent example.

22. See H.-J. Kraus, *op. cit.*, pp. 93–102, on Semler. The sense of the Scriptures is served, Semler asserted, when "der historisch Verstehende nun auch imstande ist, von diesen Gegenständen auf eine solche Weise jetzt zu reden, als es die veränderte Zeit und andere Umstände der Menschen neben uns erfordern."

With these developments, the methods of biblical hermeneutics became essentially synonymous with secular theory of
interpretation—i.e., classical philology. And at least from the
Enlightenment to the present, biblical methods of research
have been inseparably connected with philology. Thus the
phrase "Biblical hermeneutics" superseded "hermeneutics"
as a reference to scriptural theory of exegesis; "hermeneutics,"
unmodified, was virtually indistinguishable definitionally from
philological methodology. A later chapter will explore more
specifically the content of philology at the beginning of the
nineteenth century with a discussion of two great philologists
of Schleiermacher's time, Friedrich August Wolf and Friedrich Ast. It is enough here to say simply that the conception
of hermeneutics as strictly biblical gradually shaded into hermeneutics as the general rules of philological exegesis, with
the Bible as one among other possible objects of these rules.

HERMENEUTICS AS THE SCIENCE OF LINGUISTIC UNDERSTANDING

SCHLEIERMACHER HAS THE DISTINCTION of having
reconceived hermeneutics as a "science" or "art" of understanding. Since a full chapter will subsequently be devoted to
him it need only be noted here that such a conception of hermeneutics implies a radical critique of the standpoint of philology, for it seeks to go beyond the concept of hermeneutics as
an aggregate of rules and to make hermeneutics systematically
coherent, a science which describes the conditions for understanding in all dialogue. The result is not simply philological
hermeneutics but a "general hermeneutics" (*allgemeine Hermeneutik*) whose principles can serve as the foundation for
all kinds of text interpretation.

This conception of a general hermeneutics marks the beginning of the nondisciplinary "hermeneutics" so significant
for the present discussion. For the first time hermeneutics defines itself as the study of understanding itself. It might almost
be said that hermeneutics proper here emerges historically
from its parentage in biblical exegesis and classical philology.

HERMENEUTICS AS THE METHODOLOGICAL FOUNDATION FOR THE *Geisteswissenschaften*

WILHELM DILTHEY was a biographer of Schleiermacher and one of the great philosophical thinkers of the late nineteenth century. He saw in hermeneutics the core discipline which could serve as the foundation for all the *Geisteswissenschaften* (i.e., all disciplines focused on understanding man's art, actions, and writings).

To interpret a great expression of human life, whether it be a law, literary work, or sacred scripture, calls for an act of historical understanding, Dilthey asserted, an operation fundamentally distinct from the quantifying, scientific grasp of the natural world; for in this act of historical understanding, what is called into play is a personal knowledge of what being human means. What was needed in the human sciences, he believed, was another "critique" of reason that would do for the historical understanding what Kant's critique of pure reason had done for the natural sciences—a "critique of historical reason."

At an earlier stage in his thinking, Dilthey sought to ground his critique in a transformed version of psychology; yet since psychology was not an historical discipline, his efforts were hampered from the very outset. In hermeneutics—the discipline focused on interpretation, and specifically on the interpretation of an always historical object, a text—Dilthey found the more humane and historical basis for his own effort to formulate a truly humanistic methodology for the *Geisteswissenschaften.*

HERMENEUTICS AS THE PHENOMENOLOGY OF *Dasein* AND OF EXISTENTIAL UNDERSTANDING

MARTIN HEIDEGGER, in grappling with the ontological problem, turned to the phenomenological method of his mentor, Edmund Husserl, and undertook a phenomenological study of man's everyday being in the world. This study, *Being and Time* (1927), is now recognized as his masterwork and the key to any adequate understanding of his thought. He called the analysis presented in *Being and Time* a "hermeneutic of *Dasein*."

"Hermeneutics" in this context refers neither to the science or rules of text interpretation nor to a methodology for the *Geisteswissenschaften* but to his phenomenological explication of human existing itself. Heidegger's analysis indicated that "understanding" and "interpretation" are foundational modes of man's being. So Heidegger's "hermeneutic" of *Dasein* turns out, especially insofar as it presents an ontology of understanding, also to be hermeneutics; his investigation was hermeneutical in content as well as method.

Heidegger's deepening of the conception of hermeneutics and the hermeneutical in *Being and Time* marks another turning point in the development and definition of both the word and the field. At one stroke hermeneutics is connected with the ontological dimensions of understanding (and all that this implies) and at the same time is identified with Heidegger's special kind of phenomenology.

Professor Hans-Georg Gadamer, following the lead of Heidegger, has developed the implications of Heidegger's contribution to hermeneutics (both in *Being and Time* and in later works) into a systematic work on "philosophical hermeneutics" (*Wahrheit und Methode* [*Truth and Method*], 1960). Gadamer traces the development of hermeneutics in detail from Schleiermacher through Dilthey and Heidegger, providing the first adequate historical account of hermeneutics that encompasses and reflects the standpoint of Heidegger's revolutionary contribution. But *Wahrheit und Methode* is more than a history of hermeneutics; it is an effort to relate hermeneutics to aesthetics and to the philosophy of historical understanding. It presents in well-developed form the Heideggerian critique of hermeneutics in the older style of Dilthey, and reflects some of Hegel's as well as Heidegger's hermeneutical thinking in the concept of "historically operative consciousness" dialectically interacting with tradition as transmitted through the text.

Hermeneutics is carried one step further still, into the "linguistic" phase, with Gadamer's controversial assertion that "Being that can be understood is language." Hermeneutics is an encounter with Being through language. Ultimately, Gadamer asserts the linguistic character of human reality itself, and hermeneutics is plunged into the fully philosophical questions of the relationship of language to being, understanding, history, existence, and reality. Hermeneutics is put in the center of the philosophical problems of today; it cannot escape the epistemological or the ontological questions when understanding itself is defined as an epistemological and ontological matter.

HERMENEUTICS AS A SYSTEM OF INTERPRETATION: RECOVERY OF MEANING *versus* ICONOCLASM

PAUL RICOEUR, in *De l'interprétation* (1965), adopts a definition of hermeneutics which goes back to a focus on textual exegesis as the distinctive and centrally defining element in hermeneutics. "We mean by hermeneutics the theory of rules that govern an exegesis, that is to say, an interpretation of a particular text or collection of signs susceptible of being considered as a text."[23] Psychoanalysis, and in particular the interpretation of dreams, is very obviously a form of hermeneutics; the elements of the hermeneutical situation are all there: the dream is the text, a text filled with symbolic images, and the psychoanalyst uses an interpretive system to render an exegesis that brings to the surface the hidden meaning. Hermeneutics is the process of deciphering which goes from manifest content and meaning to latent or hidden meaning. The object of interpretation, i.e., the text in the very broadest sense, may be the symbols in a dream or even the myths and symbols of society or literature.

Ricoeur's study distinguishes between univocal and equivocal symbols; the former are signs with one designated meaning, like the symbols in symbolic logic, while the latter are the true focus of hermeneutics. For hermeneutics has to do with symbolic texts which have multiple meanings; they may constitute a semantic unity which has (as in myths) a fully coherent surface meaning and at the same time a deeper significance.

23. "Ainsi, dans la vaste sphère du langage, le lieu de la psychanalyse se précise: c'est à la fois le lieu des symboles ou du double sens et celui où s'affrontent les diverses manières d'interpréter. Cette circonscription plus vaste que la psychanalyse, mais plus étroite que la théorie du langage total qui lui sert d'horizon, nous l'appellerons désormais le 'champ herméneutique'; nous entendrons toujours par herméneutique la théorie des règles qui président à une exégèse, c'est-à-dire à l'interprétation d'un texte singulier ou d'un ensemble de signes susceptible d'être considéré comme un texte" (*DI* 18)

Hermeneutics is the system by which the deeper significance is revealed beneath the manifest content.

Yet the operation of finding a hidden meaning in dreams and in slips of the tongue actually demonstrates a distrust in surface or manifest reality; it is the achievement of Freud to have made us distrust our conscious understanding of ourselves, ultimately to ask us to smash our myths and illusions. Even our religious beliefs, as Freud attempts to show in *The Future of an Illusion,* are actually infantile illusions. The function of Freudian hermeneutics, then, is iconoclasm.

This leads Ricoeur to propose that there are two very different syndromes of hermeneutics in modern times: one, represented by Bultmann's demythologizing, deals lovingly with the symbol in an effort to recover a meaning hidden in it; the other seeks to destroy the symbol as the representation of a false reality. It destroys masks and illusions in a relentless rational effort at "demystification." Ricoeur singles out as examples of this latter form of hermeneutics three great demystifiers: Marx, Nietzsche, and Freud. Each of these three men interpreted surface reality as false and put forward a system of thought which demolished this reality. All three actively opposed religion; for all three, true thinking was an exercise in "suspicion" and doubt. They undermined the individual's pious confidence in reality, in his own beliefs and motives; each pleaded for a transformation of viewpoint, a new system to interpret the manifest content of our worlds—a new hermeneutic.

Because of these two antithetical approaches to the interpretation of symbols today, Ricoeur asserts, there can be no universal canons for exegesis but only separate and opposing theories concerning the rules of interpretation.[24] The demythologizers treat the symbol or text as a window to a sacred reality; the demystifiers treat the same symbols (say, the biblical texts) as a false reality that must be shattered.

Ricoeur's own approach to Freud is itself a brilliant exercise in the former type of interpretation, for he recovers and interprets Freud's significance anew to the present historical moment. Ricoeur attempts to encompass both the rationality of doubt and the faith of recollective interpretation in a reflective philosophy that does not retreat into abstractions or de-

24. *Ibid.,* 35.

generate into the simple exercise of doubt, a philosophy that takes up the hermeneutical challenge in myths and symbols and reflectively thematizes the reality behind language, symbol, and myth. Philosophy today is already focused on language; it is then already, in a sense, hermeneutics; the challenge is to make it creatively hermeneutical.

4 / The Contemporary Battle over Hermeneutics: Betti *versus* Gadamer

THE SIX INTERRELATED and often overlapping definitions of hermeneutics just discussed carry us from 1654 to the present. All six are in varying degrees still found in the spectrum of contemporary hermeneutical thinking, yet a clear polarization exists today. There is the tradition of Schleiermacher and Dilthey, whose adherents look to hermeneutics as a general body of methodological principles which underlie interpretation. And there are the followers of Heidegger, who see hermeneutics as a philosophical exploration of the character and requisite conditions for all understanding.

The preeminent representatives of these two basic positions today are Emilio Betti, author of a work on the theory of interpretation,[1] and Hans-Georg Gadamer, whose *Wahrheit und Methode* was discussed briefly in the previous chapter. Betti, in the tradition of Dilthey, aims at providing a general theory of how "objectivations" of human experience can be interpreted; he argues strongly for the autonomy of the object of interpretation and the possibility of historical "objectivity" in making valid interpretations. Gadamer, following Heidegger, orients his thinking to the more philosophical question of what understanding itself is; he argues with equal conviction that understanding is an historical act and as such is always connected to the present. To speak of "objectively valid interpretations" is naive, he asserts, since to do so assumes that it is possible to understand from some standpoint outside of history.

The demythologizing theologians — Rudolf Bultmann and

1. *TGI* and *AAMG*.

[46]

the two leaders of the New Hermeneutic, Gerhard Ebeling and Ernst Fuchs—can be grouped together as allies of Gadamer's basically Heideggerian and phenomenological approach. This identification of the New Hermeneutic with Gadamer is explicit and mutual; Gadamer cites Ebeling and Fuchs with approval in his book,[2] and the theologians advise their students to study Gadamer's book with care.[3] Also, the theological and philosophical critics of the New Hermeneutic, such as Wolfhart Pannenberg,[4] explicitly connect it with Gadamer's position. Betti has attacked Bultmann, Ebeling, and Gadamer as enemies of historical objectivity in his 1962 pamphlet, *Die Hermeneutik als allgemeine Methodik der Geisteswissenschaften,* and E. D. Hirsch has subsequently echoed and somewhat amplified the protest in his article on Gadamer's theory of interpretation.[5]

It is a debatable question, of course, as to who is attacking and who is defending, or who started the attack. It would appear that Betti and Hirsch are assailing the whole Heideggerian version of hermeneutics and the New Hermeneutic.[6] Yet they are voices of reaction and defense, for they call for a return to "objectivity," for a reaffirmation that the study of history involves leaving behind the historian's own present standpoint; hermeneutics, they claim, must function to supply the principles for objective interpretation. In his own defense, Gadamer states that he is simply engaged in describing what *is,* in every act of understanding; he is doing ontology, not methodology.[7]

The problem arises in the fact that Gadamer's ontology is such that the possibility of objective historical knowledge is

2. *WM* 313.

3. Professor Ebeling conducted a semester seminar on the book at the University of Zurich shortly after it was published. The customary *Protokol* (minutes) of the proceedings was kept, which would be of interest in assessing Ebeling's relationship to Gadamer.

4. See "Hermeneutics and Universal History," *HH* 122-52; originally *ZThK* LX (1963), 90-121.

5. *HAMG;* and Hirsch, "Gadamer's Theory of Interpretation," *RM* XVIII (1965), 488-507, reprinted in *VII* 245-64.

6. Betti discusses Bultmann, Ebeling, and Gadamer in *HAMG,* and Hirsch refers to Gadamer's *WM* as the "summa" of the New Hermeneutic in theology.

7. Letter to Betti, printed in *HAMG* 51n. This letter is later cited in Gadamer's article, "Hermeneutik und Historismus," *PhR* IX (1962), 248-49. The point is further clarified in the Preface to the 2d edition of *WM.* See also Robinson's discussion of this significant letter in *NH* 76. See Niels Thulstrup. "An Observation Concerning Past and Present Hermeneutics," *OL* XXII (1967), 24-44, for a comparison of Gadamer and Betti.

called into question. From Betti's standpoint, Heidegger and Gadamer are the destructive critics of objectivity who wish to plunge hermeneutics into a standardless morass of relativity. The integrity of historical knowledge itself is under attack and must be stoutly defended.

To understand the general thrust of the objections of Betti and Hirsch to the hermeneutics of Bultmann, Ebeling, and Gadamer, it is necessary to sketch very briefly the approaches of Bultmann and two of his disciples, Gerhard Ebeling and Ernst Fuchs.

HERMENEUTICS IN BULTMANN, EBELING, AND FUCHS

RUDOLF BULTMANN is well known as one of the major Protestant theologians of this century. Although his name is most often associated with the controversial project of demythologizing, his reputation as a great New Testament scholar was well established before he published his famous essay *Jesus Christ and Mythology* in 1941.[8] The main lines of his existentialist emphasis in theology, however, were in evidence as early as 1926 in his *Jesus*,[9] and they have since continued. This emphasis is itself an effort to confront more meaningfully the hermeneutical problem of interpreting the New Testament to twentieth-century man.

"Demythologizing" is probably an unfortunate choice of term. It tends to suggest that the New Testament as it stands is regarded as untrue (i.e., mythical) and that its message will have to be accommodated to our post-deistic world view. The picture is formed all too easily of an ingenious theologian who is ready to purge away the mythical elements as meaningless and present a reduced Bible in which only the most believable elements remain. This is emphatically not the case. On the contrary, demythologizing does not presume to delete or bypass

8. Bultmann's major works are available in translation, such as *The History of the Synoptic Tradition* (1921); *Jesus and the Word* (1926); and *Theology of the New Testament*, I (1941) and II (1951). There are also two collections of his articles: *Essays: Philosophical and Theological;* and *Existence and Faith*, trans. and ed. Schubert M. Ogden. (The dates given in parentheses are those of the original German editions and not of the translations.)

9. See esp. pp. 11-19: "Introduction: Viewpoint and Method."

the mythical elements in the New Testament but to emphasize in them the original and saving meaning. Far from being
an effort to accommodate the Gospels to modern ways of seeing,
demythologizing is directed against the shallow literalism in
the modern way of seeing, the tendency of laymen and even of
theologians to regard language as merely information rather
than as the medium through which God confronts man with
the possibility of a radically new (un-Greek, unnaturalistic,
unmodern) self-understanding. Demythologizing is not an
instrument of rationalist demystification and iconoclasm in
the manner of Freud, Nietzsche, or Marx (to mention Ricoeur's
distinction between demystification and demythologizing); it
does not seek to strike down and destroy the mythical symbol,
but regards it as a window to the sacred. To interpret the symbol is to recollect its original, authentic, but now hidden,
meaning.

The emphasis of Bultmann's demythologizing is obviously
on transforming one's self-understanding. In the matter of
existential self-understanding, Bultmann is clearly indebted
to Heidegger, with whom he was in close association in the
middle 1920's at the University of Marburg while the latter
was putting together *Being and Time.* The influence of Heidegger on Bultmann is so well known that it is sometimes vastly
overestimated. Yet while the attempt to construct a point-for-
point analogy between Heidegger's concepts and those of Bultmann (as John Macquarrie has done[10]) may be due as much to
the unconsciously religious character of Heidegger's ontological model as to Bultmann's debt, it is nevertheless fair to
say that Heidegger was a decisive force in Bultmann's thinking
on the hermeneutical problem. This reflects itself in demythologizing, which is essentially a hermeneutical project in existential interpretation.

For instance, not only is Bultmann's concept of man as a
future-oriented, historically existing being very close to that
enunciated in *Being and Time,* but there are at least three other
fairly specific respects in which Bultmannian theology follows
Heidegger. (1) There is the distinction between language used
as mere information to be interpreted objectively as fact, and
language filled with personal import and the power to command
obedience, which parallels Heidegger's concept of the deriva-

10. *An Existentialist Theology: A Comparison of Heidegger and Bultmann.*

tive character of assertions (especially logic).[11] (2) There is the
idea that God (Being) confronts man as Word, as language,
which parallels Heidegger's increasing emphasis on the linguistic character of Being as it presents itself to man. (3) There
is also the concept that *kerygma* as Word in words speaks to
existential self-understanding. The movement of the New
Testament in itself, says Bultmann, is toward a new ("authentic") self-understanding; the function of proclaiming the New
Testament is to bring about this new understanding in the
modern man it addresses today. The New Testament Word is
thus something like an actualization of the call of conscience
that Heidegger describes in *Being and Time*.[12]

Certainly the call to a new self-understanding is an affront
to one's present way of being in the world. Bultmann has no
wish to remove the "scandal" of the New Testament but to
place the scandalousness where it belongs: not on credal
affirmation of myths that are taken literally, not on believing
cosmological information that is manifestly false, but on the
call for radical obedience, openness to grace, freedom in faith.
Bultmann's discussions of the hermeneutical problem specifically indicate that for him hermeneutics is always defined in
terms of exegesis of an historically transmitted text. However
much he may be indebted to Heidegger, he still sees hermeneutics as the philosophy that should guide exegesis rather than
as understanding theory per se. In "The Problem of Hermeneutics" (1950), he reaffirms the liberal Protestant insistence on
full freedom of inquiry—the critical-historical method—and
goes so far as to say again that the Bible is subject to the same
conditions of understanding, the same philological and historical principles, as would apply to any other book.[13] The "hermeneutical problem," although always related to exegesis, is seen
not as distinctly and peculiarly theological but as resident in
all text interpretation, whether of legal documents, historical
works, literature, or the Scriptures.

Of course the crux of the problem remains the definition
of what constitutes historical understanding in reference to

11. *SZ* § 33.
12. *Ibid.*, § 60.
13. "Die Interpretation der biblischen Schriften unterliegt nicht anderen
Bedingungen des Verstehens als jede andere Literatur," *G&V* II, 231. The article first appeared as "Das Problem der Hermeneutik," *ZThK* XLVII (1950),
47-69, and later in translation in *Essays: Philosophical and Theological*, pp.
234-61.

a text. For Bultmann, the hermeneutic question is that of "how to understand historical documents delivered by tradition," which in turn rests on the question, "What is the character of historical knowledge?" [14] It is to this problem that the second half of his Gifford Lectures (1955) are devoted, and it is precisely the analysis there presented to which Betti later takes violent exception.[15]

Bultmann points out that each interpretation of history or an historical document is guided by a certain interest, which in turn is based on a certain preliminary understanding of the subject. Out of this interest and understanding, the "question" put to it is shaped. Without these, no question could arise, and there would be no interpretation. All interpretation, then, is guided by the interpreter's "preunderstanding." [16] (Again, this analysis of understanding is clearly related to Heidegger's delineation of *Vorhabe, Vorsicht,* and *Vorgriff* in *Being and Time* as preconditions for interpretation.[17] Applied to history, this means that the historian always chooses a certain viewpoint, which in turn means that he is open principally to the side of the historical process disclosed to questions arising out of that viewpoint. However objectively he may pursue his subject, the historian cannot escape his own understanding: "Already in choosing a viewpoint there is at work what I may call the existential encounter with history. History gains meaning only when the historian himself stands within history and takes part in history." [18] Bultmann then cites R. G. Collingwood to the effect that events have to be reenacted in the mind of the historian and thus are objective and known to him only because they are also subjective.[19] Since meaning arises only out of the interpreter's relation to the future, according to Bultmann, it becomes impossible to speak of objective — that is, standpointless — meaning, and since we no longer claim to know the end and goal of history, "the question of meaning in history [as a whole] has become meaningless." [20]

14. *HE* 110.
15. See *HAMG* 19-36.
16. *HE* 113. See Betti's critique of this "ambiguous word, which is best avoided," *HAMG* 20-21.
17. *SZ* § 32. *Vorhabe, Vorsicht,* and *Vorgriff* may be rendered somewhat literally as "prior having," "view," and "conception."
18. *HE* 119.
19. R. G. Collingwood, *The Idea of History,* p. 218.
20. *HE* 120.

In essence the "Heisenberg principle" or field theory in more radical form may be seen in operation here; that is, that the object being observed is itself subtly altered simply by the condition of being observed. The historian is part of the very field he is observing. Historical knowledge is itself an historical event; subject and object of historical science do not exist independently of each other.[21] This has implications for Christian faith, according to Bultmann, especially since through the eschatological moment the Christian is lifted above history and reenters it with a new future, and therefore a new meaning for history. It may be mentioned here that in the idea of eschatology Bultmann seeks to go a step beyond Collingwood to use a theological (eschatological) approach to the question of meaning in history.[22] But Bultmann's central contention is clear (the very issue which is disputed by Betti): that objective meaning in history cannot be spoken of, for history cannot be known except through the subjectivity of the historian himself.

Gerhard Ebeling and Ernst Fuchs follow Bultmann in placing the hermeneutical problem at the center of their thinking. Like him, they continue to grapple with the clear disparity between the modern view of reality and that in which the New Testament is set. They continue Bultmann's opposition to literalism in language and his effort to restore to the Word its native power. Like him, they focus on the meaning of the New Testament witness rather than on its factual character; they emphasize that the interpreter is always in the midst of the history he is to interpret, and that the meaning of history stands in a relationship to the interpreter's understanding of the future.

If anything, Ebeling and Fuchs have carried still further Bultmann's assumptions regarding history, language, and demythologizing, giving them an even more radical interpretation. If Bultmann's hermeneutics focused on man's existential self-understanding and went directly to an analysis of what this means in terms of the proclaimed Word, Ebeling and Fuchs turn to language itself and its relation to reality. The hermeneutical problem in this prespective is not simply a matter of adjusting the proclamation of the Word to the reality it conveys in terms of existential self-understanding; it is linguistic, i.e., "how a word [word event] that has taken place comes to

21. *Ibid.*, 133.
22. *Ibid.*, 136.

be understood." [23] As Ebeling asserts in "Word of God and Hermeneutics," "Existence is existence through word and in word; ... existentialist interpretation would mean *interpretation of the text with regard to the word event.*" [24]

Both Ebeling and Fuchs have made the word event the center of their theological thinking, which has been labeled "word-event theology." Hermeneutics, they assert, must take its bearings from the word event; "the object of hermeneutics," says Ebeling, "is the word event as such." [25] Hermeneutics does not, however, seek through paraphrase to make up for a deficiency of the biblical Word but to facilitate the "hermeneutical function" (of causing understanding to happen) of the word itself. The word itself is what opens up and mediates understanding: "The primary phenomenon in the realm of understanding is not understanding *of* language, but understanding *through* language." [26] Or elsewhere, to reemphasize the linguistic character of such theology: "Hermeneutics as the theory of understanding must therefore be the theory of words." [27] Fuchs puts the matter succinctly at the beginning of his *Hermeneutik:* "Hermeneutics in the realm of theology is faith's doctrine of language [*Sprachlehre*]." [28]

Two matters are of interest in this approach, from the standpoint of defining hermeneutics. First, the reference to the "hermeneutical function" of words goes back to the more primary sense of interpretation as a direct mediation of understanding, thus making the goal of hermeneutics the "removal of hindrances" to understanding. [29] This is a salutary focusing of the purpose of hermeneutics, although it does not change the fact that we tend to make use, consciously or unconsciously, of systems of interpretation even in the most direct act of mediation. The second point relates to historicism: the focus on the language event, which goes on to assert the "linguisticality of reality," takes a view of history not as a museum of facts but as a reality coming to expression in words. Thus the appropriate questions are not so much "What were the facts?" or

23. WF 313.
24. *Ibid.,* 331.
25. *Ibid.,* 319.
26. *Ibid.,* 318; cited in HAMG 36.
27. WF 319.
28. F H v.
29. WF 318–19.

"How can we explain this fact?" but "What came to expression in this fact or myth?" "What is it that is being mediated?" [30] Historicism in theology, then, originates in a misuse of language, a "depraved view of word" which abstracts it from the live word event and treats it as a matter of mere statement, resulting in the critical failure of the interpreter to understand the transmitted word in the light of its character as word event.[31]

The effect of the word event emphasis in theology is to bring philosophy of language to the very center of hermeneutics. The purpose of hermeneutics is still a practical one, that of removing hindrances to the word event, but the focus of the hermeneutical problem centers unequivocally on the interconnectedness of language, thinking, and reality. Since hermeneutics cannot be considered apart from modern epistemology, metaphysics, and philosophy of language, it clearly transcends the limits of mere practical disciplinary rules of interpretation. In its departure from the realistic objectivity of "historical facts," it has invited criticism within theology, preeminently from Wolfhart Pannenberg,[32] and outside theology, principally from Emilio Betti.

BETTI'S HERMENEUTICS

IN 1962, EMILIO BETTI, an Italian historian of law who founded in Rome, in 1955, an institute for interpretation theory,[33] published a booklet entitled *Die Hermeneutik als allgemeine Methodik der Geisteswissenschaften*. Appearing not long after Gadamer's masterwork of 1960, this essay put forward a clear and unequivocal protest against Gadamer's approach to the subject—as well as that of Bultmann and Ebeling. In simplest terms, Betti's objections to Gadamer's work are: first, that it does not serve as a methodology or aid to methodology for the humane studies and, secondly, that it jeopardizes the legitimacy of referring to the objective status of objects of interpretation and thus renders questionable the objectivity of the interpretation itself.

30. *Ibid.*, 295.
31. *Ibid.*
32. "Hermeneutics and Universal History," *HH* 122–52.
33. See *HAMG* 6–7n.

The booklet begins with a lament:

> Hermeneutics as the general problematic of interpretation, that
> great general discipline which welled up so nobly in the Romantic
> period as the common concern of all the humane disciplines, which
> commanded the attention of many great minds of the 19th cen-
> tury—like Humboldt in philosophy of language, August Wilhelm
> von Schlegel, the great literary historian, Böckh, the philologist
> and encyclopedist, Savigny, the jurist, and historians like Niebuhr,
> Ranke, and Droysen—this venerable older form of hermeneutics
> appears to be fading out of modern German consciousness.[34]

Betti was seeking to renew this older but richly significant
German tradition in his own earlier encyclopedic work, *Teoria
generale della interpretazione.*[35]

German readers had access to Betti's general thinking as
early as 1954, when he published his short "hermeneutical
manifesto," *Zur Grundlegung einer allgemeinen Auslegungslehre,*[36] a heavily documented advance notice of his *magnum
opus* of 1955, which eventually also appeared in German translation in 1967.[37] The larger work was the product of some seven
or more years of thinking which dated back to his inaugural
lecture of May 1948. The 1954 manifesto, in fact, is an enlarged
version of this earlier presentation. Betti writes with regret in
1962 that despite this 1954 publication, very little note was
taken in Germany of his work.[38] Rather, the spell of Heidegger's philosophy had continued to exert its influence on Protestant theology and philosophy, and a very different version
of hermeneutics had emerged.

This development was not in the great stream of tradition
stretching from Schleiermacher through Humboldt, Steinthal,
Lazarus, Böckh, Dilthey, Simmel, Litt, Joachim Wach, and
Nikolai Hartmann, which had occupied the attention of Betti
in his resolve to take up anew the project of formulating a
general methodological theory for interpretation.[39] Rather, it
was the influence of phenomenology and Heideggerian ontology, coupled with the general interest in philosophy of lan-

34. HAMG.
35. TGI.
36. Originally appeared in the *Festschrift für Ernst Rabel,* II, 79-168,
published the same year.
37. AAMG.
38. HAMG 6.
39. Ibid.

guage, that were the driving forces in the new German interest in hermeneutics. (Gadamer testifies that another impetus in his own thinking was his profound dissatisfaction in the 1930's with the prevailing theory in aesthetics.[40]) In theology, as we have seen, the development of hermeneutics was closely tied to demythologizing as a way of confronting the profound problem of how the Bible can be made relevant and meaningful to present-day hearers of its Word.

As an historian of law, Betti's interest did not arise out of a philosophical desire for a more adequate account of the truth of a work of art (as for Gadamer), or a desire to achieve a deeper understanding of the nature of Being (as for Heidegger), or from a compulsion to get at the saving meaningfulness of the biblical Word (as in Bultmann and Ebeling). He wished to differentiate among the various modes of interpretation in the humane disciplines and to formulate a foundational body of principles with which to interpret human actions and objects. If a distinction is to be made between the moment of understanding an object in terms of itself and the moment of seeing the existential meaning of the object for one's own life and future, then it may be said that this latter is clearly the concern of Gadamer, Bultmann, and Ebeling, while the nature of "objective" interpretation has been Betti's concern.

Betti by no means wishes to omit the subjective moment from interpretation, or even to deny that it is necessary in every humane interpretation. But he does wish to affirm that, whatever the subjective role in interpretation may be, the object remains object and an objectively valid interpretation of it can reasonably be striven for and accomplished. An object speaks, and it can be heard rightly or wrongly precisely because there is an objectively verifiable meaning in the object. If the object is not other than its observer, and if it does not, of itself, speak, why listen? [41]

Betti argues, however, that recent German hermeneutics has so occupied itself with the phenomenon of *Sinngebung* (the interpreter's function of conferring meaning on the object) that this has come to be equated with interpretation. At the

40. According to remarks by Gadamer on the genesis of *WM* in discussion following my paper, "Die Tragweite von Gadamers *WM* für die Literaturauslegung," Heidelberg, July 14, 1965.
41. *HAMG* 35.

beginning of *Die Hermeneutik als allgemeine Methodik der Geisteswissenschaften* (1962), Betti asserts that his main purpose is to clarify the essential distinction between *Auslegung* (interpretation) and *Sinngebung*. Precisely because this distinction is ignored, Betti asserts, the whole integrity of objectively valid results in the humanities (*die Objektivität der Auslegungsergebnisse*) is challenged.

A few examples of the canons of Betti's hermeneutics and his objections to Gadamer's position will illustrate Betti's defense of objectivity. For Betti, the interpretive object is an objectification of man's spirit (*Geist*) expressed in sensible form. Interpretation, then, is necessarily a recognition and reconstruction of the meaning that its author, using a special kind of unity of materials, was able to embody. This means, of course, that the observer must be translated into a foreign subjectivity and, through an inversion of the creative process, get back to the idea or "interpretation" which is embodied in the object.[42] Thus, as Betti observes, to speak of an objectivity that does not involve the subjectivity of the interpreter is manifestly absurd. Yet the subjectivity of the interpreter must penetrate the foreignness and otherness of the object, or he succeeds only in projecting his own subjectivity on the object of interpretation. Thus it is fundamental and is the first canon of all interpretation to affirm the essential autonomy of the object.[43]

A second canon is that of context of meaning, or a totality within which individual parts are interpreted. There is an inner relationship of coherence between individual parts of a speech because of the overarching totality of meaning built up of the individual parts.[44] In a third general canon, Betti acknowledges the "topicality" (*Aktualität*) of meaning, that is, the relatedness to the interpreter's own stance and interests in the present, which is involved in every understanding. The interpreter of an event in ancient times will necessarily interpret in terms of what he has experienced. On the subjective side, there is no escape from one's own understanding and experience. Betti is far from imagining that understanding is a matter of passive

42. *Ibid.*, 11–12.
43. *Ibid.*, 14.
44. "Kanon des sinnhaften Zusammenhanges (Grundsatz der Ganzheit)" or "Kanon der Totalität," *ibid.*, 15.

receptivity; rather, it is always a reconstructive process which involves the interpreter's own experience of the world.[45] It may even be said that Betti reaffirms "in principle" the concept of preunderstanding enunciated by Bultmann.

He emphatically takes issue, nonetheless, with Bultmann's conclusion that, because of the historicality of preunderstanding, the idea that it is possible to have objective historical knowledge is "an illusion of objectifying thinking" (*die Illusion eines objektivierenden Denkens*).[46] Says Betti:

> The text to which the preunderstanding gives meaning is not simply there to strengthen our previously held opinion; rather, we must assume that the text has something to say to us, which we do not already know from ourselves and which exists independently of our act of understanding. Precisely here the questionability of a subjective focus comes to light, one which is obviously influenced by contemporary existential philosophy, and one which strives to throw together explication [*Auslegung*] and understanding [*Sinngebung*], with the result that the objectivity of the results of the interpretive process in the humane studies as a whole is placed in question.[47]

Betti's criticisms of Gadamer raise strenuous objection to existential "subjectivity" and the historicality of understanding, asserting that Gadamer has failed to provide normative methods for distinguishing a right from a wrong interpretation, and that he lumps together very different modes of interpretation.[48] The historian, for instance, Betti asserts, is not concerned with a practical relation to the present so much as contemplatively immersing himself in the text he is studying; the lawyer, on the other hand, has a practical application to the present in mind in his interchange with a text. As a result, the two processes of interpretation are different in character; the assertion by Gadamer that every interpretation involves an application to the present is true enough of legal but not of historical interpretation.[49]

Gadamer answered these objections in a letter to Betti. He stated that he is not proposing a method but trying to "describe *what is.* . . . I try to think beyond modern science's concept

45. *Ibid.*, 19–22.
46. *HE* 121.
47. *HAMG* 35.
48. *Ibid.*, 43–44.
49. *Ibid.*, 45–49.

of method and to think in explicit universality what always happens." [50] Betti printed Gadamer's letter as a footnote in the same pamphlet in which he attacks Gadamer, so it is clear that Betti is hardly satisfied with this answer. For Betti, Gadamer is lost in a standardless existential subjectivity. In the Preface to the 1965 edition of *Wahrheit und Methode,* Gadamer again replies to Betti, this time emphasizing the nonsubjective character of understanding. The ontological turn of his book (which Betti deplores) leads Gadamer to view the functioning of the "historically operative consciousness" [51] not as a subjective but as an ontological process:

> The meaning of my investigation is not, in any case, to present a general theory of interpretation with differentiations to account for the different methods of special disciplines, as E. Betti has so excellently done, but to seek out what all ways of understanding have in common and to show that understanding is never a subjective procedure in relation to a given "object" but that it belongs to the operative history [*Wirkungsgeschichte*]—and this means, to the being—of what is understood. [52]

The point Gadamer is making will be further examined in Chapters 10 and 11, but at this point the fundamental contrast between Betti and Gadamer is clear. We are confronted with two very different conceptions of the scope and purpose of hermeneutics, the methods and kinds of thinking appropriate to it, and the essential character of the discipline as a field of study. With two very different definitions, resting on different philosophical foundations, the two thinkers formulate hermeneutics to fulfill very different purposes. Betti, following Dilthey in quest of a foundational discipline for the *Geisteswissenschaften,* looks for what is practical and useful to the interpreter. He wants norms to distinguish right from wrong interpretations, one type of interpretation from another. Gadamer, following Heidegger, asks such questions as: What is the ontological character of understanding? What kind of encounter with Being is involved in the hermeneutical process? How does tradition, the transmitted past, enter into and shape the act of understanding an historical text?

What is one to say of this conflict of definitions? As I shall

50. *Ibid.,* 51n.
51. "Wirkungsgeschichtliches Bewusstsein"; see *WM* 325-60.
52. *Ibid.,* Preface to 2d ed., xvii.

assert in the next chapter, the two positions are not totally antithetical. Rather, the two thinkers are working on different aspects of the hermeneutical problem. Obviously a basic choice must ultimately be made between a realistic and a phenomenological perspective; nevertheless, it can be admitted that for hermeneutics as a whole, both philosophical positions yield important approaches to the hermeneutical problem.

E. D. HIRSCH:
HERMENEUTICS AS THE LOGIC OF VALIDATION

IN 1967 E. D. HIRSCH, JR., published the first full-dress treatise in general hermeneutics written in English: *Validity in Interpretation*. In the years to come it will undoubtedly take its place among the significant American works on the theory of interpretation. In a systematic and carefully argued presentation, the book challenges some of the most cherished assumptions that have guided literary interpretation for some four decades. For instance, Hirsch maintains that the author's intention must be the norm by which the validity of any "interpretation" (explication of the verbal meaning of a passage) is measured. He argues, further, that this intention is a determinate entity about which objective evidence can be gathered and that, when the evidence is in hand, a determination of the meaning can be made which will be universally recognized as valid. Dilthey's dream of objectively valid interpretation would seem to be realized.

Of course the "verbal meaning" of a passage as determined by intensive philological analysis (both of the work and all external evidence that bears on its author's intentions) and the "significance" that same work may have today are two very different matters. But this is precisely Hirsch's point: endless confusion is created by lumping together "verbal meaning" and "significance" (meaningfulness for us), and this sin he ascribes to Gadamer, Bultmann, and the theologians of the New Hermeneutic.[53] In the language of Betti's attack on the same point, the *Bedeutung* (meaning) must be held separate from *Bedeutsamkeit* (significance),[54] or philology will fall

53. *VII* 246.
54. *HAMG* 28-29.

apart and the possibility of obtaining objective and valid results will vanish. Upon this distinction rests the integrity of philology and the possibility of objectivity.

The objective of hermeneutics, says Hirsch, is not to find the "significance" of a passage for us today but to make clear its verbal meaning. Hermeneutics is the philological discipline which sets forth the rules by which valid determinations of the verbal meaning of a passage may be achieved. Gadamer and the followers of Bultmann have not only wrongly brought in considerations that lie outside the real task of hermeneutics, but they have, Hirsch asserts, espoused a philosophical position which goes so far as to question whether it is even possible to hope for an objectively determinable meaning.

In essence, Hirsch argues that if it is held that the "meaning" of a passage (in the sense of the verbal meaning) can change, then there is no fixed norm for judging whether the passage is being interpreted correctly. Unless one recognizes the "glass slipper" of the original verbal meaning intended by the author, there is no way of separating Cinderella from the other girls.[55] This recalls Betti's objection to Gadamer's hermeneutics: that Gadamer does not provide a stable normative principle by which the "correct" meaning of a passage can be validly determined. Hirsch makes the author's intended verbal meaning the norm and goes even further to characterize verbal meaning as changeless, reproducible, and determinate. A brief quotation will show his reasoning and also give something of the Aristotelian flavor of his exposition:

> When, therefore, I say that a verbal meaning is determinate I mean that it is an entity which is self-identical. Furthermore, I also mean that it is an entity which always remains the same from one moment to the next—that it is changeless. Indeed, these criteria were already implied in the requirement that verbal meaning be reproducible, that it be always the same in different acts of construing. Verbal meaning, then, is what it is and not something else, and it is always the same. That is what I mean by determinacy.[56]

Hermeneutics here sets for itself the task of furnishing the theoretical justification for the determinacy of the object of interpretation and of setting forth norms by which the determinate, changeless, self-identical meaning can be understood.

55. *VII* 46.
56. *Ibid.*

Naturally, the task is also to say on what grounds one meaning may be chosen over another; such is the question of validity.
A hermeneutics that does not deal with validity is, in Hirsch's
view, not hermeneutics but something else. Like Betti, he
raises the objection that the Heideggerian current in hermeneutics sidesteps the issue of validity, without which there
simply cannot be a science of interpretation and a method of
arriving at correct interpretations.

To the objection that hermeneutics should deal with the
significance of the text for us today, and with the structures or
mechanisms by which the verbal meaning becomes meaningful to us, Hirsch replies that such is the province of literary
criticism and of areas other than hermeneutics.[57] Hermeneutics, strictly speaking, is "the modest, and in the old-fashioned
sense, philological effort to find out what the author meant."[58]
This is "the only proper foundation for criticism,"[59] but it is
not criticism; it is interpretation. Hermeneutics may well make
use of logical analysis, biography, and even the calculus of
probability (to determine the most probable among several
possible interpretations), but it remains essentially philology.
Even with this restriction, however, it is still broadly significant
and interdisciplinary; it is still a foundational discipline which
enunciates general principles of interpretation for any written
document, whether legal, religious, literary—or culinary.

What are we to say of this latest definition of hermeneutics
as the rules of the modest yet foundational effort to determine
the verbal meaning of a passage? The most striking thing about
it is what it leaves out; hermeneutics is not concerned with the
subjective process of understanding, as in Schleiermacher and
Dilthey, or with relating an understood meaning to the present
(criticism), but with the problem of umpiring between already
understood meanings so as to judge among conflicting possible
interpretations. It is a guide for the philologist who must decide
among several possibilities what is the most likely meaning of
a passage.

57. See esp. the crucial distinction in Chap. 4 of *VII*, titled "Understanding,
Interpretation, and Criticism." Hermeneutics as a logic of validation excludes
"understanding" on the one hand, and criticism on the other; it is a science or
set of principles for valid ascertaining of the verbal sense of the text, i.e., interpretation.
58. *Ibid.*, 57.
59. *Ibid.*

For Hirsch, then, the hermeneutical problem would not be one of "translation"—of how to span the historical distance between, say, the New Testament and today so that the meaningfulness of the text *for us* can emerge; the problem is simply a philological one of determining the verbal meaning intended by the author. Certainly Hirsch would acknowledge that relating a text to the present is a real problem, but he would deny that it belongs within the field of hermeneutics. To take this position, of course, he has to affirm that the verbal meaning is something independent, changeless, and determinate, which one can establish with objective certainty. Such a conception of verbal meaning rests on certain specifiable philosophical presuppositions, mainly realistic, or perhaps those of the early Husserl of *Logical Investigations,* whom Hirsch quotes to the effect that the same intentional object may be the focus of many different intentional acts.[60] The object, in this latter case, remains the same, an independent idea or essence.

Although it is beyond the scope of the present work to present a detailed critique of Hirsch's presuppositions, it is necessary to observe that when the hermeneutical problem is defined simply as the philological problem, then the whole complex development of twentieth-century thought on historical understanding is shoved aside as irrelevant to the practical determination of verbal meaning. Hermeneutics becomes a set of philological principles of interpretation which the English teacher, clergyman, or lawyer can use, without bothering his head about twentieth-century developments in philosophy of language, phenomenology, epistemology, or Heideggerian ontology. Who needs to trouble about Hegel, Heidegger, or Gadamer to collect data on the "real intention," the "changeless verbal meaning," of Milton's *Lycidas*? What about the problem in understanding what *Lycidas* can or should mean to us today? That, says Hirsch, is the business of the literary critic. But of course the literary critic will "not disdain" the modest technical job of work performed by the "interpreter"—"the only foundation for criticism"—even as the interpreter cherishes the pristine purity of the changeless, suprahistorical meaning in isolation from its significance for the present day.

But in fact the hermeneutical problem is not simply a philological problem, and it is not possible to relegate to limbo with

60. See Hirsch's interesting Appendix III, "An Excursis on Types," *ibid.,* 265-74.

Aristotelian definitions the bulk of understanding theory in Schleiermacher, Dilthey, Heidegger, and Gadamer, not to mention the contributions both inside and outside theology toward defining historical understanding. Hirsch argues that verbal meaning is in fact separable from significance since (1) we can in fact distinguish what the work meant to its author and what it means to us, and (2) otherwise, objective, repeatable meanings would be impossible. Yet how satisfactory is this argument? The fact that a mental object can be viewed from several perspectives does not make it historically changeless and eternal; and to argue that objectivity would otherwise be impossible is circular, since the possibility of objective and ahistorical knowledge is itself the question. Upon the validity of this distinction between meaning and significance, however, the validity of Hirsch's whole treatise on validity depends. But does understanding operate in the mechanical way Hirsch assumes? Or is this separation of meaning from significance strictly a reflexive operation, constructed *after* the act of understanding? Is not this form of hermeneutics perhaps actually textual criticism in disguise—a methodology for distinguishing reflexively between one understanding and another? Is it not merely a system or structure for the critic or philologist to use in judging whether one of Wordsworth's Lucy poems (to use an example cited by Hirsch) reflects a gloomy or affirmative view of life?

Certainly such a hermeneutical theory does not propose but presupposes a theory of how understanding itself takes place. (And it must be asked how adequate this theory of understanding is.) Rather, it begins after understanding. As Hirsch remarks: "The act of understanding is at first a genial (or a mistaken) guess, and there are no methods for making guesses, or rules for generating insights. The methodological activity of interpretation commences when we begin to test and criticize our guesses."[61] Or more pointedly, "The discipline of interpretation comprises the having of ideas and the testing of them. . . . [It] is founded not on a methodology of construction but on a logic of validation."[62] Hermeneutics is for Hirsch no longer the theory of understanding; it is the logic of validation. It is the theory by which it can be said, "This is what the author meant to say, not that."

Hirsch has succeeded brilliantly in his purpose: to construct

61. *Ibid.*, 207.
62. *Ibid.*

a single system for arriving at objectively verifiable meanings. But at what cost? First, in order to make the meaning determinate, he asserts that the norm or standard must always be the intention of the author. Second, in order to make this meaning objective, it has to be reproducible and changeless, so Hirsch asserts that verbal meaning, as meaning, is forever the same, and that it is separate and separable from its meaning for us as we encounter it in understanding. But can these assertions be accepted? Many of them rest on basically Aristotelian epistemological assumptions and a theory of meaning that must itself be defended on philosophical grounds.

Has Hirsch's redefinition of hermeneutics as the logic of validation really contributed to a grasp of the hermeneutical problem in its breadth and complexity, or has it oversimplified the problem? Ebeling asserts that "the object of hermeneutics is the word event as such"; thus hermeneutics reaches deeply into the question of reality and the nature of our participation in language. What happens to this vision of the hermeneutical problem? Can it be left to some other field, like philosophy of language? The ease with which Hirsch ignores the implications of understanding theory and philosophy of language suggests that the specialization he proposes for hermeneutics is inadvisable. How much narrower the problem of hermeneutics would be in theology today if it proposed simply to establish the author's probable verbal meaning! But immediately the question arises as to the nature of, say, Paul's meaning; was he trying to convey new self-understanding, or what? Can the norms for judging this be found in Paul himself? If such norms were allegedly found, on what basis would we decide whether these were valid? We are back in the present again. And it is just this point that needs to be emphasized; even the standards for, and of, objectivity are manufactured out of today's historical fabric. To recognize this is to recognize something of the complexity of the hermeneutical problem, a complexity which a narrowly restrictive definition of hermeneutics subtly encourages an interpreter to bypass.

So the hermeneutical debate goes on. On the one side are the defenders of objectivity and validation, who look to hermeneutics as the theoretical source for norms of validation; on the other side are the phenomenologists of the event of understanding, who stress the historical character of this "event," and consequently the limitations of all claims to "objective knowledge" and "objective validity."

5 / The Meaning and Scope of Hermeneutics

WHAT IS TO BE CONCLUDED with reference to the six definitions which have been discussed and the contemporary conflict between two radically different conceptions of the scope and purpose of hermeneutics? Can all these definitions, some of which do battle with each other, and these two especially conflicting conceptions of hermeneutics, be categorized by one term?

The answer is, I believe, yes. The six definitions light up different but important sides of the hermeneutical problem. And there is room for a hermeneutics oriented to method and validity, as well as for a hermeneutics focused on the historicality of understanding—even if the two are predicated on antithetical assumptions and do not harmonize on the issue of objectivity. There may be differences among the several forms of hermeneutics, but there are also many underlying similarities. The diverse directions in hermeneutical theory illustrate in themselves a hermeneutical principle: interpretation is shaped by the question with which the interpreter approaches his subject. It is best to acknowledge that the various directions of development in hermeneutics are thematizations of responses to questions the several interpreters themselves have raised.

Since Hirsch seeks the kind of hermeneutics that will furnish valid interpretations, from the outset the issue of validity shapes the course of his questioning. But what if the guiding question is no longer "How can I obtain valid interpretations?" but "What is the nature of understanding itself?" The preoccupation with valid judgments causes the question of what elements are involved in all understanding to be passed over; conversely, a focus on the essential nature of all understanding will tend to leave aside the necessary development of systems of distinguishing valid from invalid interpretations. Both questions are worthy, and their exploration makes a contribution to understanding the hermeneutical problem.

The hermeneutical problem as a whole, I believe, is too important and too complex to become the property of a single school of thought. One-sided and restrictive definitions of hermeneutics may serve limited purposes, but care should be taken not to make them absolute. Certainly debate on specific issues, like the character of historical understanding and historical objectivity, is in order; but the demand by Betti and Hirsch that Gadamer's hermeneutics should furnish an objective norm for distinguishing valid from invalid interpretations fails to take account of the basic intention of Gadamer's thinking: to examine the dynamics of understanding itself. Gadamer, had he wished to show a parallel lack of objectivity, could have asked why Betti neglects to discuss the ontological character of language, or why Hirsch presents no adequate account of the complex event of understanding itself. Such criticisms, which would ask a theory to do what it never proposed to do in the first place, are essentially indirect debates on the nature and scope of hermeneutics itself. They do not in themselves render the opposing theory invalid. Hermeneutics, in spite of the contemporary conflict, must remain a field of study and continuing problem area open to contributions from many different and sometimes conflicting traditions.

THE DOUBLE FOCUS OF HERMENEUTICS: EVENT OF UNDERSTANDING AND THE HERMENEUTICAL PROBLEM

THE HISTORICAL DEVELOPMENT OF HERMENEUTICS as an independent field seems to hold within itself two separate foci: one on the theory of understanding in a general sense, and the other on what is involved in the exegesis of linguistic texts, the hermeneutical problem. These two foci need not be either self-canceling or absolutely independent, yet they are best held in sufficient separateness for one to instruct the other.

Hermeneutics is true to its great past in Schleiermacher and Dilthey when it takes its bearings from a general theory of linguistic understanding. It must be willing to think through the nature of understanding and in the broadest possible terms to ask: What is understanding? What happens when I say, "I understand"? This latter question is specifically to emphasize the event-character of understanding. A theory of understanding is most relevant to hermeneutics when it takes lived experience, the event of understanding, as its starting point. In this way, thinking is oriented to a fact, an event in all its concreteness, rather than to an idea; it becomes a phenomenology of the event of understanding. Such a phenomenology of understanding is not to be conceived in a narrow and doctrinaire way, however, but as open to all other fields which can contribute to a fuller grasp of what and how understanding happens, such as epistemology, ontology, phenomenology of perception, learning theory, philosophy of symbols, logical analysis, and so on.

The second focus, designated as the "hermeneutical problem," is a specific instance of the event of understanding: it always involves language, the confronting of another human horizon, an act of historical penetration of the text. Hermeneutics needs to go ever more deeply into this complex act of understanding; it must struggle to formulate a theory of linguistic and historical understanding as it functions in text interpretation. Such a theory must be harmonized with and related to a general phenomenology of understanding; at the same time, it will itself contribute to such a general field.

This broad interpretation of the hermeneutical problem sees the event of understanding a text as including always a moment of relationship to the present; indeed, the absence of this relationship would immediately become a hermeneutical problem. The view of the hermeneutical problem presented by Hirsch would leave aside the moment of understanding itself and focus on the need to judge among several understandings; hermeneutics then becomes not the phenomenology of understanding but the logic of validation. The purpose of hermeneutics would then be narrowed to merely determining "what the author meant" and exclude the question of how this becomes meaningful to us. While the logic of validation must be considered a legitimate part of the hermeneutical problem, the hermeneutical problem understood in the wider sense poses the more fundamental challenge of grasping and being grasped by the meaningfulness of the text. The deeper problem, then, is that of achieving meaningful dialogue with a text in the first place, and must be based on the fullest possible definition of what understanding a text means; it is not simply that of arbitrating among competing interpretations.

THE POTENTIAL CONTRIBUTION OF OTHER FIELDS TO HERMENEUTICS

WHEN THE FOCI OF HERMENEUTICS are defined to include a general phenomenology of understanding and a specific phenomenology of the event of text interpretation, then the scope of hermeneutics becomes vast indeed. As has been said, however, the scope of the hermeneutical problem is such that hermeneutics cannot isolate itself as a closed and specialized field. Indeed, one of the great impediments to the historical development of nonspecialized hermeneutics has been that it has no home in an established discipline. The stepchild of theology, the ungainly offspring of philology, nontheological hermeneutics is only now coming of age as a field. However, with the interest in the subject being presently stirred by the New Hermeneutic, Betti, Gadamer, Hirsch, Ricoeur, and the later Heidegger, there is reason to hope for a brighter future.

If so, hermeneutics may indeed be in a fairly early stage of its development as a general discipline. Certainly the exploration of what other fields could contribute to hermeneutical theory has hardly begun in any systematic way. Ricoeur's brilliant study of Freud suggests the fruitful contribution which an exploration of an interpretive system can yield. Betti's monumental work covers a cross-section of interpretive disciplines in the humanities. Gadamer's essay in philosophical hermeneutics may be taken as showing the fruitful impact of Heidegger's ontological analysis of understanding.

Yet many other fields need to be explored as to the significance they might have for hermeneutical theory. For instance, there are the many areas of study concerned with language, such as linguistics, philosophy of language, logical analysis, translation theory, information theory, and theory of oral interpretation (speech). Literary criticism—not only the phenomenological variety in France and in the works of Roman

Ingarden but also contextualist New Criticism and myth criticism—needs to be explored for its significance for general interpretation theory. And phenomenology of language is indispensable for hermeneutical theory, not only the recent work by Merleau-Ponty, Gusdorf, Kwant, and others but also the contribution of Husserl, including the early *Logische Untersuchungen*.

Of course, many fields not specifically concerned with language have great potential importance for hermeneutics. The whole development of philosophy of mind and the debate in epistemology in our century cannot be ignored. Cassirer's work in this field, as well as his general philosophy of symbolic forms, is important to hermeneutical theory. Various forms of phenomenology—of perception, of musical understanding, of aesthetics—are helpful in showing the temporality and existential roots of understanding.

The philosophy of legal, historical, and theological interpretation—especially the recent New Hermeneutic and the earlier project of demythologizing—all bring out important elements in the phenomenon of interpretation. The questions of novelty and creativity in aesthetics as explored by Hausman and others are contributions relevant to the hermeneutical task of understanding what lies outside one's present horizon of understanding. The whole question of methodology in the philosophy of science, the experiments with participant-observation methods in sociology, the psychology of learning and of imagination—all are richly suggestive for new directions in thinking about this process we call interpretation. Many other areas could be named, but these are sufficient to suggest that hermeneutics could become an interdisciplinary crossroads for significant thought that might enable some of these fields to view their own problem areas in a more comprehensive context. Many concrete studies are needed to develop and clarify the significance of these fields for hermeneutical theory. The present work cannot undertake this, but a few books in the fields mentioned above have been included in Section C of the Bibliography.

In the chapters that follow I propose to clarify somewhat the breadth and complexity of the hermeneutical problem, and to point to a conception of hermeneutics broader than any that has hitherto been available in English. Professor Hirsch's book makes available a highly restricted definition of interpretation in terms of the logic of validation. The several recent books explaining the New Hermeneutic tend to treat hermeneutics largely in a theological context. The appearance of Gadamer's book in English will do much to broaden the current conception of hermeneutics. Yet the present essay will, I hope, help to clarify the significance of this anticipated event, for hermeneutics must be seen as more than a logic of philological validation, and as more than a vital new movement within contemporary theology. It is a comprehensive field focused on the event of textual understanding in all its ramifications. The present treatments of the subject fail also to suggest the possibilities of a basically phenomenological hermeneutic, as suggested by the phenomenological turn of the field in Heidegger and Gadamer. Through an expository presentation of hermeneutics in four thinkers who point toward the broader approach I have in mind, perhaps the foundation will be laid both for a more comprehensive conception of the field and for a dawning appreciation of its potential significance.

PART II
Four Major Theorists

6 / Two Forerunners
of Schleiermacher

IN ORDER TO APPRECIATE the nature and magnitude of Schleiermacher's contribution to the development of hermeneutical theory, it is necessary to consider the state of hermeneutics in his time, and in particular the conceptions of the field advanced by two of the great luminaries in the philology of the day, Friedrich Ast and Friedrich August Wolf.

Schleiermacher developed his concept of hermeneutics from its earliest groping formulations as aphorisms in 1805 and 1806 in more or less explicit critical dialogue with Ast and Wolf. His call for a new conception of hermeneutics which opened his lectures on the subject in 1819 refers in its first sentence to the two famous philologists,[1] and the title of his *Akademiereden* of 1829 was "On the Concept of Hermeneutics in Relation to F. A. Wolf's Indications and Ast's Manual."[2] So a knowledge of something of the work of Wolf and Ast is a prerequisite for understanding Schleiermacher. As we shall see, however, many of their conceptions are of continuing importance to hermeneutics, worthy in themselves of the attention of anyone seeking to penetrate the variant directions and complexity of hermeneutics as a whole.

1. "Die Hermeneutik als Kunst des Verstehens existirt noch nicht allgemein sondern nur mehrere specielle Hermeneutiken. Asts Erkl., S. 172, Wolf S. 37" (*H* 79).
2. "Ueber den Begriff der Hermeneutik, mit Bezug auf F. A. Wolfs Andeutungen und Asts Lehrbuch," *ibid.*, 123.

FRIEDRICH AST

FRIEDRICH AST (1778-1841) published two major works in philology in 1808: *Grundlinien der Grammatik, Hermeneutik und Kritik (Basic Elements of Grammar, Hermeneutics and Criticism)* and *Grundriss der Philologie (Outlines of Philology)*. Since Schleiermacher makes reference to the former, the present discussion will focus on it. *Grundlinien der Grammatik, Hermeneutik und Kritik* was conceived originally as an introduction to the larger *Grundriss*, and makes clear the aims and objects of philological study. For Ast, the basic aim is grasping the "spirit" of antiquity, which is most clearly revealed in the literary heritage.[3] The outer forms of antiquity all point to an inner form, an inner unity of being, harmonious in its parts, that may be called the *Geist* of antiquity. Philology is not a matter of dusty manuscripts and dry pedantry about grammar; it does not treat the factual and empirical as ends in themselves but as means to grasp the outer and inner content of a work as a unity. This unity points to the higher unity of "spirit," the source of the inner unity of individual works—an idea obviously derived from Herder's concept of *Volksgeist*, here the *Volksgeist* of Greek or Roman antiquity. Because of this encounter with "spirit," the study of philology has "spiritual" values; it serves a "pedagogical-ethical purpose": to become more like the Greeks. "Antiquity is not only the paradigm (*Muster*) of artistic and scientific cultivation *but of life in general*."[4]

But the spirit of antiquity cannot be grasped without looking at its words; language is the prime medium for the transmission of the spiritual. We must study the writings of antiquity, and to do this we need grammar, which accounts for the first term in the title: *Grammatik*. In addition, reading an ancient writer presupposes certain fundamental principles to understand and explain him correctly, "thus, the study of ancient languages must always be bound up with hermeneutics."[5] Hermeneutics is here clearly separated from the study of grammar. It is the theory of extracting the *geistige* (spiritual) meaning of the text. Our common participation in *Geist* is the reason

3. V I, 33. The brief discussions here of Ast and Wolf are largely indebted to Joachim Wach's chapters in V I: 31-62 on Ast, and 62-82 on Wolf.

4. *Ibid.*, 36.

5. *Ibid.*, 37.

that we can apprehend the meaning of writings transmitted from antiquity. *Geist* is the focal point of all life and its permanent formative principle.[6] Ast asks: "Would it be possible for us to understand the strangest and previously most unknown viewpoints, feelings, and ideas, *if* all that is and can be were not in some primordial way bound up in *Geist*? And then it is so unfolded, like the one eternal Light breaking into a thousand colors. . . ."[7]

The conception of the spiritual unity of the humanities (*Einheit des Geistes*) is the basis of Ast's conception of the hermeneutical circle. That is, because *Geist* is the source of all development and all becoming, the imprint of the spirit of the whole (*Geist des Ganzen*) is found in the individual part; the part is understood from the whole and the whole from the inner harmony of its parts.[8] Applied to antiquity, this means, according to Ast, "One can only rightly grasp the combined unity of the spirit of antiquity if one grasps the individual revelations of it in individual ancient works, and on the other hand, the *Geist* of an individual author cannot be grasped apart from placing in its higher relationship [to the whole]."[9]

The task of hermeneutics, then, becomes the clarification of the work through the development of its meaning internally and the relationship of its inner parts to each other and to the larger spirit of the age.[10] This task is explicitly divided by Ast into three parts, or forms, of understanding: (1) the "historical," that is, understanding in relation to the content of the work, which could be artistic, scientific, or general; (2) the "grammatical," that is, understanding in relation to the language; and (3) the "*geistige*," that is, understanding the work in relation to the total view of the author and the total view (*Geist*) of the age. The first two "hermeneutics" in their various relationships and possibilities had already been developed, as we have noted, by Semler and by Ernesti respectively.[11] It is the third which is Ast's distinctive contribution, and which is further

6. *GGHK* 7; quoted in V I, 38.
7. *GGHK* 166; V I, 38-39.
8. Schleiermacher properly credits Ast with asserting the basic principle of the hermeneutical circle, *H* 141. *GGHK* 178; V I, 41.
9. *GGHK* 179; V I, 44.
10. *GGHK* 174-75; V I, 45.
11. Semler and Ernesti, along with other Enlightenment writers on hermeneutics, are treated in F. W. Farrar, *History of Interpretation*, and more briefly in Robert M. Grant, *A Short History of the Interpretation of the Bible*.

developed in Schleiermacher and in the great nineteenth-century philologist August Böckh. In Ast we already find some of the basic conceptions in Schleiermacher's hermeneutic: the hermeneutical circle, the relation of the part to the whole, the metaphysics of genius or individuality. Individuality? Yes, for the *geistige*, according to Ast, makes us aware not only of the general spirit of the age but of the specific individual's spirit (genius), the spirit of the author.

Applied to a Pindaric ode, the threefold pattern is as follows: The first level (the historical) refers to the object (*Gegenstand*), which in this particular Pindaric ode is the *Kampfspiele*, (contest), of which the poet sings; the second level (the grammatical) refers to the plastic presentation in language (not mere grammatical analysis); the third level (the *geistige*) refers to its spirit glowing with love of country, with courage and heroic virtue. The historical, grammatical, and *geistige* levels are essentially what we would call the matter, form, and the spirit of the work. And the spirit of the work reveals both the general spirit of the age and the individuality (the "genius") of its author; indeed, it is a composite of these, interacting with and mutually illuminating each other.[12]

Ast makes a distinction between levels of understanding, as just discussed, and levels of explanation. Paralleling the historical, grammatical, and *geistige* levels of understanding, therefore, are three levels of explanation: the hermeneutic of the letter (*Hermeneutik des Buchstabens*), the hermeneutic of the sense (*Hermeneutik des Sinnes*), and the hermeneutic of the spirit (*Hermeneutik des Geistes*). The hermeneutic of the letter is fairly broadly conceived, for it includes both the explanation of words (which would seem to involve grammatical understanding) and the explanation of the factual context (*Verstehen der Sache*) as well as of the historical setting (historical understanding). This first hermeneutic requires not only a factual acquaintance with the historical milieu but also a knowledge of the language, its historical transformations and individual characteristics. The hermeneutic of the sense or of the "meaning" refers to the exploration of the genius of the age and of the author. It determines the meaning as it takes a specific direction because of the place in which it occurs (*die Bedeutung in dem Zusammenhang einer gegebenen Stelle*). For instance,

12. *GGHK* 183–84; V I, 48.

a statement in Aristotle may have a different meaning than a literally very similar statement in Plato,[13] and even within the same work two literally similar passages may vary in their sense or meaning with their placement in relation to the work as a whole. For the intricacies of such determinations, it is necessary to have a knowledge of literary history, of the particular form being used, and of the life and other works of the author in order to capture accurately the sense of a given passage.

The third level, the hermeneutic of the spirit, seeks out the controlling idea (*Grundidee,* foundational idea), the view of life (*Anschauung,* viewpoint, especially in "historical" authors), and the basic conception (*Begriff,* especially in philosophical works) which finds expression or embodiment in the work. In the case of seeking the "view of life," there is a multiplicity in the unfolding of life; when the "basic conception" is sought, however, we find the unity of form behind the multiplicity. For Ast, the concept of a controlling idea represents a combination of both the other moments of meaning, but only the greatest authors and artists achieve this full and harmonious synthesis in which conceptual content and view of life stand in balanced complement within the controlling idea.

Since the emphasis on the idea is a very familiar aspect of German romantic thought, it is not surprising to find it in Ast's hermeneutics. Worthy of critical note is the fact that, for Ast, the harmonious reconciliation of view of life in the "ground idea" leads to *transcendence* of the temporal: "All temporality is dissolved in *geistige* explanation." [14] Thus the romantic interest in history is subordinated to the idea, just as is the romantic admiration of genius and individuality; all are manifestations of *Geist.* The twentieth-century Heideggerian assertion of the radically historical character of human reality (and thus reality itself) is foreign to the idealistic presuppositions of Ast. Neither in the context of the Enlightenment rationalistic presuppositions nor in those of the Romantics does history become really historical; it is only the raw material for deducing an atemporal truth or an atemporal *Geist.*

One other idea in Ast's thinking heralds things to come in hermeneutics: the concept of the process of understanding

13. *GGHK* 195-96; V I, 56.
14. *GGHK* 199; V I, 57.

itself as *Nachbildung*, reproduction. In the *Grundlinien*, Ast views the process of understanding as a repetition of the creative process. This view of the way understanding takes place is essentially similar to that of Schlegel, Schleiermacher, and, later, Dilthey and Simmel. The hermeneutical significance of this lies in relating explication to the creative process as a whole: interpretation and interpretive problem must obviously now be related to the processes of knowledge and creativity. With this concept of understanding as *Nachbildung*, hermeneutics steps significantly beyond the philological and theological hermeneutics of the preceding age. It is now connected with the side of the understanding process related to the theory of artistic creation, for understanding repeats the artist's process of creation. Previously interpretation had not been seen in connection with any theory of artistic creation. Joachim Wach goes so far as to say that to make this connection was one of Ast's main contributions to the development of hermeneutical theory.[15]

The bogey of psychologism should not frighten us away from considering the relation of the theory of artistic creation to the theory of literary understanding and, therefore, to literary interpretation. While we may not agree with Ast that, in understanding, the artist's creative processes are repeated—the creation has already taken place—it may be asserted that the experience communicated in the work must somehow rise again as event for the reader. In the rationalist hermeneutics of the Enlightenment there is no basis for relating the artist's creative process to that of the reader, then, while in the idealist hermeneutics of Romanticists Ast and Schleiermacher the processes are clearly grounded in the fundamental operations of understanding. Similarly, in the realist literary interpretation practiced by English and American critics today, the question of the process of creation by which a literary work came into existence is irrelevant, whereas for the phenomenological hermenuetics of the present day, both creation and interpretation are grounded in understanding. We see from this parallel

15. "Herder führt zuerst in grösserem Stil eine literarkritisch-ästhetische Betrachtung der Bibel durch. . . . Bis dahin allerdings hatte man wenig auf die Zusammenhänge von Interpretation und Theorie des Schaffens geachtet: hier hat vor *Boeckh* vor allem *Humboldt* gewirkt. Ich sehe gerade darin einen Teil von Asts Bedeutung für die Geschichte der hermeneutischen Theorie, dass er—ohne dass ich philologische Vorgänger zu nennen wüsste—auf diese Zusammenhänge hingewiesen hat" (V I, 52).

how decisive is our underlying theory of knowledge and our theory of the ontological status of a work, for they determine in advance the shape of our theory and practice in literary interpretation.

FRIEDRICH AUGUST WOLF

FRIEDRICH AUGUST WOLF (1759-1824) was the more colorful and well known of the two philologists. He was also less systematic, for though Ast's *Grundlinien* constitute something of a system, Wolf cared little for system. In his *Vorlesung über die Enzyklopädie der Altertumswissenschaft*, he defined hermeneutics as "the science of the rules by which the meaning of signs is recognized." [16] The rules would naturally vary with the object, and thus there is a hermeneutic for poetry, for history, or for laws. Wolf asserted that every rule should be arrived at through practice; hermeneutics is thus basically a practical rather than a theoretical endeavor. It is a collection of rules.

The aim of hermeneutics, according to Wolf, is "to grasp the written or even spoken thoughts of an author as he would have them to be grasped." [17] Interpretation is dialogue, dialogue with an author. It is surely not falling into psychologism to suggest that a work *is* an effort at communication, and that the aim of hermeneutics is perfect communication, that is, to grasp the subject or idea of the author as he would have it grasped. Wolf asserts that the interpreter must be "temperamentally suited" to understanding the subject in order to explain it to others. He must have a general talent for empathizing with the thoughts of others; he must have "that lightness of soul" which "quickly attunes itself to foreign thoughts." [18] Without an aptitude for dialogue, for entering into the mental world of another person, explanation—therefore, hermeneutics—is impossible.

As with Ast, explanation must be grounded in understanding, and understanding is distinguished from explanation. The meaning of an image is directly grasped in understanding.

16. "Die Wissenschaft von den Regeln, aus denen die Bedeutung der Zeichen erkannt wird" (*VEA* 290; *V* I, 67).
17. "[Die] geschriebene oder auch bloss mündlich vorgetragene Gedanken eines ander ebenso zu fassen, wie er sie gefasst haben will" (*VEA* 293; *V* I, 68).
18. *VEA* 273; *V* I, 72.

A further step is taken in giving an oral or written explanation of it. We understand for ourselves but we explain to others, according to Wolf. As soon as we determine that explanation is our task, we must also know for whom the explanation must be designed. The form and the content of an explanation will vary depending on whether the interpretation is for the enthusiastic beginner, the disinterested reader, or the discerning scholar interested in minor shades of difference. But as Wolf puts it in a picturesque mixture of Latin and German: *"Niemand kann interpretari, nisi subtiliter intellexerit."* [19] Hermeneutics inevitably has two sides, then: the understanding *(verstehenden)* and the explaining *(erklarenden)*.

Wolf, like Ast, propounds a threefold hermeneutics; but it lacks Ast's metaphysics of *Geist* in the third stage. Rather, it is more practical. The three levels or kinds of hermeneutics are: *interpretatio grammatica, historica,* and *philosophica.* [20] The grammatical deals with all that the understanding of language can furnish to aid interpretation. The historical is concerned not only with the historical facts of the time but also with the factual knowledge of the author's life, so as to arrive at a knowledge of what the author knew. Naturally, the general historical facts are important, even to the point of knowing the physical and geographical characteristics of the country. In short, the interpreter should have as much historical knowledge as possible. The philosophical level of interpretation serves as a logical check or control on the other two levels. Everywhere in Wolf there is the strong emphasis on the practical and factual; yet in the welter of rules for meeting different problems, there is no basic systematic unity. The rules remain an aggregate of observations on specific difficulties in interpretation.

This brief treatment of the hermeneutics of Ast and Wolf helps to introduce the philological hermeneutics of Schleiermacher's time. Although the prominent Ernesti and his follower, Morus, wrote in Latin, both Ast and Wolf wrote in German. The elements of "grammatical" interpretation laid down by Ernesti are still foundational in Ast and Wolf; but almost as if owing to the use of German, the grasp of the historical is more nuanced and the interest in it more profound. With the

19. *VEA* 273; *V I,* 74.
20. *VEA* 290–95; *V I,* 77–78.

transition into German, there is a deepening of the historical and philosophical levels of interpretation. This trend toward the philosophical is carried over into Schleiermacher, where the grammatical interpretation is still foundational, yet the insistence on philosophical consistency is still more pronounced as hermeneutics moves toward psychological interpretation and toward being based on a systematic conception of the operations of human understanding in dialogue.

7 / Schleiermacher's Project
of a General Hermeneutics

"HERMENEUTICS AS THE ART OF UNDERSTANDING does not exist as a general field, only a plurality of specialized hermeneutics."[1] This programmatic assertion, with which Schleiermacher opened his lectures on hermeneutics in 1819, enunciates in one sentence his fundamental aim: to frame a general hermeneutics as the art of understanding. This art, Schleiermacher contended, is in its essence the same whether the text be a legal document, a religious scripture, or a work of literature. Certainly there are differences among these various kinds of texts, and for this reason each discipline develops theoretical tools for its peculiar problems, but beneath these differences lies the more fundamental unity. The texts are in language and thus grammar is used to find the meaning of a sentence; a general idea interacts with the grammatical structure to form the meaning, no matter what the type of document. If the principles of all understanding of language were formulated, these would comprise a general hermeneutics. Such a hermeneutics could serve as the basis and core of all "special" hermeneutics.

But such a hermeneutics, Schleiermacher asserted, did not yet exist! Instead, there were diverse special "hermeneutics," primarily the philological, the theological, and the legal. And even within philological hermeneutics, there was no systematic coherence. On the contrary, Friedrich August Wolf asserted that a different hermeneutic was needed for history, poetry, religious texts, and by extension for subvarieties within each of these classifications. Hermeneutics, for Wolf, was a very

1. *H* 79. See Chap. 6, note 1.

practical thing: a body of wisdom for meeting specific problems of interpretation. There were rules and advice for the most diverse problems of interpretation, tailored to the particular linguistic and historical difficulties posed by ancient texts in Hebrew, Greek, and Latin. Hermeneutics was a body of theory to assist in the task of translating ancient texts, but the theory had simply accumulated as more and more elements were seen to be important to the understanding of ancient texts. The great Astius' hermeneutics had a more philosophical bent but still tried to be encyclopedic and based itself on a metaphysical idealism unacceptable to Schleiermacher. Still missing was the disposition to examine the foundational act of all hermeneutics: the act of understanding, the act of a living, feeling, intuiting human being.

In 1799 Schleiermacher had already, in his famous tract addressed to the cultured despisers of religion, decisively rejected metaphysics and morals as a basis for the phenomenon of religion. Religion had to do not with man living according to some rational ideal but rather living, acting, and feeling in relation to his creaturely dependence on God. Similarly, hermeneutics was held by Schleiermacher to be related to. the concrete, existing, acting human being in the process of understanding dialogue. When we start with the conditions that pertain to all dialogue, when we turn away from rationalism, metaphysics, and morality and examine the concrete, actual situation involved in understanding, then we have the starting point for a viable hermeneutics that can serve as a core for special hermeneutics, such as the biblical.

Even the art of explanation, which had constituted a large part of hermeneutical theory, was held by Schleiermacher to fall outside of hermeneutics. "As soon as explication becomes more than the outside of understanding, it becomes the art of presentation. Only what Ernesti calls the *subtilitas intelligendi* [acuteness of understanding] genuinely belongs to hermeneutics." [2] Explication imperceptibly becomes the art of rhetorical

2. "Eigentlich gehört nur das zur Hermeneutik was Ernesti Prol. 4 [*IINT*] subtilitas intelligendi nennt. Denn die [subtilitas] explicandi sobald sie mehr ist als die äussere Seite des Verstehens ist wiederum ein Object der Hermeneutik und gehört zur Kunst des Darstellens" (*H* 31). This aphorism probably dates from 1805 and is among Schleiermacher's earliest written comments on the subject of hermeneutics. At the same time it is one of his most significant insights, for it marks hermeneutics as the art of understanding rather than of explaining.

formulation instead of the art of "understanding." In the conditions of dialogue, it is one operation to formulate something and bring it to speech; it is quite another and distinct operation to understand what is spoken. Hermeneutics, Schleiermacher contended, dealt with the latter. This fundamental distinguishing of speaking and understanding formed the basis for a new direction in hermeneutics, and it opened the way to a systematic basis for hermeneutics in the theory of understanding. If hermeneutics is no longer basically devoted to clarifying the varying practical problems in interpreting different kinds of texts, then it can take the act of understanding as its true starting point: hermeneutics becomes in Schleiermacher truly the "art of understanding."

And so Schleiermacher takes as the starting point of his hermeneutics this general question: How is all or any utterance, whether spoken or written, really "understood"? The understanding situation is one of a dialogical relationship. In every such relationship, there is a speaker, who constructs a sentence to express his meaning, and a hearer. The hearer receives a series of mere words, and suddenly through some mysterious process can divine their meaning. This mysterious, even divinatory, process is the hermeneutical process. It is the true locus of hermeneutics. Hermeneutics is the art of hearing. We now turn to some of the principles of this art or process.

UNDERSTANDING AS A RECONSTRUCTIVE PROCESS

FOR SCHLEIERMACHER, understanding as an art is the reexperiencing of the mental processes of the text's author. It is the reverse of composition, for it starts with the fixed and finished expression and goes back to the mental life from which it arose. The speaker or author constructed a sentence; the hearer penetrates into the structures of the sentence and the thought. Thus interpretation consists of two interacting moments: the "grammatical" and the "psychological" (in the larger sense of everything encompassed by the psychic life of the author). The principle upon which this reconstruction stands, whether grammatical or psychological, is that of the hermeneutical circle.

THE HERMENEUTICAL CIRCLE

UNDERSTANDING is a basically referential operation; we understand something by comparing it to something
we already know. What we understand forms itself into systematic unities, or circles made up of parts. The circle as a
whole defines the individual part, and the parts together form
the circle. A whole sentence, for instance, is a unity. We understand the meaning of an individual word by seeing it in reference
to the whole of the sentence; and reciprocally, the sentence's
meaning as a whole is dependent on the meaning of individual
words. By extension, an individual concept derives its meaning
from a context or horizon within which it stands; yet the
horizon is made up of the very elements to which it gives meaning. By dialectical interaction between the whole and the part,
each gives the other meaning; understanding is circular, then.
Because within this "circle" the meaning comes to stand, we
call this the "hermeneutical circle."

Of course the concept of the hermeneutical circle involves a
logical contradiction; for, if we must grasp the whole before
we can understand the parts, then we shall never understand
anything. Yet we have asserted that the part derives its meaning
from the whole. And surely, on the other hand, we cannot start
with a whole, undifferentiated into parts. Is the concept of the
hermeneutical circle therefore invalid? No; rather, we must
say that logic cannot fully account for the workings of understanding. Somehow, a kind of "leap" into the hermeneutical
circle occurs and we understand the whole and the parts together. Schleiermacher left room for such a factor when he saw
understanding as partly a comparative and partly an intuitive
and divinatory matter. To operate at all, the hermeneutical
circle assumes an element of intuition.

With its spatial image, the hermeneutical circle suggests
an area of shared understanding. Since communication is a
dialogical relation, there is assumed at the outset a community
of meaning shared by the speaker and the hearer. This seems to
involve another contradiction: what is to be understood must
already be known. But is this not the case? Is it not vain to speak
of love to one who has not known love, or of the joys of learning
to those who reject it? One must already have, in some measure, a knowledge of the matter being discussed. This may be

termed the minimal preknowledge necessary for understanding, without which one cannot leap into the hermeneutical
circle. Take a common example, the experience of initial
unintelligibility in reading a great author, say Kierkegaard,
Nietzsche, or Heidegger: the problem is that of acquiring a
grasp of the whole direction of the author's thought without
which individual assertions and even whole works do not speak
meaningfully. Sometimes a single sentence will illuminate
and draw all that was previously without coherence into a
meaningful whole, precisely because it suggests "the whole
thing" about which the author has been speaking.

The hermeneutical circle, then, operates not only on the
linguistic level but also on the level of the "matter" being
discussed. Both the speaker and the hearer must share the
language and the subject of their discourse. Both on the level
of the medium of discourse (language) and the material of
discourse (the subject) the principle of preknowledge—or the
hermeneutical circle—operates in every act of understanding.

GRAMMATICAL INTERPRETATION AND, PSYCHOLOGICAL INTERPRETATION

IN SCHLEIERMACHER'S LATER THINKING there is
an increasing tendency to separate the sphere of language from
the sphere of thought. The former is the province of "grammatical" interpretation, while the latter Schleiermacher first
called "technical" (*technische*) and then later "psychological."
Grammatical interpretation proceeds by locating the assertion
according to objective and general laws; the psychological
side of interpretation focuses on what is subjective and individual. According to Schleiermacher, "Just as every speech has
a twofold relationship, both to the whole of the language and to
the collected thinking of the speaker, so also there exists in
all understanding of the speech two moments: understanding
it as something drawn out of language and as a 'fact' in the
thinking of the speaker." [3] To the moment of language belongs
the "grammatical" interpretation, and Schleiermacher regarded
this as essentially a negative, general, rather boundary-setting
procedure in which the structure within which the thought

3. *Ibid.*, 80.

operates is set forth. The psychological interpretation, however, seeks the individuality of the author, his peculiar genius. For this, a certain congeniality with the author is required; this is not a boundary-setting operation but the truly positive side of interpretation.

Of course both sides of interpretation are necessary and in fact constantly interact. Individual usages of language bring about changes in the language itself, yet an author finds himself over against language and obliged to stamp his own individuality upon it. The interpreter understands the individuality of the author in reference to the general but also in a positive, almost direct and intuitive way. Just as the hermeneutical circle involves the part and the whole, the grammatical and psychological interpretation as a unity involve the specific and the general; this latter kind of interpretation is general and boundary-setting as well as individual and positive. The grammatical interpretation shows the work in relation to language, both in the structure of sentences and in the interacting parts of a work, and also to other works of the same literary type; so we may see the principle of parts and whole at work in grammatical interpretation. Likewise, the individuality of the author and work must be seen in the context of the larger facts of his life and in contrast to other lives and works. The principle of the interaction and reciprocal illumination of the part and the whole is basic to both sides of interpretation.

All of this presupposes the goal of hermeneutics as the reconstruction of the mental experience of the text's author, a point that is especially clear in the statement of 1819: "The art [of interpretation] can develop its rules only out of a positive formula, and this is: the historical and divinatory, objective and subjective reconstructing of a given utterance." [4] Schleiermacher obviously wishes to reexperience what the author experienced and does not see the utterance apart from its author. Yet it is well to emphasize that this reexperiencing need not be seen as "psychoanalysis" of the author; rather, it merely asserts that understanding is an art of reconstructing the thinking of another person. In other words, the objective is not to assign motives or causes for the author's feelings (psychoanalysis) but to reconstruct the thought itself of another person through interpretation of his utterance.

4. *Ibid.*, 87.

In fact, the full reconstruction of the individuality of an author can never proceed through analysis of causes; this would remain hopelessly general. For the heart of psychological interpretation, a basically intuitive approach is required. A grammatical approach can use the comparative method and proceed from the general to the particularities of the text; the psychological approach uses both the comparative and the "divinatory." "The divinatory [method] is that in which one transforms oneself into the other person in order to grasp his individuality directly."[5] For this moment of interpretation, one goes out of himself and transforms himself into the author so that he can grasp in full immediacy the latter's mental process. Nevertheless, the objective is not ultimately to "understand" the author from a psychological standpoint; rather it is to gain fullest access to that which is meant in the text.

HERMENEUTICAL UNDERSTANDING AS UNDERSTANDING OF STYLE

THE DISCUSSION of Schleiermacher's emphasis on the psychological and intuitive may cause us to forget the strong insistence on the centrality of language which is present from the beginning to the end of his speculations on hermeneutics. Not only is grammar an indispensable element in guiding the focus of our interpretation, but the psychological revelation of individuality is expressed in a fundamental way in the author's particular style. Thus no matter how deep the special "talent" for the individual knowledge of other human beings, unless this talent is combined with the talent of linguistic insight both as the grammatical boundary-setting and the psychological penetration of the individuality of the author through his style, no adequate understanding will result. We know man in all his individuality through style; in 1819 Schleiermacher summed up the importance of style pungently: "The fulfilled understanding of style is the whole goal of hermeneutics."[6]

5. *Ibid.*, 109.
6. *Ibid.*, 108.

HERMENEUTICS AS A SYSTEMATIC SCIENCE

SCHLEIERMACHER'S HERMENEUTICAL SPECULATION has the objective of making the loosely organized "aggregate of observations" into a unity with systematic coherence. Indeed, his intentions went further than this: first to posit the idea that understanding operates according to laws that may be discovered, and then to enunciate some of the laws or principles by which understanding occurs. This hope may be summed up in the word "science"; what he sought was not a set of rules, as in earlier hermeneutics, but a set of laws by which understanding operates—a science of understanding, which could guide the process of extracting meaning from a text.[7]

FROM A LANGUAGE-CENTERED TO A SUBJECTIVITY-CENTERED HERMENEUTICS

UNTIL AS RECENTLY AS 1959, the prevailing conception of Schleiermacher's hermeneutics was necessarily based on a posthumously published volume in his collected works, edited by his friend and student, Friedrich Lucke.[8] This volume, published in 1838, was only in part taken from the author's own manuscripts, most of it being pieced together from student notes. Although Schleiermacher left behind him notes in his own hand dating from 1805, the 1838 volume contained little from these notes before 1819. In the late 1950's Heinz Kimmerle carefully went through Schleiermacher's unpublished papers in the Berlin Library and put together in chronological order all the writings on hermeneutics in Schleiermacher's own hand. For the first time it became possible to trace with accuracy and confidence the development of Schleiermacher's

---

7. Understanding as such remains an art, of course. As Richard R. Niebuhr rightly observes in his illuminating treatment of Schleiermacher's hermeneutics (pp. 72-134 in his *Schleiermacher On Christ and Religion*): The act of interpreting was for Schleiermacher "something personal and creative as well as scientific, an imaginative reconstitution of the selfhood of the speaker or writer. Such an effort of empathy must always go far beyond the principles of philological science into the realm of art" (p. 79). In this regard, see *H* 82.
   8. *H&K.*

own thinking on the project of a "general hermeneutics." [9]

What emerges in this edition is not merely a fuller picture of Schleiermacher's hermeneutics but a hitherto unknown part of Schleiermacher—the earlier, language-centered and less psychological Schleiermacher. In some twenty pages of aphorisms on hermeneutics dating between 1805 and 1809 and in the first tentative drafts during the period 1810-1819 Schleiermacher proposes a fundamentally language-centered hermeneutics. From the beginning, apparently, Schleiermacher had in mind a general, foundational hermeneutics divided into two basic parts: the grammatical (objective) and the technical (subjective). Of course the decisive turning-away from philological objectivity and starting from the conditions pertaining to dialogue still prevail in the pre-1819 writings. Sometime in the period between 1810 and 1819, Schleiermacher wrote that the task of hermeneutics "proceeds from two different points: understanding in language and understanding into the speaker." [10] An earlier aphorism had stated that one must have an understanding of man himself in order to understand what he speaks, and yet one comes to know what man is from his speech. [11] Hermeneutics is the art of understanding the speaker in what is spoken, but language is still the key. In another early aphorism, he asserts: "Everything to be presupposed in hermeneutics is only language and everything to be found also; that wherein the other objective and subjective presuppositions belong must be found through [or from out of] language." [12]

The decisive element in the move away from a language-centered hermeneutics to a psychologically oriented hermeneutics, according to Kimmerle, was the gradual relinquishment of the conception of the identity of thought and language. The reason for this, says Kimmerle, was a philosophical one: Schleiermacher saw as his task the mediation between the innerness of transcendental speculative philosophy and the externalness of positive, empirical science. He presupposed a discrepancy between the ideal, inner essence and the outer appearance. Thus the text could not be seen as the direct mani-

---

9. See the valuable introduction in H 9-24, and his article, "Hermeneutical Theory or Ontological Hermeneutics," HH 107-21.

10. H 56.

11. Ibid., 44.

12. Ibid., 38.

festation of inner mental process but something given up to the empirical exigencies of language. Ultimately, then, the task of hermeneutics came to be that of transcending language in order to get at the inner process. It is still necessary to go through language, but language is no longer seen as fully equivalent to thought. On the other hand, as late as 1813 Schleiermacher had asserted: "Essentially and inwardly, thought and its expression are completely the same." [13] And the fact that Schleiermacher did not refer to his hermeneutics as a methodology *(Kunstlehre)* until 1829 is evidence of his own reluctance to abandon the fundamental conception of the identity of thought and expression.

Yet he did in fact abandon it, and thus the mental process reconstructed in hermeneutics is no longer conceived of as intrinsically linguistic but as some sort of elusive inner function of individuality separate from the individuality of language. At this point strength is added to the contemporary view, voiced by Kimmerle and Gadamer, that Schleiermacher goes astray and gives up the more fruitful possibility of a truly language-centered hermeneutics and falls into bad metaphysics. [14] Of course Schleiermacher was pushed toward these conclusions not only by his own idealistic metaphysics [15] but also by the assumption that the aim of hermeneutics is the reconstruction of the mental process of the author. But this assumption is questionable, for a text is understood not by reference to some vague inner mental process but by reference to the subject, the matter, to which the text is referring. Schleiermacher in his earlier hermeneutical thinking had held a position closer to present conceptions by firmly maintaining that an individual's thinking, and indeed his whole being, is essentially determined through language, in which an understanding of his self and world is given. Only in the face of a direct contradiction to his larger systematic position did Schleiermacher give up this insight, to the detriment of his own project. The fruitful new starting point apparent in his early thinking—a truly language-

13. *Ibid.*, 21.
14. See "Schleiermachers Entwurf einer universalen Hermeneutik," *WM* 172-85, esp. 179-83. See also the paper titled "The Problem of Language in Schleiermacher's Hermeneutics" which Gadamer read at the Consultation on Schleiermacher, Commemorating the 200th Anniversary of his Birth, February 29, 1968, at Vanderbilt Divinity School.
15. See *WM* 179 regarding the concepts of individuality and genius in relation to Schleiermacher's hermeneutics.

centered hermeneutics based on the actual conditions for understanding a partner in dialogue—is surrendered. Hermeneutics becomes psychological, the art of determining or reconstructing a mental process, a process which is no longer seen as essentially linguistic at all. Style is still considered a key to the individuality of an author, but it is seen as pointing to a nonlinguistic individuality of which it is merely an empirical manifestation.

THE SIGNIFICANCE OF SCHLEIERMACHER'S PROJECT OF A GENERAL HERMENEUTICS

REGARDLESS OF THE PSYCHOLOGIZING ELEMENT in the later Schleiermacher, his contribution to hermeneutics marks a turning point in its history. For hermeneutics is no longer seen as a specifically disciplinary matter belonging to theology, literature, or law; it is the art of understanding any utterance in language. A luminous early aphorism states that hermeneutics is precisely the way a child grasps the meaning of a new word.[16] The sentence structure and the context of meaning are the guides for the child and are the systems of interpretation for a general hermeneutics. Hermeneutics is seen as starting from the conditions of dialogue; Schleiermacher's was a dialogical hermeneutic which regrettably did not realize the creative implications of its dialogical nature but was blinded by its own desire for laws and systematic coherence.[17] Yet just this defect (from our present point of view) pointed hermeneutics in a new direction, toward becoming a science.

As we shall see, Dilthey continued this direction in his quest for "objectively valid" knowledge and in his assumption that the task of hermeneutics is discovering the laws and principles of understanding. These assumptions could be criti-

16. "Jedes Kind kommt nur durch Hermeneutik zur Wortbedeutung" (*H* 40). Gadamer calls attention to Schleiermacher's assertion that "Hermeneutik ist die Kunst, Missverstand zu vermeiden" (*H & K* 29; *WM* 173).
17. See Niebuhr, *op. cit.*, pp. 81 ff., regarding the dialogical character of thinking itself according to Schleiermacher. Niebuhr emphasizes the relation of Schleiermacher's hermeneutics to his *Dialektik* and to his interest in ethics; since the interpreter "feels into" the moral being of an author, interpretation itself becomes a moral act (p. 92).

cized for a shortcoming in historical understanding, since they assume that it is possible to occupy a point above or outside of history from which atemporal "laws" can be devised. But the movement toward a hermeneutics which takes the understanding problem as its starting point was a fruitful contribution to interpretive theory. Only after many years would the assertion be advanced that the universals in understanding which Schleiermacher saw in scientific terms could better be seen in historical terms, that is, in terms of the intrinsically historical structure of understanding and more specifically the importance of preunderstanding in all understanding. Schleiermacher, and even hermeneutical theorists before him, pointed to this latter conception in enunciating the principle of the hermeneutical circle within which all understanding takes place.

Thus Schleiermacher moved decisively beyond seeing hermeneutics as methods accumulated by trial and error and asserted the legitimacy of a general art of understanding prior to any special art of interpretation. This raises the question of the proper relationship of present-day literary interpretation to some implicit or explicit general theory of understanding. Perhaps it may be asserted that we today should interpret without trying to know what interpretation is, but this merely claims the right to do something without really knowing what is being done. We can imagine this attitude on the part of the artisans confronted by Socrates as he walked about Athens inquiring whether they knew what it was they were doing. Such willful ignorance has its attractions, but it can hardly help to lead American literary interpretation, for instance, beyond the pyrotechnics of the New Criticism or the contradictions of present "myth criticism." What is needed now is a new principle for weighing what is and is not germane to interpretation, and for this what interpretation is and does must be ascertained more adequately. Present-day literary interpretation certainly should consider more carefully its relation to the general nature of all linguistic understanding.

It is too easy, as an example of this, to pass off as psychologizing the concern with what happens when a hearer understands an utterance. Psychologizing, properly defined, refers to the effort to go behind the utterance to its author's intentions and mental processes. Certainly Schleiermacher was guilty of this, but his contribution may not be passed off as invalid because of this one portion. Certainly it can be conceded that airy speculations about the mental processes of the speaker of an utterance are illegitimate; but Schleiermacher is correct, I believe, in seeing the interpretive problem as inseparable from the art of understanding in the hearer. Just this assertion helps to go beyond the illusion that the text possesses an independent, real meaning separable from every event of understanding it. Such a naive view may assume the essential transparency and unhistoricality of understanding; it may assume that we have privileged access to the meaning of the text outside of time and history. Precisely these assumptions, however, need to be questioned.

Another significant element in Schleiermacher's hermeneutics is the concept of understanding "out of a relationship to life." This will be the starting point for Dilthey's and for Heidegger's hermeneutical thinking. For Dilthey took as his goal to understand "from out of life itself," and Heidegger took this same goal and tried to reach it in a different and more radically historical way. A thought complex is not interesting as a clue to its author's mental process, but as something in itself, an experience which is understood in reference to our own horizon of experience. We need not fall into psychologizing in order to assert that understanding cannot be conceived of apart from meaningful relationships to our own previous experience.

There are other consequences of Schleiermacher's hermeneutics, however, which are cause for some concern. For instance, to take understanding as a starting point may lead wrongly to lumping poetry and prose together, or to embracing theories of fundamental psychology and a fundamental human nature which are open to severe question. Nor is the tendency to gloss over the problem of translating a foreign language and penetrating a distant time to be taken lightly; Schleiermacher's focus on the art of understanding, however, tends to make these seem less problematical than understanding itself. Gadamer calls attention to these and other problems in Schleiermacher's hermeneutics, concluding with a striking assertion: "The problem for Schleiermacher was not that of the obscurities of history but of the obscurity of the thou." [18] Such a concentration on the psychological conditions of dialogue can lead to

18. WM 179.

slurring over the historical element in interpretation and even the centrality of language for hermeneutics. The concentration on dialogue along with the erroneous view that the understanding process is one of "imitation" or "reconstruction" led him the more easily to the misconceptions in his later hermeneutics.

Schleiermacher, nevertheless, is properly regarded as the father of modern hermeneutics as a general study. Joachim Wach notes that hermeneutical theorists of the later nineteenth century in many different disciplines and directions of thought were indebted to the hermeneutical thinking of Schleiermacher, so much so that most important hermeneutical theories in nineteenth-century Germany bear his imprint. Among these we shall discuss only the preeminently significant contribution of Wilhelm Dilthey.

8 / Dilthey: Hermeneutics
as Foundation
of the *Geisteswissenschaften*

AFTER SCHLEIERMACHER'S DEATH in 1834, the project of developing a general hermeneutics languished. Certainly the hermeneutical problem in various aspects occupied the attention of great minds in different fields, for example, Karl Wilhelm von Humboldt, Heymann Steinthal, August Bockh, Leopold von Ranke, S. G. Droysen, and Friedrich Karl von Savigny. But the consideration of the problem tended to lapse back into the confines of one particular discipline and to become historical, philological, or judicial interpretation rather than a general hermeneutics as the art of understanding. Near the end of the century, however, the gifted philosopher and literary historian Wilhelm Dilthey (1833-1911) began to see in hermeneutics the foundation for the *Geisteswissenschaften*—that is, all the humanities and social sciences, all those disciplines which interpret expressions of man's inner life, whether the expressions be gestures, historical actions, codified law, art works, or literature.

It was Dilthey's aim to develop methods of gaining "objectively valid" interpretations of "expressions of inner life." At the same time, he reacted sharply to the tendency in the humane studies simply to take on the norms and ways of thinking of the natural sciences and apply them to the study of man. Nor was the idealist tradition a viable alternative, for under the influence of August Comte and from his study under Ranke he determined that concrete experience and not speculation must be the only admissible starting point for a theory of the

Geisteswissenschaften. Such was the quality of Dilthey's mind that he truly perceived the epistemological inconsistency of the claim of the German "historical school" to "objectivity" as an uncritical mixture of the idealist and realist perspectives. Concrete, historical, lived experience must be the starting and ending point for the *Geisteswissenschaften.* Life itself is that out of which we must develop our thinking and toward which we direct our questioning. We do not try to go behind it to a realm of ideas: "Behind life itself our thinking cannot go." [1]

There is a romantic tinge to this emphasis on a return to life itself, and it is not surprising that Dilthey published studies on the German "Storm and Stress" movement, Novalis, Goethe, and Schleiermacher. Such was his immersion in the heritage of Romanticism, then, that the failure of positivism and realism, in their various forms, to come to grips with the fullness, immediacy, and variegatedness of living experience itself was all too apparent. We sense in Dilthey some of the fundamental conflicts in nineteenth-century thinking: the romantic desire for immediacy and totality even while seeking data that would be "objectively valid." His restless mind struggled against historicism and psychologism and partially transcended them, for there emerges in his thinking an understanding of history far deeper than that of the historical school in Germany, and in his turn to hermeneutics in the 1890's he was going decisively beyond the psychologizing tendency he had adopted from his study of Schleiermacher's hermeneutics. As H. A. Hodges notes in his book on Dilthey, two great philosophical traditions, largely separate until then, met in Dilthey: Anglo-French empirical realism and positivism, and German idealism and life philosophy.[2] Dilthey's attempt to forge an epistemological foundation for the *Geisteswissenschaften* became a meeting place for two fundamentally conflicting views of the proper way to study man.

In order to understand Dilthey's hermeneutics, we must first clarify the context of problems and aims within which he was struggling in his effort to find a methodological basis for the *Geisteswissenschaften.* This involves understanding the project in relation to (1) Dilthey's view of history, and (2) his "life-philosophical" orientation.

1. *GS* V, 5; VIII, 184.
2. *PhWD*, Chap. 2.

THE PROBLEM OF FINDING A METHODOLOGICAL BASIS FOR THE *Geisteswissenschaften*

THE PROJECT of formulating a methodology appropriate to sciences focused on understanding man's expressions—social and artistic—is first seen by Dilthey in the context of a need to get away from the reductionist and mechanistic perspective of the natural sciences, and to find an approach adequate to the fullness of phenomena. For this reason a recent work on Dilthey's literary theory has called it a "phenomenological approach." [3] Thus the task of finding the basis for such a methodology was seen as (1) an epistemological problem, (2) a matter of deepening our conception of historical consciousness, and (3) a need to understand expressions from out of "life itself." When these factors have been understood, the distinction is clear between the approach of the "human sciences" (*Geisteswissenschaften*) and that of the natural sciences.

For Dilthey any kind of metaphysical basis for describing what happens when we understand a humanly created phenomenon is rejected at the outset, for it could hardly produce results that would universally be recognized as valid. Rather, the problem is to specify what kind of knowledge and what kind of understanding is specifically appropriate to intepreting human phenomena. He asks: What is the nature of the act of understanding which is the basis for all study of man? In short, he sees the problem not in metaphysical but in epistemological terms.

In a sense Dilthey is continuing the "critical idealism" of Kant even though he was not a neo-Kantian but a "life philosopher." Kant had written a *Critique of Pure Reason* which laid the epistemological foundations for the sciences. Dilthey consciously set for himself the task of writing a "critique of historical reason" which would lay the epistemological foundations for the "human studies." He did not question the adequacy of the Kantian categories for the natural sciences, but he saw in space, time, number, etc., little possibility for understanding the inner life of man; nor did the category of "feeling" seem to do justice to the inner, historical character of human sub-

---

3. Kurt Müller-Vollmer, *Towards a Phenomenological Theory of Literature: A Study of Wilhelm Dilthey's "Poetik."*

jectivity. Dilthey asserted: "This is a matter of [further] developing the whole Kantian-critical attitude; but in the category of self-interpretation [*Selbstbesinnung*] instead of theory of knowledge, a critique of historical instead of 'pure' reason." [4]

"Not through introspection but only through history do we come to know ourselves." [5] The problem of understanding man was for Dilthey one of recovering a consciousness of the "historicality" (*Geschichtlichkeit*) of our own existence which is lost in the static categories of science. We experience life not in the mechanical categories of "power" but in complex, individual moments of "meaning," of direct experience of life as a totality and in loving grasp of the particular. These units of meaning require the context of the past and the horizon of future expectations; they are intrinsically temporal and finite, and they are to be understood in terms of these dimensions—that is, historically. (This historicality will be discussed later in connection with Dilthey's hermeneutics itself.)

The problem of formulating a theory of the human sciences was seen in the horizon of Dilthey's life philosophy. Life philosophy is most commonly associated with three late-nineteenth-century philosophers, Nietzsche, Dilthey, and Bergson. Professor O. F. Bollnow's helpful book[6] on the development of life philosophy traces this general trend of thought back to the eighteenth-century protests against formalism, antiseptic rationalism, and indeed all abstract thought which passes over the whole person, the living, feeling, willing personality in its fullness. Thus Rousseau, Jakobi, Herder, Fichte, Schelling, and other eighteenth-century thinkers anticipated life philosophy in their efforts to get at the experiential fullness of human existence in the world. In these various thinkers may be seen the life philosopher's struggle for a reality unfalsified by externalities and culture. The word "life" was even then a battle cry against the fixedness and determinations of convention. Says Bollnow, "It ["life"] referred to the collected inner powers of man, especially the irrational powers of feeling and passion as over against the prevailing power of rational understanding." [7] Friedrich Schlegel referred to the "philosophy of life" as the living presentation of human consciousness and

4. *GS* V, xxi.
5. *Ibid.*, VII, 279 and elsewhere.
6. *L.*
7. *Ibid.*, 5.

human living as over against the abstract and unintelligible speculations of "school philosophy." And Fichte took as the ground of his whole philosophy the antithesis between the fixedness of Being and the powerful flowing forth of life.

The list of thinkers with affinities for life philosophy could be extended indefinitely, including such figures as William James, Marx, Dewey, Pestalozzi, Plessner, and Scheler. Bollnow singles out for specific attention Georg Simmel (1858-1918), Ludwig Klages (1872-1956), and José Ortega y Gasset (1883-1955).[8] In all of these there is the general tendency to try to return to the fullness of lived experience; and for the most part this is at the same time an opposition to the formal, mechanical, abstract tendencies of technological civilization. The forces of Mind (*Geist*, in Scheler's sense of the word) or Being (*Sein*, in Fichte's sense of the word) stood for the rigid and deadening; the forces of life (*Leben*) were the dynamic, inexhaustible sources for all forms of creativity and meaning.

In Dilthey this antithesis expressed itself as a critique of naturalistic, causality-oriented thought forms when applied to the task of understanding the inner life and experience of man. Dilthey held that the dynamics of man's inner life are a complex matter of cognition, feeling, and will, and that these cannot be made subject to the norms of causality and the rigidness of mechanistic, quantifying thinking. To invoke the categories of thought from the *Critique of Pure Reason* for the task of understanding man actually imposes from outside of life a set of abstract categories in no way derived from it. These categories are static, atemporal, abstract – the opposite of life itself.

The object of the human sciences should not be to understand life in terms of categories extrinsic to it but from intrinsic categories, ones derived from life. Life must be understood from the experience of life itself. Dilthey remarked scornfully that "in the veins of the 'knowing subject' constructed by Locke, Hume, and Kant, runs no real blood."[9] There is a distinct tendency in Locke, Hume, and Kant to restrict "knowing" to the cognitive faculty in separation from feeling and will. Furthermore, cognition is often treated as if it were separable from the essentially historical context of man's inner life; the fact is,

8. *Ibid.*, 144-50.
9. *GS* V, 4; also *L* 121.

however, that we perceive, think, and understand in terms of
the past, present, and future, in terms of our feelings and moral
demands and imperatives. The obvious need is to return to the
meaningful unities present in lived experience.

To return to "life" does not mean, for Dilthey, to return to
some mystical ground or source for all life both human and
nonhuman, or to some sort of foundational psychic energy.
Rather, life is seen in terms of "meaning"; life is "human experience known from within." [10] We feel Dilthey's antimetaphysical sentiment in his refusal to treat the phenomenal
world as mere appearance: "Behind life, thinking cannot go." [11]
The categories of life are not rooted in a transcendental reality
but in the reality of lived experience. Hegel had expressed his
intention to understand life from life itself; Dilthey put this
intention in an antimetaphysical context—perhaps neither a
realistic nor an idealistic but a phenomenological context.
Dilthey follows Hegel in asserting that life is an "historical"
reality; history for Dilthey, however, is not an absolute goal or
a manifestation of absolute spirit but an expression of life.
Life is relative, and it expresses itself in many forms; in human
experience it is never an absolute.

The "Human Sciences" *versus* the "Natural Sciences"

What does the foregoing discussion mean in
terms of methods of studying man? Dilthey contended that
the "human studies" or "human sciences" *(Geisteswissenschaften)* had to forge new models for the interpretation of
human phenomena. These had to be derived from the character
of lived experience itself; they had to be based on categories
of "meaning" instead of "power," history instead of mathematics. Dilthey saw a fundamental distinction between all
human studies and the natural sciences.[12]

The human studies do not deal with facts and phenomena
which are silent about man but with facts and phenomena

10. *L* 12; see *GS* VIII, 121: "Leben erfasst hier Leben."
11. *GS* VIII, 184.
12. See Carl Michalson, *The Rationality of Faith,* for a careful exploration
of the contrasting kinds of understanding appropriate to these two areas. See
also *GS* V, 242-68; VII, *passim.*

which are meaningful only as they shed light on man's inner processes, his "inner experience." The methodology appropriate to natural objects is not adequate to the understanding of human phenomena except in their status as natural objects. The human studies, however, have available to them something unavailable in the natural sciences—the possibility of understanding the inner experience of another person through a mysterious process of mental transfer. Dilthey asserts: "Exactly because a real transposition can take place [when man understands man], because affinity and universality of thought . . . can image. forth and form a *social-historical world,* the inner events and processes in man can be distinguished from those of animals." [13] Because of this "real transposition" which can take place through objects that embody inner experience, man can achieve a degree and depth of understanding impossible in relation to any other kind of object. Obviously such a transposition can only take place because a likeness exists between the facts of our own mental experience and those of another person. This phenomenon brings with it the possibility of finding in another person the profoundest depths of our own experience; from the encounter can come the discovery of a fuller inner world. [14]

Dilthey, following Schleiermacher, sees this transposition as a reconstruction and reexperiencing of another person's inner world of experience. The interest is not in the other person, however, but in the world itself, a world seen as a "social-historical" world; it is the world of inner moral imperatives, a shared community of feelings and reactions, a common experience of beauty. We are able to penetrate this inner, human world not through introspection but through interpretation, the understanding of expressions of life; that is, through deciphering the imprint of man on phenomena.

The difference between the human studies and the natural sciences, then, does not necessarily lie either in a different kind of object in the human studies or in a different kind of perception; the essential difference lies in the context within which the perceived object is understood. [15] The human studies will sometimes make use of the same objects or "facts" as the natural sciences, but in a different context of relationships,

13. *GS* V, 250.
14. *Ibid.*
15. *Ibid.*, 248.

one which includes or refers to inner experience. The absence of reference to human experience is characteristic of the natural sciences; the presence of reference to the inner life of man is inevitably present in the human studies. "Accordingly," Dilthey states, "the difference between the natural and human sciences is not fundamentally determined in respect to a *special way of knowing* but differs in content." [16] The same object and the same fact can contain different systems of relationship; the human studies should take the object or fact and use it in new, nonscientific "categories" derived from life itself. For instance, an object might be explained in terms of purely causal categories (i.e., in a scientific way) or in relation to what it tells us about the inner life of man, or more objectively about man's social-historical world, which is both the fabric and manifestation of man's inner experience. Natural sciences cannot use mental facts (*geistige Tatsachen*) without ceasing to be natural sciences; the human studies can use physical facts, but the external world is treated only in relation to feeling and willing men, and facts are significant only as they affect behavior and help or hinder human purposes.

The key word for the human studies, Dilthey believed, was "understanding." Explaining is for the sciences, but the approach to phenomena which unites the inner and outer is understanding. The sciences explain nature, the human studies understand expressions of life.[17] Understanding can grasp the individual entity, but science must always see the individual as a means of arriving at the general, the type. Especially in the arts we value the particular for its own sake, and we linger lovingly in the understanding of the phenomenon in its individuality. This absorbing interest in the individual inner life stands in fundamental contrast to the attitude and procedure of the natural sciences. The human studies must, Dilthey contends, attempt to formulate a methodology of understanding that will transcend the reductionist objectivity of the sciences and return to the fullness of "life," of human experience.

This gives us a general conception of Dilthey's view of the human studies. Can his description of the separation of the

16. *Ibid.*, 253.
17. "Die Natur erklären wir, das Seelenleben verstehen wir" (*ibid.*, 144).

human and natural sciences be defended? Even some of Dilthey's stoutest supporters have had to say no. His literary executor, Georg Misch, early recognized that a productive reconciliation of the two approaches is possible and desirable. Bollnow, too, rightly observes that as helpful as these distinctions are in the theoretical self-understanding of the two great branches of knowledge, it must be admitted that "understanding" is not limited to the human studies nor explanatory procedures to the natural sciences. Rather, both work together in varying degrees in every true act of knowledge. Ironically, from the present vantage point, it is possible to see the extent to which scientific conceptions, and even the historicism that Dilthey strove to overcome, do creep into his conception of the human studies, for his quest for "objectively valid knowledge" was itself an expression of the scientific ideal of clean, clear data. And this imperceptibly guided his thinking toward the atemporal, spatialized metaphors and images of mental life compatible with scientific thinking. On the other hand, the heritage of Schleiermacher led him into a conception of understanding as reconstruction and into a tendency to psychologizing from which he only slowly and laboriously extricated himself as he turned toward basing his theory on hermeneutics rather than on a new kind of psychology.

Yet the project of understanding life in terms of life itself, the drive to deepen the historical aspect of understanding, the sharp critique of creeping scientism in the human studies—all these have played a major part in hermeneutics since Dilthey. We see in him some of the fundamental problems and aims of hermeneutics laid open as problems. Heidegger was to build on these aims, and he clearly went back to Dilthey in an effort to move beyond the scientific tendencies in his teacher, Edmund Husserl.[18]

DILTHEY'S HERMENEUTICAL FORMULA: EXPERIENCE, EXPRESSION, UNDERSTANDING

"A SCIENCE BELONGS TO THE HUMAN STUDIES," says Dilthey, "only if its object becomes accessible to us through a procedure based on the systematic relation between

18. See SZ § 77.

life, expression, and understanding."[19] This formula of "experience-expression-understanding" is far from self-explanatory, for each term has a fairly distinct meaning in terms of Dilthey's life philosophy. Let us explore each of these terms separately.

1 / *Experience*

There are two words in German for "experience": *Erfahrung* and the more technical and recent *Erlebnis*.The former refers to experience in general, as when one refers to his "experience" in life. Dilthey uses the more specific and limited term *Erlebnis,* coined from the verb *erleben* (to experience, especially in individual instances). The verb *erleben* is itself a fairly recent word, formed by adding the prefix *er-* (which generally is used as an emphatic prefix, deepening the meaning of the main word). Thus the word "experience" is in German a cognate of the verb "to live," an emphatic form which suggests the immediacy of life itself as we meet it. *Erlebnis* as a singular noun was virtually nonexistent in German before Dilthey's use of it in a highly specific sense, although the plural form, *Erlebnisse,* appears in Goethe, from whom Dilthey undoubtedly took the term.

An *Erlebnis* or "lived experience" is defined by Dilthey as a unit held together by a common meaning:

> That which in the stream of time forms a unity in the present because it has a unitary meaning is the smallest entity which we can designate as an experience. Going further, one may call each encompassing unity of parts of life bound together through a common meaning for the course of life an "experience"—even when the several parts are separated from each other by interrupting events.[20]

In other words, a meaningful experience of a painting, for instance, may have involved many encounters separated by time and still be called an "experience" (*Erlebnis*). An experience of romantic love is not based on one encounter but brings together events of various kinds, times, and places; but their unity of meaning as "an experience" lifts them out of the stream of life and holds them together in a unit of meaning, i.e., an experience.

19. *GS* VII, 86; quoted in *PhWD* 249.
20. *GS* VII, 194.

What is the character of this unit of meaning? Dilthey goes into the question in considerable detail, and to understand what this thing called "experience" consists of is basic to understanding his hermeneutics. First, experience is not to be construed as the "content" of a reflexive act of consciousness, for then it would be something of which we are conscious; rather, it is the act itself. It is something we live in and through, it is the very attitude we take toward life and in which we live. In short, it is experiencing as such, as it is prereflexively given in meaning. Experience can subsequently become an object of reflection, but then it is no longer immediate experience but the object of another act of encounter. Thus experience is not so much a matter of content as an act of consciousness; it is not to be construed as something which consciousness stands over against and apprehends.[21]

This means that experience does not and cannot directly perceive itself, for to do so would itself be a reflexive act of consciousness. And it is not a "datum" of consciousness, for to be such it would stand over against the subject as an object given to it. Thus experience exists before the subject-object separation, which separation is itself a model used by reflexive thought. Experience is, in fact, not distinguished from perceiving or apprehending (*innewerden*) itself. *Erlebnis* represents that direct contact with life which we may call "immediate lived experience."

The descriptive analysis of this elusive realm prior to reflexive thought must be foundational for both the human studies and the natural sciences, but it is particularly important to the former, for the very categories of humanistic and hermeneutical understanding must be derived from it. Just this realm of prereflexive consciousness is that staked out by Husserl's and Heidegger's phenomenology. As Dilthey seeks to implement his methodological project in close coordination with his life philosophy, as he makes a clear separation between mere "thinking" and "life" (or experience), he is laying the foundations for twentieth-century phenomenology.

Dilthey asserts, for instance,

The way in which "lived experience" presents itself to me [literally, "is there-for-me"] is completely different from the way in which images stand before me. The consciousness of the experi-

21. *Ibid.*, 139; *PhWD* 38–40.

ence and its constitution are the same: there is no separation between what is there-for-me and what *in* experience is there-for-me. In other words, the experience does not stand like an object over against its experiencer, but rather its very existence for me is undifferentiated from the *whatness* which is present for me in it.[22]

Yet it would be a grave mistake to think of experience as pointing to some kind of merely subjective reality, for experience is precisely the reality of what is there-for-me before experience becomes objective (and therefore admits of a separation from the subjective). This prior unity is that out of which Dilthey tries to forge categories that will contain rather than separate the elements of feeling, knowing, and will, which are held together in experience—such categories, perhaps, as "value," "meaningfulness," "texture," and "relationship." In the formulation of these categories, Dilthey encounters great difficulties, yet the task itself is of highest importance. His selection was governed by his aim to gain objectively valid knowledge, and just this aim tends to place uncalled-for limitations on his thinking. At the same time, we must admire the restless way he pressed for categories which would express "the freedom of life and of history."[23] His fruitful insight lay in seeing experience as a realm before subject and object, a realm in which the world and our experience of it are given together. He saw with clarity the poverty of the subject-object model of human encounter with the world and the shallow separation of feelings from objects, sensations from the total act of understanding. "We live and move," he points out scornfully, "not in a sphere of 'sensations' but of objects presenting themselves to us, not in a sphere of 'feelings' but of value, meaning, and so on."[24] How absurd, he said, to separate one's sensations and feelings from the total context of relationships held together in the unity of experience.

A further fruitful emphasis in Dilthey is on the temporality of the "context of relationships" given in "experience." Experience is not a static matter; on the contrary, in its unity of meaning it tends to reach out and encompass both recollection of the past and anticipation of the future in the total context of "meaning." Meaning cannot be imagined except in terms of what the

22. *GS* VII, 139.
23. *Ibid.*, 203.
24. *GS* VI, 317.

future is expected to be, nor can it free itself from dependence upon the materials which the past supplies. The past and the future, then, form a structural unity with the presentness of all experience, and this temporal context is the inescapable horizon within which any perception in the present is interpreted.

Dilthey goes to great lengths to prove that the temporality of experience is not something imposed reflexively by consciousness (the position Kantians would take: the mind is the active agent imposing a unity on perception) but rather that it is already implicit in experience itself as given to us. In this respect, Dilthey may be called a realist rather than an idealist: the temporality of experience is, as Heidegger would say, "equiprimordial" with experience itself. It is never something added to experience. Suppose one tries in a reflexive act consciously to grasp the course or progression of one's life (*das Lebensverlauf*). The unity in this particular exercise is instructive, for it is almost a mirror of the way this unity is actually given in consciousness on a prereflexive level. Dilthey describes his own effort to do this:

> What happens when "experience" (*das Erlebnis*) becomes the object of my reflection? I lie awake at night [for example] worrying over the possibility of completing in my old age the work I have begun; I think over what to do. There is in this "experience" a structural set of relationships: an objective grasping of the situation forms the basis of it, and on this is based a stance [*Stellungnahme*] as concern-towards and pain-over-the-objectively-grasped fact, along with a striving to go *beyond* the fact. And all this is there-for-me in this its [the fact's] structural context. Of course, I have brought the situation now to discriminating consciousness, and I have brought into relief the structural relationship—I have "isolated" it. But everything which I have here so brought out is really contained in experience itself and has merely been brought to light in this act of reflection.[25]

The "meaning" of an "objectively grasped fact" is given with the fact itself, and the meaning is intrinsically temporal, defined in terms of one's life context. Dilthey continues the passage above by claiming that this means something fundamentally significant for all study of human reality: "The component parts of what comprises our view of the progression

25. *GS* VII, 139-40; paraphrased, not literally translated.

of our life [*Anschauung des Lebensverlaufes*] are all contained together in *living itself.*" [26] We may call this the inner temporality or historicality which is not imposed on life but intrinsic to it. Dilthey is asserting a fact that is of the greatest importance to hermeneutics: *Experience is intrinsically temporal* (and this means *historical* in the deepest sense of the word), *and therefore understanding of experience must also be in commensurately temporal* (historical) *categories of thought.*

Dilthey has, then, with the insistence on the temporality of experience asserted the foundation of all subsequent efforts to affirm the "historicality" of human being-in-the-world. Historicality does not mean being focused on the past, or some kind of tradition-mindedness that enslaves one to dead ideas; historicality (*Geschichtlichkeit*) is essentially the affirmation of the temporality of human experience as we have just described it. It means we understand the present really only in the horizon of past and future; this is not a matter of conscious effort but is built into the structure of experience itself. But to bring this historicality to light does have hermeneutical consequences, for the nonhistoricality of interpretation can no longer be assumed and leave us satisfied with analysis that remains firmly in scientific categories fundamentally alien to the historicality of human experience. It makes brutally plain that experience is not to be understood in scientific categories. The task is clear: to work out the "historical" categories appropriate to the character of lived experience.

2 / *Expression*

The second term in the experience-expression-understanding formula—*Ausdruck*—may be translated as "expression." The use of this term should not automatically associate Dilthey with expression theories of art, for such theories are framed in subject-object terms. For instance, we link the term "expression" almost automatically with "feeling"; we "express" our feelings and an expression theory of art generally sees the work as symbolic representation of feelings. Wordsworth, an exponent of the expression theory of poetic creation, sees a poem as the spontaneous overflow of powerful feelings.

26. *Ibid.*, 140.

When Dilthey uses *Ausdruck*, he is not principally referring either to overflow or to feeling but to something far more encompassing. An expression, for Dilthey, is not primarily an embodiment of one person's feelings but rather an "expression of life"; an "expression" can refer to an idea, a law, a social form, language—anything that reflects the imprint of the inner life on man. It is not primarily a symbol of feeling.

Ausdruck could be translated perhaps not as "expression" but as an "objectification" of the mind—knowledge, feeling, and will—of man. The hermeneutical significance of objectification is that because of it understanding can be focused on a fixed, "objective" expression of lived experience instead of struggling to capture it through introspection. Introspection could never serve as the basis for the human studies, Dilthey recognized, for direct reflection on experience produces either (1) an intuition that cannot be communicated, or (2) a conceptualization which is itself an expression of inner life. Introspection, then, is an unreliable way to either self-knowledge or knowledge of man in the human studies. The human studies must necessarily focus on "expressions of life"; these studies, focused on an objectification of life, are intrinsically hermeneutical. On what kinds of objects may the human studies focus? Dilthey is very definite on their scope: "Everything in which the spirit of man has objectified itself falls in the area of the *Geisteswissenschaften*. Their circumference is as wide as understanding, and understanding has its true object in the objectification of life itself." [27]

3 / *The Art Work as Objectification of Lived Experience*

If the circumference of the human studies is so vast, where does the understanding of the art work, and specifically the literary work of art, fit? Dilthey classified the various manifestations of life or human inner experience ("life" is for Dilthey not a metaphysical thing, not a deep source behind lived experience itself; human experience is that behind which reflection should not presume to go) into three major categories: (1) *Ideas* (i.e., "concepts, judgments, and larger thought-forms") are "mere thought content," which are independent of the place, time, and person in which they appear, and for

27. *Ibid.*, 148.

this reason have a certain accuracy and are easily communicated. (2) *Actions* are more difficult to interpret because in an action there is a certain goal, but only with great difficulty can we determine the factors at work in the decision which led to the act. A law, for instance, is a public or community act, but the same difficulty applies; it cannot be known, for instance, what was decided *against* in making the act. (3) There are, lastly, *expressions of lived experience,* which extend from the spontaneous expressions of inner life, such as exclamation and gesture, to the consciously controlled expressions embodied in art works.

Dilthey generally refers to the first two categories—ideas and actions—as "manifestations of life" *(Lebensäusserungen),* but for the third he tends to reserve the more specific term "expressions of lived experience" *(Erlebnisausdrücke).* It is in this third category that human inner experience comes to fullest expression, and in it understanding meets its greatest challenge:

> How completely different [from idea or act] is the expression of lived experience! A special relationship exists between it as expression of life itself and understanding, which brings it about. The expression can contain more of the context of inner life [*seelischen Zusammenhang*] than any introspection can perceive, for it rises up out of the depths which consciousness never lights up.[28]

The art work, of course, goes vastly beyond mere gestures or exclamations in its flexibility and reliability, since gestures can be counterfeited but art points to or expresses experience itself and thus is not subject to counterfeiting:

> In the great works of art a vision [*ein Geistiges*] is set free [*sich loslöst*] from its creator, the poet, the artist, or the writer, and we step into a realm where deception by the expressor ends. No truly great work of art can try to mirror a reality foreign to the inner content [*geistigen Gehalt*] of its author. Indeed, it does not wish to say anything at all about its author. True in itself, it stands there fixed, visible enduring . . .[29]

Gone is the problem of counterfeiting which is present in gestures and in any human act or human situation with its interplay of conflicting interests, for the art work does not point to its author at all but to life itself. Precisely for this reason the

28. *Ibid.,* 207.
29. *Ibid.*

art work is the most reliable, enduring, and fruitful object of the human studies. With this fixed, objective status there becomes possible a secure, artistic understanding of the expression. "So arises in the confines between knowing and act a circle or realm in which life discloses itself in a depth inaccessible in observation, reflection, or theory." [30]

Of all art works, those in language have perhaps the greatest power to disclose the inner life of man. Because of the presence of these fixed, unchanging objects, in this case literary works, there has already arisen a body of theory about interpretation of texts: *hermeneutics*. The principles of hermeneutics, Dilthey asserted, can light the way to a general theory of understanding, for "above all . . . the grasping of the structure of the inner life is based on the interpretation of *works,* works in which the texture of inner life comes fully to expression." [31] Thus, for Dilthey, hermeneutics takes on a new and larger significance: it becomes the theory not merely of text interpretation but of how life discloses and expresses itself in works.

The "expression" in this case, however, is not of an individual and purely personal reality, for then it could not be understood by another person; when the expression is in writing, it uses language, a medium held in common with the understander. Likewise, experience is held in common with the understander, and understanding comes by virtue of analogous experience. Thus it is possible to posit the existence of generally held structures in and through which objective understanding takes place. And expression is therefore not of a person at all, as in psychologizing, but of a social-historical reality disclosed in experience, the social-historical reality of experience itself.

4 / *Understanding*

"Understanding" *(Verstehen),* like the other two key words in Dilthey's experience-expression-understanding formula, is used in a special sense. Thus "understanding" does not refer to understanding a rational conception such as a mathematical problem. "Understanding" is reserved to designate the operation in which the mind grasps the "mind" *(Geist)* of the other

30. *Ibid.*
31. *Ibid.,* 322.

person. It is not a purely cognitive operation of the mind at all but that special moment when life understands life: "We explain by means of purely intellectual processes, but we understand by means of the combined activity of all the mental powers in apprehending."[32] In his terser and more famous statement of this thought: "We explain nature; man we must understand."[33] Understanding, then, is the mental process by which we comprehend living human experience. It is the act which constitutes our best contact with life itself. Like lived experience *(Erlebnis)*, understanding has a fullness that escapes rational theorizing.

Understanding opens to us the world of individual persons, and thereby also possibilities in our own nature.[34] Understanding is not a mere act of thought but a transposition and reexperiencing of the world as another person meets it in lived experience. It is not a conscious, reflexive act of comparison but an operation of silent thought which accomplishes a prereflexive transposition of oneself into the other person. One rediscovers himself in the other person.[35] A further fact that emphasizes the way in which understanding contrasts with all merely scientific comprehension and explanation is that the understanding has value in itself aside from all practical considerations. It is not a means to something else, necessarily, but is an inherent good. Only through understanding are the specifically personal and nonconceptual sides of reality encountered. "The secret of the 'person' attracts [us] for its own sake to ever newer and deeper efforts to understand. And in such understanding arises the realm of the individual, which encompasses man and his creations. Herein lies the understanding function most proper to the human studies."[36] Like Schleiermacher before him, Dilthey affirms that the human studies linger lovingly over the particular for its own sake. Scientific explanations are seldom valued in themselves but for the sake of something else; when certain treatises are enjoyed in themselves, as in the case of Lucretius' *De rerum natura,* we see them as clues to man's inner nature — we move, in other words, into the human studies and the categories of understanding rather than mere explanation.

32. *GS* V, 172.
33. *Ibid.*, 144.
34. *GS* VII, 145, 215-16; see *D* 170-71.
35. *GS* VII, 191.
36. *GS* V, 212-13.

THE MEANING OF "HISTORICALITY" IN DILTHEY'S HERMENEUTICS

DILTHEY REPEATEDLY ASSERTED that man is "an historical being" (*ein geschichtliches Wesen*). But what does the word "historical" denote here? The answer is significant not only for understanding Dilthey's hermeneutics but for the influence it has had on subsequent hermeneutical theory.

Dilthey does not conceive history as something past that stands over against us as an object. Nor does historicality point to the already objectively clear fact that man is born, lives, and dies in the course of time. It does not refer to the fleetingness and ephemerality of human existence, which is a subject for poetry. Historicality (*Geschichtlichkeit*) means two things:

(1) Man understands himself not through introspection but through objectifications of life. "What man is only history can tell him." [37] Elsewhere, in more detail, "What man is and what he wills, he experiences only in the development of his nature through the millennia and never completely to the last syllable, never in objective concepts but always only in the living experience which springs up out of the depths of his own being." [38] Man's self-understanding, in other words, is not direct but indirect; it must take a hermeneutical detour through fixed expressions dating back over the past. Dependent on history, it is essentially and necessarily *historical*.

(2) Man's nature is not a fixed essence; man is not in all his objectifying simply painting endless murals on the walls of time in order to find out what his nature has always been. On the contrary, Dilthey would agree with another life philosopher, Nietzsche, that man is the "not-yet-determined animal" (*noch nicht festgestellte Tier*), the animal who has not yet determined what he is. [39] Moreover he is not simply trying to find out; he has not yet decided what he will be. What he will be is waiting for his historical decisions. He is not so much the rudder man on an already finished ship as rather the architect of the ship itself. (This is what Ortega y Gasset later called man's "ontological privilege." [40]) As man is continually taking possession of the formed expressions which constitute his

37. *GS* VIII, 224.
38. *GS* VI, 57; IX, 173; also D 219.
39. *L* 42.
40. *L* 44.

heritage, he becomes creatively historical. This grasping of the past is not a form of slavery but of freedom, the freedom of ever fuller self-knowledge and the consciousness of being able to will what one is to become. Since man has the power to alter his own essence, it could be said that he has the power to alter life itself; he has true and radical powers of creation.

A further consequence of historicality is that man does not escape from history, for he is what he is in and through history. "The totality of man's nature is only history." [41] For Dilthey, this resulted in an historical relativism. He asserted that "It is in no way possible to go back behind the relativity of historical consciousness. . . . The type 'man' dissolves and changes in the process of history." [42] History is ultimately a series of world views, and we have no firm and fixed standards of judgment for seeing the superiority of one world view over another.[43]

All this only reinforces what was said earlier about the intrinsic temporality of understanding: meaning always stands in a horizonal context that stretches into the past and into the future. Gradually this temporality becomes an intrinsic part of the concept of "historicality" so that the term comes to refer not only to man's dependence on history for his self-understanding and self-interpretation, and to his creative finitude in determining his own essence historically, but also to the inescapability of history and the intrinsic temporality of all understanding.

The hermeneutical consequences of "historicality" are everywhere evident in Dilthey, so much so that Bollnow rightly notes that, along with the conception of the unity of life and expression, the conception of historicality is central to understanding Dilthey.[44] When Dilthey is differentiated from other life philosophers, it is just this historicality which marks him off from Bergson and others. Dilthey gave the real impetus to the modern interest in historicality. As Bollnow rightly observes: "All recent efforts to understand human historicality find in Dilthey their decisive beginning." [45] He is, in short, the father of modern conceptions of historicality. Neither Dilthey's

41. *GS* VIII, 166.
42. *Ibid.*, 6.
43. *GS* I, 123 ff.; V, 339 ff.; VIII, *passim;* all discuss his doctrine of world views. An expository treatment in English can be found in *PhWD* 85–95.
44. *D* 221.
45. *L* 6.

own hermeneutics nor that of Heidegger or Gadamer, which will be considered shortly, is conceivable except in terms of historicality, especially the temporality of understanding. In hermeneutical theory, man is seen as dependent on constant interpretation of the past, and thus it could almost be said that man is the "hermeneutical animal," who understands himself in terms of interpreting a heritage and shared world bequeathed him from the past, a heritage constantly present and active in all his actions and decisions. In historicality, modern hermeneutics finds its theoretical foundations.

THE HERMENEUTICAL CIRCLE AND UNDERSTANDING

THE OPERATIONS OF UNDERSTANDING are seen by Dilthey to take place within the principle of the hermeneutical circle already enunciated by Ast and Schleiermacher. The whole receives its definition from the parts, and, reciprocally, the parts can only be understood in reference to a whole. The crucial term here in Dilthey is "meaning": meaning is what understanding grasps in the essential reciprocal interaction of the whole and the parts.

As previously indicated, the sentence furnishes a clear example of the interaction of the whole and parts and the need for both: out of the meaning of individual parts is yielded an understanding of the sense of the whole, which in turn changes the indeterminateness of the words into a fixed and meaningful pattern. Dilthey cites this example and then asserts that the same relationship exists between the parts and the whole of one's life. The meaning of the whole is a "sense" derived from the meaning of individual parts. An event or experience can so alter our lives that what was formerly meaningful becomes meaningless and an apparently unimportant past experience may take on meaning in retrospect. The sense of the whole determines the function and the meaning of the parts. And meaning is something historical; it is a relationship of whole to parts seen by us from a given standpoint, at a given time, for a given combination of parts. It is not something above or outside history but a part of a hermeneutical circle always historically defined.

Meaning and meaningfulness, then, are contextual; they are part of the situation. The meaning, for instance, of the statement "I am come to bid my king and master aye good night" is only in a trivial sense clear or meaningful without its situation. The meaning of the statement is different if it is said by (1) the old servant in *The Cherry Orchard*, (2) the famulus in *Faust*, (3) Smerdyakov in *The Brothers Karamazov*, or the literal source in this case, (4) Kent in *King Lear*.

Let us look briefly at the meaning of this sentence in its context. In the last act of the play, after the battle is over and the bastard Edmund struck down and dying, the faithful Kent enters. He expresses his magnificent loyalty in simple and moving words of leave-taking. What a world of meaning the word "master" expresses here! We hear in it not only Kent's relation to Lear but in resonance the theme of simple loyalty in the hierarchical order of things. Of course, these words do more than merely express the character of Kent and his relationship to Lear; they have a functional significance, for this simple sentence is immediately followed by the question: "Is he not here?" which triggers the final tragic action of the play. At once, attention is focused on the ominous absence of Lear and Cordelia, which prompts Edmund to tell them he has commissioned their deaths and to make a futile effort to rescind the order. And then the aged "master" enters, now master of himself but not master of the events his fateful failure in true mastery set in motion; he enters, bearing in his arms the treasure he had once cast from himself as worthless. How vastly the meaning of "love" and "loyalty" have changed for Lear in the course of the play! How frightfully have events changed the meaning of his decision to partition the kingdom!

Meaning is historical: it has changed with time; it is a matter of relationship, always related to a perspective from which events are seen. Meaning is not fixed and firm. Even the "meaning" of *King Lear* as a play changes. For us, standing in a post-hierarchical, deistic universe and in a very different social context, the meaning is obviously different from what it must have been for Shakespeare's contemporaries. The history of stage interpretations of Shakespeare shows that there is a seventeenth-, an eighteenth-, a nineteenth-, and a twentieth-century Shakespeare, just as there is an Aristotelian version of Plato, an early Christian Plato, a medieval Plato, a sixteenth-, nineteenth-, and even a twentieth-century Plato. Interpretation always stands in the situation in which the interpreter himself stands; meaning hinges on this, no matter how self-

contained within a play, poem, or dialogue it may seem. Thus
we see the correctness of Dilthey's assertion that meaning may
be of different kinds but it is always a kind of cohesion, relationship, or binding force; it is always in a context (*Zusammenhang*).

While meaning is surely a matter of relationship and context, this does not mean that it "hangs in air" like some free-
floating artistic construction. It is not something self-contained
and over against us like an object; it is the nonobjective something that we partially objectify in rendering *a* meaning explicit. Says Dilthey, "Meaningfulness fundamentally grows
out of the relation of part to whole that is grounded in the nature of living experience." [46] In other words, meaning is immanent in the texture of life, that is, in our participation in
lived experience; it is ultimately "the encompassing, fundamental category under which life become graspable." [47] As
stated earlier, "life" is not something metaphysical but "lived
experience." In a typical utterance, Dilthey tells of this basic
datum, life: "Life is the basic element or fact [*Grundtatsache*]
which must form the starting point for philosophy. It is known
from within. It is that behind which we cannot go. Life cannot
be brought before the bar of reason." [48] Our access to an understanding of "life" lies deeper than reason, for life is rendered
understandable through its objectifications. Here in the realm
of objects there can be built up a world of real relationships
which are grasped by individuals in the presentness of lived
experience. Meaning is not subjective; it is not a projection of
thought or thinking onto the object; it is a perception of a real
relationship within a nexus prior to the subject-object separation in thought. To understand meaning involves entering into
a real, not imaginary, relationship with the forms of objectified
"spirit" found everywhere about us. It is a matter of interaction of the individual person and the objective *Geist* within a
hermeneutical circle which presupposes both acting together.
Meaning is the name given to different kinds of relationships
in this interaction.

The circularity of understanding has another consequence
of greatest importance to hermeneutics: there is really no true
starting point for understanding, since every part presupposes

46. *GS* VII, 233.
47. *Ibid.*, 232.
48. *Ibid.*, 359.

the others. This means that there can be no "presuppositionless" understanding. Every act of understanding is in a given context or horizon; even in the sciences one explains only "in terms of" a frame of reference. Understanding in the human studies takes as its context "lived experience," and understanding that has no relationship to lived experience is not appropriate to the human studies *(Geisteswissenschaften)*. An interpretive approach which ignores the historicality of lived experience and applies atemporal categories to historical objects can only with irony claim to be "objective," for it has from the outset distorted the phenomenon.

Since we understand always from within our own horizon, which is part of the hermeneutical circle, there can be no nonpositional understanding of anything. We understand by constant reference to our experience. The methodological task of the interpreter, then, is not that of immersing himself totally in his object (which would be impossible, anyway) but rather that of finding viable modes of interaction of his own horizon with that of the text. As will be shown, this is the question to which Gadamer gives considerable attention: how we can achieve, within the admitted use of our own horizon, an openness to the text which does not impose in advance our own categories upon it.

THE SIGNIFICANCE OF DILTHEY FOR HERMENEUTICS: CONCLUSION

DILTHEY'S CONTRIBUTION was to broaden the horizon of hermeneutics by placing it in the context of interpretation in the human studies. His thinking on the hermeneutical problem started very much in the shadow of Schleiermacher's psychologism, and only gradually did he conceive of interpretation as focused on the expression of "lived experience" without reference to its author. But when he did, hermeneutics and not psychology had to become the foundation of the human studies. This satisfied two of Dilthey's most basic objectives. First, it focused the problem of interpretation on an object which had a fixed, enduring, objective status; thus the human studies could envision the possibility of objectively valid knowledge, since the object was relatively unchanging in itself. Second, the object clearly called for "historical" rather than scientific modes of understanding; it could only be understood through reference to life itself in all its historicality and temporality. The ever deeper penetration of the meaning of expressions of life could come only through historical understanding.

The consequences of this for literary theory are that one can again speak meaningfully of the "truth" of a work of literature, and, as a corollary, that form is not seen as an element in itself but as a symbol of inner realities. Art, for Dilthey, is the purest expression of life. Great literature is rooted in the lived experience of the riddles of life: the why and how of birth and death, joy and sorrow, love and hate, the power and the frailty of man, his ambiguous place in nature. As Bollnow notes, "When one values art for its achievement of expressing life, then one denies the idea that one values it solely for its own sake." [49] Thus, although the art work is a good in itself and its encounter is not a means to any other end, the work is not silent about man but speaks to his inner nature and is related to something beyond itself. Art is not, in other words, the pure, aimless play with forms that some aestheticians suppose; it is a form of spiritual nourishment which brings to expression the wellsprings of the life in which we move. At the head of Dilthey's *The Three Epochs of Modern Aesthetics and Its Present Task* (1892) stands as a motto the saying of Schiller: "Would that at last the demand for beauty might be given up and wholly and completely replaced by the demand for truth." [50] Art is not poetic fantasy and delight but expression of the truth of lived experience. "Truth" here is, of course, not used in a metaphysical sense but as the loyal representation of inner reality.

The interpretation of the literary work of art, then, is in Dilthey set in the context of the historicality of man's self-understanding. It is historical not only in that it must interpret an historically inherited object but in that one must understand the object in the horizon of one's own temporality and position in history. Because the expressive work involves man's self-understanding, it opens a reality that is neither "subjective" nor truly "objective" (i.e., separate from the horizon of our self-understanding). Methodologically, this confronts interpretation with the problem of understanding meaning in some way outside the subject-object dichotomization characteristic of scientific thinking.

49. *L* 74.
50. "Die drei Epochen der modernen Ästhetik und ihre heutige Aufgabe," *GS* VI.

Much has changed in hermeneutics since Dilthey. We note from our vantage point that he did not fully succeed in extricating himself from the scientism and objectivity of the historical school which he had undertaken to transcend. We see more clearly today that the quest for "objectively valid knowledge" was itself a reflection of scientific ideals wholly contrary to the historicality of our self-understanding. We may even assert that "life" is itself a category suspiciously close to Hegel's "objective Spirit," however much Dilthey protested against absolute idealism and tried to ground hermeneutics in empirical facts free of all metaphysics.[51] We may criticize the fact that Dilthey saw understanding—as did Schleiermacher—as reexperiencing *(Nacherleben)* and reconstruction of the author's experience and therefore analogous to the act of creation. For our act of understanding of Beethoven's *Ninth Symphony* is of course very different in character from the act on Beethoven's part of creating it. The work speaks in its totality of impact; the processes of creating it involve knowledge we need not have in order to "understand" what is "said" in the work.

Yet Dilthey renewed the project of a general hermeneutics and significantly advanced it. He placed it in the horizon of historicality, within which it has subsequently undergone important development. He laid the foundations for Heidegger's thinking on the temporality of self-understanding. He may properly be regarded as the father of the contemporary hermeneutical "problematic."

51. Dilthey's defense, in essence, is that "Hegel constructed metaphysically; I analyze the given" (*GS* VII, 150), but the principle would seem to be the same: the historical objectifications of mind reveal man to himself.

9 / Heidegger's Contribution to Hermeneutics in *Being and Time*

HUSSERL AND HEIDEGGER: TWO TYPES OF PHENOMENOLOGY

JUST AS DILTHEY saw hermeneutics in the horizon of his own project of finding an historically oriented theory of method for the *Geisteswissenschaften,* so Heidegger used the word "hermeneutics" in the context of his larger quest for a more "fundamental" ontology. It cʊuld be said that Heidegger defended the claims of *Leben* against *Geist* in the tradition of those two great life philosophers, Nietzsche and Dilthey, but in a different mode and on a different level. Like Dilthey, Heidegger wanted a method that would disclose life in terms of itself, and in *Being and Time* (1927) he quoted with approval Dilthey's aim of understanding life from out of life itself.[1] From the beginning Heidegger sought a method of going behind and to the root of Western conceptions of Being, a "hermeneutics" that would enable him to render visible the presuppositions on which they have been based. Like Nietzsche, he wished to call the whole Western metaphysical tradition into question.

In the phenomenology of Edmund Husserl, Heidegger found conceptual tools unavailable to Dilthey or Nietzsche, and a method which might lay open the processes of being in human existence in such a way that being, and not simply one's own ideology, might come into view. For phenomenology had opened up the realm of the preconceptual apprehending of

1. *SZ* 398.

[124]

phenomena. This new "realm" had a quite different significance to Heidegger than to Husserl, however. Whereas Husserl had approached it with an idea of bringing into view the
functioning of consciousness as transcendental subjectivity,
Heidegger saw in it the vital medium of man's historical being-
in-the-world. In its historicality and temporality, he saw clues
to the nature of being; being as it discloses itself in lived
experience escapes the conceptualizing, spatializing, and
atemporal categories of idea-centered thinking. Being was the
concealed prisoner, almost forgotten, of Western static categories, that Heidegger hoped to release. Could phenomenological method and theory provide the means?

It did in part; yet such was Heidegger's debt to Dilthey and
Nietzsche, and such was the character of his quest for a critique of Western metaphysics, and specifically of ontology, that
he was profoundly uneasy about Husserl's willingness to trace
all phenomena back to human consciousness, that is, to transcendental subjectivity. Heidegger held that the facticity of
being is a still more fundamental matter than human consciousness and human knowledge, while Husserl tended to
regard even the facticity of being as a datum of consciousness.[2]
Such a standpoint grounded in subjectivity did not provide the
framework within which the kind of critique Heidegger had
in mind could be fruitfully undertaken. While it was sufficient
for a far-reaching revision in epistemology, the ramifications
of which are still being felt in many fields today,[3] it was not in
itself what Heidegger could use to re-ask the question of being.

It is significant for the definition of hermeneutics that the
kind of phenomenology that Heidegger developed in *Being
and Time* is sometimes called hermeneutic phenomenology.[4]
This designation is more than a subdivision within the field
that Husserl had in mind; rather, it points to two very different
types of phenomenology. Heidegger's debt to Husserl was far
from minimal, and it is surprising how many of his early conceptions can be traced to Husserl; yet they are placed in a new
context and in the service of a different purpose. Thus it would
be a mistake to see "phenomenological method" as a doctrine
formulated by Husserl and used by Heidegger for another
purpose. On the contrary, Heidegger rethought the concept

2. WM 241.
3. See Herbert Spiegelberg, *The Phenomenological Movement.*
4. As in *ibid.,* I, 318-26, 339-49.

of phenomenology itself, so that phenomenology and phenomenological method take on a radically different character.

This difference is epitomized in the word "hermeneutic"
itself. Husserl never used it in reference to his work, while
Heidegger asserted in *Being and Time* that the authentic
dimensions of a phenomenological method make it hermeneutical; his project in *Being and Time* was a "hermeneutic of
Dasein." Heidegger's selection of the term "hermeneutic"—a
word laden with associations, from its Greek roots to its modern
use in philology and theology—suggests the antiscientific bias
which forms a marked contrast to Husserl. This same strain
is carried over into Hans-Georg Gadamer's "philosophical
hermeneutics," stamping the word itself with overtones of
antiscientism.

The contrasting attitudes toward science may be taken as
a key to the differences between Husserl and Heidegger, which
seem to follow logically from the earlier training of the former
in mathematics and the latter in theology. For Husserl, philosophy needs to become a "rigorous science," [5] a "higher empiri-
cism"; for Heidegger, all the rigor in the world could not make
scientific knowledge a final goal. Husserl's scientific leanings
are reflected in his quest for apodictic knowledge, his reductions, his tendency to search out the visualizable and conceivable through eidetic reduction; Heidegger's writings make
virtually no mention of apodictic knowledge, transcendental
reductions, or the structure of the ego. After *Being and Time,*
Heidegger turns increasingly to reinterpreting earlier philosophers—Kant, Nietzsche, Hegel—and the poetry of Rilke, Trakl,
or Hölderlin. His thinking becomes more "hermeneutical"
in the traditional sense of being centered on text interpretation. Philosophy in Husserl remains basically scientific, and
this is reflected in the significance it has for the sciences today;
in Heidegger, philosophy becomes historical, a creative recovery
of the past, a form of interpretation.[6] Even had Heidegger never
designated his analysis of *Dasein* as a "hermeneutic," he could
still on the strength of his whole later way of proceeding be
designated as a hermeneutical philosopher par excellence.

The lines between the two types of phenomenology are

5. See Husserl's fairly early *Philosophie als strenge Wissenschaft.*
6. The two antithetical kinds of interpretation described by Ricoeur—
récollection du sens (demythologizing) and *exercice du soupçon* (demystification)—are both at work in Heidegger, although the former predominates.
See *DI* 36-44.

clearly drawn on another issue: historicality (*Geschichtlich-keit*). Husserl had observed the temporality of consciousness and furnished a phenomenological description of internal time consciousness, yet his eagerness for apodictic knowledge led him to translate this temporality back into the static and presentational terms of science — essentially to deny the temporality of being itself and assert a realm of ideas above the flux. Thus Heidegger asserted in 1962 that Husserl's phenomenology elaborated "a pattern set by Descartes, Kant, and Fichte. The historicality of thought remains completely foreign to such a position." [7] At the same time Heidegger felt that his analysis in *Being and Time* "was, as I still believe today [1962], a materially justified holding fast to the principle of phenomenology." [8] Phenomenology need not be construed as necessarily a laying-open of consciousness; it can also be a means of disclosing being, in all its facticity and historicality. To understand the meaning of this, we turn to Heidegger's discussion of phenomenology in § 7 of *Being and Time*.

PHENOMENOLOGY AS HERMENEUTICAL

IN THE SECTION OF *Being and Time* entitled "The Phenomenological Method of Investigation" Heidegger explicitly refers to his method as a "hermeneutic." While it may be asked what this does to phenomenology, there is another question equally important for the present study: What does this do to hermeneutics? Before we face this question, however, it is necessary to explore Heidegger's redefinition of phenomenology.

Heidegger goes back to the Greek roots of the word: *phaino-menon* or *phainesthai*, and *logos*. *Phainomenon*, Heidegger tells us, means "that which shows itself, the manifested, revealed [*das Offenbare*]." The *pha* is akin to the Greek *phōs*, meaning light or brightness, "that in which something can become manifest, can become visible." [9] Phenomena, then, are "the collection of what is open to the light of day, or can be brought to light, what the Greeks identified simply with *ta onta, das Seiende*, what is." [10]

7. Letter to W. J. Richardson in April, 1962, printed as a preface to Richardson's *TPhT* xv.
8. *Ibid.*
9. *SZ* 28.
10. *Ibid.*

This "becoming manifest," or form of revealing something "as it is," should not be construed, Heidegger says, as a secondary form of referring—as when something "seems to be something else." Nor is it like a symptom of something, pointing to another more primary phenomenon. Rather, it is a showing or bringing to appearance of something as it is, in its manifestness.

The -ology suffix in phenomenology goes back, of course, to the Greek word *logos*. *Logos*, Heidegger tells us, is that which is conveyed in speaking; the deeper sense of *logos* then is itself to let something appear. It is not defined by Heidegger as something like "reason" or "ground" but rather suggests the speaking function, which makes both reason and ground possible. It has an apophantic function—it points to phenomena. In other words, it has an "as" function, since it lets something be seen *as* something.

Yet this function is not free but a matter of disclosing, or bringing to manifestness, what a thing is; it brings it out of concealment into the light of day. The mind does not project a meaning onto the phenomenon; rather, what appears is an ontological manifesting of the thing itself. Of course, through dogmatism a thing can be forced to be seen only in the desired aspect. But to let a thing appear as what it is becomes a matter of learning to allow it to do so, for it gives itself to be seen. *Logos* (speaking) is not really a power given to language by its user but a power which language gives to him, a means of being seized by what is made manifest through it.

The combination of *phainesthai* and *logos*, then, as phenomenology means letting things become manifest as what they are, without forcing our own categories on them. It means a reversal of direction from that one is accustomed to: it is not we who point to things; rather, things show themselves to us. This is not to suggest some primitive animism but the recognition that the very essence of true understanding is that of being led by the power of the thing to manifest itself. This conception is an expression of Husserl's own intention to return to things themselves. Phenomenology is a means of being led by the phenomenon through a way of access genuinely belonging to it.

Such a method would be of highest significance to hermeneutical theory, since it implies that interpretation is not grounded in human consciousness and human categories but in the manifestness of the thing encountered, the reality that comes to meet us. But Heidegger's concern was with metaphysics and the question of being. Could such a method put an end to the subjectivity and speculative character of metaphysics? Could it be applied to the question of being? Unfortunately the task is complicated by the fact that being is not really a phenomenon at all but something more encompassing and elusive. It can never truly become an object for us, since we are being in the very act of constituting any object as object.

Yet in *Being and Time* Heidegger finds a kind of access in the fact that one has with his existence, along *with* it, a certain understanding of what fullness of being is. It is not a fixed understanding but historically formed, accumulated in the very experience of encountering phenomena. Being can perhaps, then, be interrogated by an analysis of how appearing occurs. Ontology must become phenomenology. Ontology must turn to the processes of understanding and interpretation through which things appear; it must lay open the mood and direction of human existence; it must render visible the invisible structure of being-in-the-world.

How does this relate to hermeneutics? It means that ontology must, as phenomenology of being, become a "hermeneutic" of existence. But this kind of hermeneutic is certainly not old-fashioned philological methodology, or even the general methodology of the *Geisteswissenschaften* envisioned by Dilthey. It lays open what was hidden; it constitutes not an interpretation of an interpretation (which textual explication is) but the primary act of interpretation which first brings a thing from concealment.

> The methodological meaning of phenomenological description is *interpretation* [*Auslegung,* laying open]. The *logos* of a phenomenology of *Dasein* has the character of *hermēneuein* [to interpret], through which are made known to *Dasein* the structure of his own being and the authentic meaning of being given in his [preconscious] understanding of being. Phenomenology of *Dasein* is hermeneutics in the original sense of the word, which designated the business of interpretation.[11]

Hermeneutics, with one step, has become "interpretation of the being of *Dasein*."[12] Philosophically, it sets forth the basic structures of possibility for *Dasein;* it is "an analysis of the

11. *Ibid.,* 37.
12. *Ibid.* .

existentiality of *Existenz*," [13] that is, of the being's authentic possibilities for being. Hermeneutics, says Heidegger, is that fundamental announcing function through which *Dasein* makes known to himself the nature of being. Hermeneutics as methodology of interpretation for the humanities is a derivative form resting on and growing out of the primary ontological function of interpreting. It is a regional ontology which must be based on the more fundamental ontology.

In effect, hermeneutics becomes an ontology of understanding and interpretation. While some critics of Heidegger on behalf of the philological discipline of hermeneutics may view with alarm this desertion of the received definition, it really deepens and extends the historical tendency to define hermeneutics in an ever more comprehensive way. For hermeneutics in Schleiermacher had looked for a foundation in the conditions pertaining to all dialogue, and Dilthey attempted to see understanding as a power of man through which life meets life. Yet understanding in Dilthey was not universalized, for he cherished the idea of an "historical" understanding separate from the scientific. Heidegger takes the final step and defines the essence of hermeneutics as the ontological power of understanding and interpretation which renders possible the disclosure of being of things and ultimately of the potentialities of *Dasein's* own being.

It might be put another way: Hermeneutics is still the theory of understanding, but understanding is differently (ontologically) defined.

THE NATURE OF UNDERSTANDING: HOW HEIDEGGER MOVES BEYOND DILTHEY

UNDERSTANDING (*Verstehen*) is a special term in Heidegger, meaning neither what the English word ordinarily denotes, nor what the term meant in Dilthey. In English "understanding" suggests sympathy, the capacity to feel something of what another person is experiencing. We speak of an "understanding look" and suggest by this more than mere objective knowledge; it is something like participation in the thing understood. One can have vast knowledge and little understanding, for understanding seems to reach into what is essential and, in

13. *Ibid.*, 38.

some usages, personal. In Schleiermacher, understanding was grounded in his philosophical affirmation of the identity of inner realities *(Identitätsphilosophie)* so that in understanding, one vibrated in unison with the speaker as one understood; understanding involved both comparative and divinatory phases. In Dilthey, understanding referred to that deeper level of comprehension involved in grasping a picture, a poem, or a fact — social, economic, or psychological — as more than a mere datum, as an "expression" of "inner realities" and ultimately of "life" itself.

All of these conceptions of understanding bring with them associations quite foreign to Heidegger's definition. For Heidegger, understanding is the power to grasp one's own possibilities for being, within the context of the lifeworld in which one exists. It is not a special capacity or gift for feeling into the situation of another person, nor is it the power to grasp the meaning of some "expression of life" on a deeper level. Understanding is conceived not as something to be possessed but rather as a mode or constituent element of being-in-the-world. It is not an entity in the world but rather the structure in being which makes possible the actual exercise of understanding on an empirical level. Understanding is the basis for *all* interpretation; it is co-original with one's existing and is present in every act of interpretation.

Understanding is thus ontologically fundamental and prior to every act of existing. A second side of it lies in the fact that understanding always relates to the future; this is its projective character *(Entwurfscharakter)*. But projection must have a base, and understanding is also related to one's situation *(Befindlichkeit)*. Yet the essence of understanding lies not in simply grasping one's situation but in the disclosure of concrete potentialities for being within the horizon of one's placement in the world. For this aspect of understanding Heidegger uses the term "existentiality" *(Existenzialität)*.

An important characteristic of understanding, as Heidegger sees it, is that it always operates within a set of already interpreted relationships, a relational whole *(Bewandtnisganzheit)*. The implications of this for hermeneutics are far-reaching, especially when connected with Heidegger's ontology. Dilthey had already asserted that meaningfulness is always a matter of reference to a context of relationships *(Strukturzusammenhang)*, an instance of the familiar principle that understanding always operates within a "hermeneutical circle" rather than proceeding in an ordered progression from simple and self-sufficient parts to a whole. Heidegger's phenomenological hermeneutics, however, goes one step farther: it explores the implications of the hermeneutical circle for the ontological structure of all human existential understanding and interpretation. Of course, understanding should not be conceived as something metaphysical, above the sentient existence of man, but as inseparable from it; Heidegger does not negate Dilthey's experience-oriented view so much as place it in an ontological context. This is seen in the fact that understanding is not separable from mood, nor on the other hand is it imaginable without "world" or "meaningfulness." The key point is that understanding in Heidegger has become ontological. A consideration of Heidegger's concept of world will clarify this.

WORLD AND OUR RELATIONSHIP
TO OBJECTS IN THE WORLD

THE TERM "WORLD" in Heidegger does not mean our environment, objectively considered, the universe as it appears to a scientific gaze. It is closer to what might be called our personal world. World is not the whole of all beings but the whole in which the human being always finds himself already immersed, surrounded by its manifestness as revealed through an always pregrasping, encompassing understanding.

To conceive of world as separate from the self would be totally antithetical to Heidegger's conception, for this would presuppose the very subject-object separation which itself arises within the relational context called world. World is prior to any separation of self and world in the objective sense. It is prior to all "objectivity," all conceptualizing; it is therefore also prior to subjectivity, since both objectivity and subjectivity are conceived within the subject-object schema.

World cannot be described by trying to enumerate the entities within it; in this process world would be passed over, for world is just what is presupposed in every act of knowing an entity. Every entity in the world is grasped as an entity *in terms of* world, which is always already there. The entities which comprise man's physical world are not themselves world but in a world. Only man has world. World is so encompassing, and at the same time so close, that it eludes notice. One sees right through it, yet one could not see anything in its own manifestness without it. Unnoticed, presupposed, encompassing, world is always present, transparent and eluding every attempt to grasp it as object.

A new realm—world—is thus opened for exploration. It will not be easy to approach, for neither the empirical description of entities within it nor even the ontological interpretation of their individual being as such will encounter the phenomenon of world.[14] World is something sensed "alongside" the entities that appear in the world, yet understanding must be through world. It is fundamental to all understanding; world and understanding are inseparable parts of the ontological constitution of *Dasein's* existing.

Corresponding to the unobtrusiveness of world is the unobtrusiveness of certain objects in the world to which one daily relates his existing. The tools used daily, the movements of the body performed without thought, all become transparent. Only when some breakdown occurs are they noticed. At the point of breakdown, we may observe a significant fact: the *meaning* of these objects lies in their relation to a structural whole of interrelated meanings and intentions. In breakdown, for a brief moment the meaning of the objects is lighted up, emerging directly from world.

How different such an understanding of an object is from a mere intellectual comprehension! To use a familiar example from *Being and Time*, a hammer that is merely present is something that can be weighed, catalogued as to properties, compared to other hammers; a broken hammer at once shows what a hammer is.[15] This experience suggests a hermeneutical principle: that the being of something is disclosed not to the contemplative analytical gaze but in the moment in which it suddenly emerges from hiddenness in the full functional context of world. Likewise, the character of understanding will best be grasped not through an analytical catalogue of its attributes, nor in the full flush of its proper functioning, but when

14. *Ibid.,* 64.
15. *Ibid.,* 69. W. B. Macomber sees the broken hammer as a key image in Heidegger's thinking; see his lucid study of Heidegger's notion of truth, *The Anatomy of Disillusion.*

it breaks down, when it comes up against a wall, perhaps when
something it must have is missing.

PREPREDICATIVE MEANINGFULNESS, UNDERSTANDING, AND INTERPRETATION

THE PHENOMENON OF BREAKDOWN that momentarily
lights up the being of a tool *as* tool points, as we have just seen,
to the largely inconspicuous "world" in which we exist. This
world is more than simply the realm of the preconscious operations of the mind in perception; it is the realm in which the
actual resistances and possibilities in the structure of being
shape understanding. It is the realm where the temporality
and historicality of being are radically present, and the place
where being translates itself into meaningfulness, understanding, and interpretation. It is, in short, the realm of the
hermeneutical process, the process by which being becomes
thematized as language.

As has been mentioned, understanding operates in a fabric
of relationships (*Bewandnisganzheit*). Heidegger coins the
term "meaningfulness" (*Bedeutsamkeit*) to designate the
ontological ground for the intelligibility of that fabric of relationships. As such, it provides the ontological possibility that
words can have meaningful signification; it is the basis for
language. The point Heidegger is making here is that meaningfulness is something deeper than the logical system of language;
it is founded on something prior to language and embedded in
world—the relational whole. However much words may shape
or formulate meaning, they point beyond their own system to a
meaningfulness already resident in the relational whole of
world. Meaningfulness, then, is not something man gives to an
object; it is what an object gives to man through supplying the
ontological possibility of words and language.

Understanding must be seen as embedded in this context,
and interpretation is simply the rendering explicit of understanding. Interpretation, then, is not a matter of sticking a
value on a naked object, for what is encountered arises as already seen in a particular relationship. Even in understanding,
things in the world are seen *as* this or *as* that. Interpretation
renders explicit this word "as." Prior to every thematic statement lies the foundation of understanding. Heidegger puts it

succinctly: "All prepredicative simple seeing of the invisible world of the ready-to-hand is in itself already an 'understanding-interpreting' seeing." [16]

When understanding becomes explicit as interpretation, as language, a further extrasubjective factor is at work, for "language already conceals within itself a developed mode of ideation," an "already shaped way of seeing." [17] Understanding and meaningfulness together are the basis for language and interpretation. In later works the connection of language to being is stressed even more, so that being itself is linguistic: Heidegger notes in the *Introduction to Metaphysics,* for instance, that "words and language are not wrappings in which things are packed for the commerce of those who write and speak. It is in words and language that things first come into being and are." [18] This is the sense in which the more familiar saying of Heidegger, "Language is the house of being," must be interpreted. [19]

Thus understanding has a certain "prestructure" which comes into play in all interpretation. This becomes very clear in Heidegger's analysis of the threefold prestructure of understanding. We need not here go into an exposition of it, however, since its essential character and significance are implicit in what we have already said about world and meaningfulness. [20]

THE IMPOSSIBILITY OF PRESUPPOSITIONLESS INTERPRETATION

THE PRESTRUCTURE OF UNDERSTANDING, always already interpreting and embedded in world, goes beyond the older model of the interpretive situation in terms of subject and object. In fact, it raises grave questions about the basic

16. "Alles vorprädikative schlichte Sehen des Zuhandenen ist an ihm selbst schon verstehend-auslegend" (SZ 149).
17. "Die Sprache je schon eine ausgebildete Begrifflichkeit in sich birgt" (*ibid.,* 157).
18. *IM* 13.
19. *PL-BH* 53. The *Letter* begins on p. 53; thus citations from preceding pages are from *PL* and succeeding ones are from *BH.*
20. See *SZ* 150-53, esp.: "Die Auslegung von Etwas als Etwas wird wesenhaft durch Vorhabe, Vorsicht und Vorgriff fundiert" (p. 150); and "Sinn ist das durch Vorhabe, Vorsicht und Vorgriff [the threefold structure of preunderstanding] strukturierte Woraufhin des Entwurfs, aus dem her etwas als etwas verständlich wird" (p. 151).

validity of describing interpretation in terms of the subject-object relationship. Likewise it raises questions as to what can be meant by so-called objective interpretation, or interpretation "without presuppositions." Heidegger puts the matter plainly: "Interpretation is never a presuppositionless grasping of something given in advance." [21]

The hope of interpreting "without prejudice and presupposition" ultimately flies in the face of the way understanding operates. What appears from the "object" is what one allows to appear and what the thematization of the world at work in his understanding will bring to light. It is naive to assume that what is "really there" is "self-evident." The very definition of what is presumed to be self-evident rests on a body of unnoticed presuppositions, which are present in every interpretive construction by the "objective" and "presuppositionless" interpreter. This body of already given and granted presuppositions is what Heidegger uncovers in his analysis of understanding.

In literary interpretation, this means that the most "presuppositionless" interpreter of a text of lyric poetry has preliminary assumptions. Even as he approaches a text, he may already have seen it as a certain kind of text, say, a lyric, and is placing himself in the posture he interprets to be appropriate to such a text. His encounter with the work is not in some context outside time and space, outside his own horizon of experiences and interests, but rather in a particular time and place. There is, for instance, a reason he is turning to this text and not some other, and thus he approaches the text questioningly, not with a blank openness.

It is important to remember, then, that the prestructuredness of understanding is not simply a property of consciousness over against an already given world. To see it in this way would be to fall back into the very subject-object model of interpretation which Heidegger's analysis transcends. Prestructure rests, rather, in the context of world, which already contains subject and object. Heidegger is describing understanding and interpretation in such a way as to place them prior to the subject-object dichotomy. He is discussing how things themselves come into view through meaning, understanding, and interpretation. He is discussing what might be called the ontological structure of understanding.

21. *Ibid.*, 150.

Hermeneutics as a theory of understanding is, in consequence, really a theory of ontological disclosure. Since human existing is itself a process of ontological disclosure, Heidegger will not allow us to see the hermeneutical problem apart from human existing. Hermeneutics in Heidegger, then, is a fundamental theory of how understanding emerges in human existence. His analysis weds hermeneutics to existential ontology and to phenomenology, and it points to a ground for hermeneutics not in subjectivity but in the facticity of world and in the historicality of understanding.

THE DERIVATIVE CHARACTER OF ASSERTIONS

A FURTHER CONSEQUENCE of the considerations we have been discussing and one which is of hermeneutical importance is contained in Heidegger's discussion of logical assertions—and, by extension, of logic itself. For Heidegger, a "statement" (*Aussage*) is not a fundamental form of interpretation but rests on the more primary operations of understanding and interpretation in preunderstanding. Without these, assertions would have no meaning.

Heidegger gives an example: "The hammer is heavy." In the assertion itself, he says, an already shaped way of conceiving is at work, that of logic. Before any really apparent interpretation or analysis, the situation has been structured into logical terms to fit the structure of an assertion. The hammer has already been interpreted as a thing with properties, in this case heaviness. The sentence structure of the assertion, with its pattern of subject, copulative, and predicate adjective, has already placed the hammer over against one as an object, as something possessing properties.

But the fundamental processes of interpreting the world do not occur in logical assertions and theoretical statements. Often words are absent, as when one tests a hammer and lays it aside without words. This is an interpretive act but not an assertion. Continuing with the hammer example, Heidegger asks how an assertion emerges:

The hammer possessed in fore-having is ready-to-hand as a tool. When this being becomes an "object" of an assertion, with the very construction of the assertion a shift occurs in the fore-having. The ready-to-hand tendency to think "with what?" becomes the "about

what?" of a referential assertion. The view of the object in preunderstanding is now focused on what is merely "on hand" in the ready-
to-hand. . . . And readiness-to-hand as such passes into concealment.[22]

The disclosing of the hammer as object is at the same time a
concealing of it as tool. The hammer as object is severed from
its living context, and its essence as a tool which can do ham-
mering is covered over.

The example of the hammer may be used to clarify Heidegger's distinction between the "apophantic" and "hermeneutical" forms of the word "as." In the context of being ready-to-
hand, the hammer disappears as object into the function of
being a tool; we do not approach it *as* an object but *as* a tool.
The "as" which merely interprets the hammer as object on
hand, as something before one's gaze and to which one points,
is the "apophantic as." The hammer disappearing into its
function *as* tool represents the "existential-hermeneutical
as." The "apophantic as" signals a subtle shift in preunderstanding to a stance of objective pointing, a pointing which
no longer connects the hammer with the primordial totality
of a lived, relational context (the *Bewandtnisganzheit*); it
cuts it off from the realm of meaningfulness in the ready-to-
hand and puts the phenomenon forward as something merely
to be looked at.

Heidegger calls for going further into the more original
"as." "We should examine more carefully," he says, "what
Aristotle meant by 'binding and separating' in their unity, and
along with this the phenomenon of something *as* something."[23]
According to this structure, something is taken together with
that from which it is understood, so that interpreting and
articulating form a unity. To shatter the original unity and
ignore the more original "as" opens the way to a mere "theory
of judgments" (*Urteilstheorie*), one which sees assertions as
the mere binding and separating of ideas and concepts, one
which always remains on the shallow level of objective, on-
hand realities.[24] To affirm the more primary "existential-hermeneutical as" is to recognize that all assertions are really
derived from and rooted in a more primary level of interpreta-

22. *Ibid.*, 157–58.
23. *Ibid.*, 159.
24. *Ibid.*

tion. It is to see that assertions cannot meaningfully be considered apart from their roots in existence.

The significance of this distinction can be appreciated by examining the way in which language tends to be treated today in the "sciences" of language. This is especially evident in the inadequacy of all definitions of language which remain on the level of assertions and logic, or which take an instrumental view of language as merely consciousness manipulating statements and ideas. For the true foundation of language is the phenomenon of speaking, where something is brought to light; this is the (hermeneutical) function of language. In taking speaking as the starting point, one goes back to the event in which word functions as word, one goes back to the living context of language. Gerhard Ebeling echoes Heidegger's viewpoint when he says: *"The word itself has a hermeneutical function."* [25] Indeed, the primary, *hermeneutical* function of language becomes a central factor in the later Heidegger and in the theological New Hermeneutic. This view of language means that understanding, again as Ebeling has put it, "is not understanding *of* language, but understanding *through* language." [26] The importance of this view theologically can hardly be overestimated, since it restores the emphasis on the speaking function.[27]

Language as speaking is no longer an objective body of words which one manipulates as objects; it takes its place in the world of what is ready-to-hand. It can, of course, pass into the objectivity of merely being before one as an object, but fundamentally language is found by man as something ready-to-hand, transparent, contextual.

Language as speaking, however, is not to be seen as expression of some "inner reality." It is a situation coming to explicitness in words. Even poetic speaking is not a conveying of pure interiority but a sharing of world. As a disclosure not of the speaker but of the being of the world, it is neither a subjective nor an objective phenomenon but both together, for world is prior to and encompasses both.

25. *WF* 318; *NH* 93-94.
26. *Ibid.*
27. See Chap. 2 on the meaning of *hermēneuein* as "to say" or "to announce." This primary dimension is emphasized in Heidegger. See also Gerhard Ebeling, *Theology and Proclamation*, where the word "proclamation" carries this meaning.

10 / Heidegger's Later Contribution to Hermeneutical Theory

HAD HEIDEGGER WRITTEN NOTHING AFTER *Being and Time*, his contribution to hermeneutics would have been decisive, for he had there placed the question of understanding in a radically new context. As a foundational mode of existing, it transcended the definitional limits placed on it by Dilthey in conceiving it as the historical over against the scientific form of understanding. Heidegger went further to assert that all understanding is temporal, intentional, historical. He went beyond previous conceptions in seeing understanding not as a mental but as an ontological process, not as a study of conscious and unconscious processes but as disclosure of what is real for man. Before, one simply assumed a prior definition of what was real and then asked how mental processes brought this reality to stand; now Heidegger probes understanding one earlier step to point to the reality-founding, reality-disclosing act by which the prior definition was achieved. A theme in later Heidegger will be the effort to go back behind the reality-founding event on the basis of which being itself is today thematized.

"Every great poet poetizes out of a single poem," Heidegger says in *Unterwegs zur Sprache*,[1] and since original thinking is essentially poetical, every great thinker enunciates a single thought that remains never fully spoken. In a sense, then, Heidegger's later writings may be seen as a series of footnotes to *Being and Time*, essaying over and over again the same quest for an access to being, deepening and rendering more radical

1. *US* 37.

[140]

the insights of his masterwork. He becomes perhaps the most poetical, the most hermeneutical philosopher since Plato; the basic quest in his thinking, however, does not change but simply becomes more fully explicated. In fact, when the central focus in Heidegger on understanding and its articulation is perceived, it can be understood why the later writings become preoccupied with "thinking," and why Heidegger defines thinking in terms of responsiveness rather than manipulation of ideas. It is common to distinguish a "turn" in Heidegger's thought, yet in reality his thought is of a piece when surveyed from the vantage point of today. *Being and Time* is the soil out of which the later thought grows. From beginning to end Heidegger is concerned with the hermeneutical process by which being can be brought to light. This was approached in *Being and Time* as a phenomenology of *Dasein,* and in subsequent works it became an exploration of nonbeing, of the word "being" itself, of Greek and modern conceptions of being and truth, of thinking, and of language. Admittedly, Heidegger becomes more poetical, obscure, and prophetic in his later writings, but disclosure of being remains his constant theme.

In the later writings, the hermeneutical character of Heidegger's thought takes on other dimensions, but it becomes more rather than less hermeneutical, and even becomes hermeneutical in the sense of concerning itself with exegesis. His theme is still how being came to be understood and articulated in static and essentialist terms, but the object of interpretation shifts from a generalized description of *Dasein's* everyday contact with being to metaphysics and poetry. Increasingly he turns to text interpretation; few thinkers in the history of Western philosophy have made the exegesis of texts, especially ancient fragments, so much a part of their way of philosophizing. Even had Heidegger not made his decisive philosophical contribution to understanding theory in *Being and Time,* he might still be called the most "hermeneutical" of Western philosophers.

Perhaps this development is owing to the intrinsically hermeneutical nature of the effort to deal with "being" if it is approached in the context of the understanding process by which things come to light. And it becomes more hermeneutical if we wish to go behind the "text" of Western thinking to the questions which gave rise to that tradition. Then, there is the effort to draw out the hidden meaning of the text, and not simply to remain satisfied with exploring the whole system on its own terms. This Heidegger attempts to do and at the same time gives his own view as to the proper hermeneutical stance for man in reference to being and to the tradition. A detailed exposition of Heidegger's later thought far exceeds the possible scope of this chapter;[2] a few major themes and their significance for hermeneutical theory will, however, be outlined briefly in the remaining sections.

THE CRITIQUE OF PRESENTATIONAL THINKING, SUBJECTISM, AND TECHNOLOGY

HEIDEGGER, IN *Being and Time*, had already suggested the direction of his later criticisms of presentational thinking in his discussion of the derivative character of "assertions" as they tend to present things in such a way as simply to be looked at. He showed there how, within the prestructure of understanding, the view of the object tended subtly to be ordered to the demands of logical and conceptual thought, and how the hammer, as an example, was ripped out of its living context (*das Zuhandene*) and placed in the abstract realm of presentational thought. In later writings Heidegger attempts to review how Western thinking came to define thinking, being, and truth in essentially presentational terms.

In "Plato's Doctrine of Truth," Heidegger turns to the famous cave allegory. In the overall allegory, there is a suggestion that truth is unconcealment, for one climbs up out of the cave into the light and goes back down into the cave; but the conception of truth as "correspondence" came to predominate over the more dynamic conception of unconcealment. Truth became correct seeing, and thinking became a matter of placing an idea before the mind's eye, that is, it became the proper manipulation of ideas.

With this view of thinking and truth, the stage is set for the whole Western development of metaphysics, for the approaching of life theoretically—ideologically, in terms of ideas:

2. See, however, W. B. Macomber's *The Anatomy of Disillusion*, as well as Richardson's detailed discussion in *TPhT*; in German, Otto Pöggeler, *Der Denkweg Martin Heideggers*, is especially to be recommended. Useful discussions in English are available by Kockelmans, Langan, Versényi, and others, listed in the Bibliography.

The essence of the idea lies in appearance and visibility. This brings to fulfillment the presence of the "what" that each being is. In the "what-being" of the being, it comes to presence. Being "present" however is as such seen to be the nature of being. For this reason, being for Plato had its authentic nature in "what-being." Later terminology puts it that the *quidditas* is the true *esse;* the *essentia,* and not the *existentia.* So what is brought into view as "idea" for the contemplator is the disclosure of the thing as it appears. So the thing disclosed is from the beginning and only grasped as what is perceived when we perceive the idea of something, the what that is known in the act of knowing.[3]

As everything comes to be ordered to the conception of ideas and ideation, and most importantly the concept of reason, Heidegger asserts, the earlier conception of truth as disclosure is lost. Western man no longer senses being as constantly emerging and receding from his grasp but as in the form of a static presence of an idea. Truth becomes something seen: "*orthotes,* correctness of perception and assertion."[4] This means that thinking aimed at truth is grounded not in existence but in perceiving an idea; being is conceived not in terms of living experience but in terms of idea—statically, as a constant, atemporal presentness.

On this rock, it might be said, the West has built its metaphysics and theology. As early as 1921, in his (unpublished) lectures on "Augustinus und der Neuplatonismus," Heidegger had traced the conflict evident in the *Confessions,* Book X, between the Christianity that arises out of the facticity of lived experience, with its fulfillment not so much in *knowing* God as in living in Him, and, on the other hand, a Christianity oriented to "enjoyment" of God as the *summum bonum* (i.e., the idea of *fruitio Dei*). This latter more static and presentational conception of being and of experiencing God is directly traceable to Neo-Platonism. When the experience of God is defined as *fruitio Dei,* and when God is enjoyed as the "peace" that stills the restlessness in the heart, then He is pressed out of the flux of factical-historical life and His vitality as a God of lived experience is stilled. He is no longer living, temporal, finite, ready-to-hand. He is merely "on hand" to be contemplated and enjoyed; God becomes an Eternal Being outside and above time, place, and history.[5]

3. *PL-BH* 35.
4. *Ibid.,* 42.
5. Pöggeler, pp. 38–45; *Ho* 338–39.

In a lecture given in June, 1938, under the title "The Founding of the Modern Image of the World through Metaphysics," Heidegger traces the effect of such a general approach to truth and thinking when combined with the Cartesian standpoint, for in Descartes, Western thinking had taken another decisive · turn. Truth, to Descartes, is more than merely the conformity between the knower and the known, it is the *subject's rational certainty* of this conformity. The consequence of this is that the human subject is seen as the ultimate reference point for the status of all that is seen. This means that every being is such only in terms of the subject-object polarity of consciousness and the objects of consciousness. What is known is not seen ultimately as an ontologically independent entity presenting itself as it "is," as disclosing and manifesting itself to us in its own power of being; rather, what is known is seen as an object, as something which the conscious subject presents to itself. Because the status of the world is firmly anchored in human subjectivity, it becomes subject-centered, and philosophy becomes consciousness-centered. This syndrome Heidegger calls modern "subjectism" (*Subjektität*).[6]

Subjectism is a broader term than subjectivity, for it means that the world is regarded as basically measured by man. In this view the world has meaning only with respect to man, whose task is to master the world. The consequences of subjectism are many. First, the sciences take preeminence, for they serve man's will to master. Yet since in subjectism man recognizes no goal or meaning that is not grounded in his own rational certainty, he is locked in the circle of his own projected world. Art objects are seen as merely "objectifications" of subjectivity, or "expressions" of human experience. A culture can only be the collective objectification of what human subjects value, a projection of the groundless activity of man.

6. Subjectism is distinguished from subjectivity, for it constitutes both the objectivity of the object and the subjectivity of the subject. Subjectivity implies necessarily that the human ego is the presentative subject, and this subjectivity is the form that subjectism takes in Descartes. But Heidegger sees subjectism as resident in any philosophical position which takes the human phenomenon as its ultimate reference point, whether it be collectivism, absolutism, or individualism. Subjectism is latent in the Platonic interpretation of being, since an idea is something seen by someone. But with Descartes the situation is made explicit that man is not the receiver of emanations of being more primary than he himself is (i.e., man is no longer creature), but rather that he is a creating being, the ground of a world that he himself forms and projects. See *TPhT* 320–30.

Neither cultural nor individual human activity can be seen, in this framework, as a response to the activity of God (or of Being), since everything is grounded in man. Ultimately even God is redefined as "the infinite, unconditioned, and absolute," and the world is de-divinized; man's relation to God is approached as merely his own "religious experience." While the older concept of *fruitio Dei* refined God out of the flux of daily living, subjectism makes God a projection of man and relationship to Him a human feeling of dependence.[7]

Modern "value philosophies" are but another consequence of the metaphysics of subjectism. Values are a stopgap concept meant to supply "things" (now that their value is subjectively grounded) with the meaning they lost in coming into the framework of subjectism. The sense of the sacredness of things, with or without man, is lost; the status of things is reduced to their usefulness to man. When man "assigns" values to objects, it is only a short step, philosophically, to see values themselves as objects. A value is then something one throws like a coat of paint over objects in his world. Science and humanism become the watchwords in an age in which man is truly the center and measure of all things.

How can thinking be defined in such a framework? Again, in presentational terms that go back to Plato. How can truth be conceived? In terms of correctness, certainty that the statement about something corresponds with the way the object is presented to us. This presentation cannot really be a self-disclosure of something, since it is caught up in the overpowering act of objectification by the subject. Therefore, says Heidegger, the great metaphysical systems become expressions of will, whether phrased in terms of reason (Kant), freedom (Fichte), love (Schelling), absolute spirit (Hegel), or will-to-power (Nietzsche).[8]

The will to power that is grounded in subjectism knows no ultimate value, only the thirst for more power. In the present day this expresses itself in the frenzy for technological mastery. Yet the impact of technological thinking is more subtle and pervasive than this, for gradually we have come to consider thinking itself in terms of mastery. Thought becomes technological, shaped to the requirements of concepts and ideas that will give control over objects and experience. Thinking

7. Ho 70.
8. VA 114–22; TPhT 381.

is no longer a matter of open responsiveness to the world but of restless efforts to master it; it does not conserve and act as guardian of the riches of the earth, but exhausts the world in trying to restructure it to man's purposes. A river, for instance, has no intrinsic worth any more, and man redirects its course to suit his purposes, building great dams, dumping poisonous refuse in it. The gods have fled, and the earth is relentlessly being consumed. Such, according to Heidegger, is the melancholy denouement of a development of thinking from Plato through Descartes and Nietzsche into the present day.

Hermeneutics, as the theory of what understanding and interpretation are, is directly affected by these considerations, for when the interpretive problem is approached within the context of technological thinking, interpretation provides the means for conceptual mastery of the object. When thinking is defined as the manipulation of ideas and concepts, it is no longer creative but manipulative and inventive. When subjectism lies at the base of the interpretive situation, what is being interpreted but an objectification? The concept of truth as correspondence fits logically with these approaches, and truth becomes merely "correctness."

For the theory of interpretation, then, it makes a great difference whether thinking is conceived strictly in ideational terms, for then interpretation itself is dealing not with an unknown matter which has to be brought to light but with the clarification and evaluation of already known data. Then its task is not the primary "showing" of the thing but that of achieving correctness among several possible interpretations. Such presuppositions tend to keep one always in the clear light of what is already known instead of bridging the gap between light and darkness. Language comes to be conceived as a system of signs applied to an already known set of objects.

But for Heidegger this whole set of definitions – of language, truth, and thinking – and the concept of understanding and interpretation built on them, represents a thematization of Plato's doctrine of truth. Western thinking, and especially metaphysics, since Plato represents the "text" of this thematization. Heidegger found his hermeneutical task to interpret this text by going behind it. In Kant, in Hegel, in Nietzsche,

Heidegger finds hints of the older Greek approach to truth as unconcealment briefly asserting its claims, only to be overshadowed and lost. From the beginning, then, Heidegger defined his philosophical task in essentially hermeneutical terms. Hermeneutics, in this context, does not mean simply interpretation in terms of correctness and agreement; hermeneutics carries its deeper traditional overtones of bringing out a *hidden* meaning, of bringing what is unknown to light: revelation and disclosure. Thus when Heidegger "interprets" Kant he is not merely saying what the author intended, for to do so would be to stop short at the very point when true interpretation must begin. He asks, rather, what the text did *not* say; he asks why Kant made certain revisions between the first and second editions of the *Critique of Pure Reason*. He goes behind the text to ask what the author did not and could not say, yet which in the text comes to light as its innermost dynamic.[9] The finished and final text is not the sole object of interpretation but rather the inner violence and struggle which were at work in the creation of the text.

This brings up two traditionally familiar issues in hermeneutics: (1) doing violence to the text, and (2) understanding the author better than he understood himself. When truth is conceived as something which both emerges and plunges back into concealment, when the hermeneutical act places the interpreter on the border of that creative emptiness out of which the work emerged, then interpretation must be creatively open to the as yet unsaid. For "nothingness" is the creative backdrop of every positive creation; yet this nothingness is meaningful only in the context of being, in its positivity. When the art work is seen not as an objectification of human subjectivity but as a disclosure of being, or a window to the sacred realm, then one's encounter is a receiving of a gift, not a subject's act of grasping its subjectivity.

Interpretation of a great work is not an antiquarian exercise, nor is it the effort, familiar in humanism, to take the Greeks as a model of how to live. It is, rather, a repetition and retrieval of the original event of disclosure. It tries to get beneath the accumulated crust of misinterpretation (Heidegger loves to "polish" words until their original luster shines through again) and take a stand in the center of what is said and unsaid.

9. *KPM* 181; in the English trans., 206.

Yet it is not a simple return to the past but a *new* event of disclosure; to try to resurrect Kant just as he was would be a foolish restoration. Thus every interpretation must do violence to the explicit formulations in the text.[10] To refuse to go beyond the explicitness of the text is really a form of idolatry, as well as of historical naïveté.

Does one, then, really understand an author better than the author understood himself? No, for the author was in the full circle of considerations which animated his composition; one does not understand an author better but differently. In *Unterwegs zur Sprache*, Heidegger, in his famous conversation with a Japanese, explains that his aim is to "think Greek thought in a more deeply Greek way."[11] He is asked if this means to understand the Greeks better than they understood themselves. No, not so much that as to go back into not only what was thought and spoken but what was unthought. Heidegger wishes to penetrate the backdrop of Greek thinking as it came to appearance: in the creative emptiness and nonbeing behind its positive emergence may lie a clue to another kind of thinking, another grasp of being, truth, and language. Until this is done, things will be mere objects, and the world man's plaything. What is needed is not more steps forward in the development of presentational thought but a "step back out of the merely ideational, i.e., explaining, type of thinking" to a meditative (*andenkende*) thinking.[12]

ON THE WAY TO THINKING

IT IS COMMONLY SAID that Heidegger was formulating a devastating critique of Western metaphysics or posing again the ontological question, but it is also quite correct to say that virtually all of his later writings are concerned with the hermeneutical process by which man, in "essential" and other kinds of thinking, bridges the boundary between being and nonbeing. The crucial question regarding being is not merely the nature of being but how to *think* being and how being comes to appearance; much consideration, for instance, is given to man's stance in this hermeneutical event in which being comes to

10. *KPM* 181–83; English trans., 206–8.
11. *US* 134.
12. *VA* 180.

stand, or comes to be "understood" in a certain way. To attempt
to trace the theme of "thinking" would be a complex and many-
sided endeavor, one which fortunately has already been done
in English by Father W. J. Richardson.[13] It suffices here to emphasize the generally hermeneutical character of such a theme,
and to touch on a few aspects of it which have particular significance to hermeneutics.

It is significant that in the dialogue with a Japanese, and
precisely at the point to which we have just referred above,
Heidegger asserts that man stands in a "hermeneutical relationship" *(ein hermeneutischer Bezug)* in which he is the
message-bringer, the enunciator of being.[14] Man is the being
who bridges the gap between concealment and disclosure of
being, between nonbeing (in other words) and being. Man, in
speaking, interprets being. True thinking is defined by Heidegger not as the manipulation of what has already been
brought into disclosure, but as disclosing what was hidden.
Yet in the text that is spoken by a thinker or by a great poet,
much remains concealed and as yet unspoken; a thinking
dialogue with the text will itself, therefore, bring further disclosure. This becomes hermeneutics in the more traditional
sense (and Heidegger's writings contain many such dialogues).
Yet this secondary act of interpretation must continually go
back to a loving repetition of the original disclosure, must keep
itself on the border between what is concealed and revealed.

How does a creative dialogue with a text proceed? In the
later writings, during the 1940's and 1950's, such as *Gelassenheit,*[15] the *Letter on Humanism,* or *What Calls Thought
Forth?*, the stance of man seems almost a devotional passivity
which will be completely open to the voice of being. In the
earlier *Introduction to Metaphysics,* however, there is a hermeneutically significant discussion of the nature of questioning when it seeks to be creative, one which brings together a
number of significant strains in Heidegger's later thinking.

Introduction to Metaphysics begins with a question. For
Heidegger, questioning need not be mere cross-examination
but can be a way of being open. The initial question of the
essay—"Why are there beings rather than nothing?"—leads
to a second question which addresses itself to the questioner:

13. *Ibid.*
14. *US* 125–27, 135–36.
15. Trans. as *DT.*

"How stands it with being?" The questioner at once finds himself transported to a standpoint different from that of the opening question, for the question is such as to turn back to the
questioner. In the process of asking such a question, says
Heidegger, "we seem to belong entirely to ourselves. Yet it is
this questioning that moves us into the open, provided that, in
questioning, it transform itself (which all true questioning
does), and cast a new space over everything and into everything." [16]

Questioning, then, is a way that man contends with and
draws being into showing itself. It bridges the ontological difference between being and the being of beings. Questioning
which remains purely on the level of the being of beings and
makes no attempt to move into the (negative) ground of such
being is not true questioning but manipulation, calculation, explanation. Characteristically, Heidegger remarks: "The paraly-
sis of all passion for questioning has long been with us. . . .
Questioning as a fundamental element of historical being has
receded from us." [17]

The essence of man's being-in-the world is precisely the
hermeneutical process of questioning, a kind of questioning
which in its true form reaches into unmanifest being and
draws it out into a concrete, historical occurrence. Through
questioning, then, being becomes history. The interrelation-
ship of being, history, and selfhood becomes clear in the following passage from the *Introduction to Metaphysics:*

1. The determination of the essence of man is never an answer
but essentially a question.
2. The asking of this question is historical in the fundamental
sense that this questioning first creates history. . . .
4. Only where being discloses itself in questioning does history
happen and with it the being of man. . . .
6. Only as a questioning, historical being does man come to
himself; only as such is he a self. Man's selfhood means this: he
must transform the being that discloses itself to him into history
and bring himself to stand in it.

In later writings the emphasis shifts from man's questioning to
the need for wakeful openness to being. Being is still historical,

16. *IM* 29–30.
17. *Ibid.,* 143.

but its occurrence is a gift from the side of being rather than a product of man's inquiry and grasping.[18]

Yet one must be wary of seeing any radical transition or turning here, for Heidegger is not contradicting but supplementing his earlier position; he attempts in the later works to emphasize his nonsubject-centered stance, and for this reason the image shifts from showing man questioningly "contending" with being to man as a "shepherd of being." Yet even as the shepherd of being, man's guardianship is referred to in terms of "thinking" and "poetizing"; these are both actions on man's part, albeit in response to being, and they retain their historical character. In the *Letter on Humanism*, Heidegger asserts:

> Insofar as thinking, as historically recollective, heeds the destiny of being, it has already bound itself to the fateful, that is commensurate with destiny. . . . The fateful character [*Geschicklichkeit*] of the saying of being as gift of truth—this is the first law of thinking, not the rules of logic. . . . Being *is* as the fateful occurrence [*Geschick*] of thinking. This event is in itself historical. Its history is already come to language in the thinker's act of *saying*.[19]

As shepherd of being, man loses the Prometheanism which is suggested in Sophocles' "Ode on Man" (*Antigone*),[20] to which Heidegger gives attention in *Introduction to Metaphysics;* in *Gelassenheit* Heidegger even asserts that "we should *do* nothing, but rather wait." [21]

In *What Calls Thought Forth?* thinking is described as a response to the calling and enjoining voice of being. It is something coming from the inmost core of man, in which "everything that remains to be thought is hidden and concealed." [22] Not questioning but response is the key word. Yet man is still the being who, in response, reaches into the negativity of being, into the undisclosed, the mystery.

The discussion of questioning has led into some of the major themes in later Heidegger: historicality, the ontological difference, poetry and thinking, and the stance of responsive openness necessary to allow one to "move into the Open" and

18. *Ibid.*
19. *PL-BH* 118.
20. *IM* 146–65.
21. *G* 37; *DT* 62.
22. *VA* 139; see *TPhT* 599–601.

be addressed. All of these suggest a hermeneutical stance that differs radically from the distanced and objective attitude that is a consequence of seeing interpretation as a primarily conceptual act, as something like analysis.

LANGUAGE AND SPEAKING

IN THE PASSAGE FROM THE *Letter on Humanism* cited above, the reference to "the thinker's act of saying" suggests another important theme in Heidegger's later writings: the linguisticality of being. Heidegger's interest in language dates from the very beginning of his career with his dissertation "The Doctrine of Judgment in Psychologism: A Critical and Positive Contribution to Logic" [23] and his dissertation on Duns Scotus' doctrine of categories and meaning. In the latter, Heidegger asserted the need to lay open the theoretical foundations of language.[24] Of this early period Heidegger speaks in his recent "Dialogue with a Japanese." Significantly, his remarks are connected with why he chose to use the word "hermeneutics" in *Being and Time*:

> The title "hermeneutics" was familiar to me from my theological studies. At that time I was especially taken with the question of the relation between the scriptural word and speculative theological thought. It was, if you wish, the same relationship—namely that between language and being, only then hidden and inaccessible to me—which I vainly was seeking to find a clue to down paths and bypaths.[25]

The analysis of *Dasein's* situational, understanding-interpreting way of being in the world in *Being and Time* placed language in a new context. It was the articulation of existential understanding. So intimately connected with understanding and intelligibility was it that logical thinking and all conceptual manipulation of objects in the world became secondary and derivative compared to language in the living context of primary articulation of understanding.[26] As early as *Being and Time* the

23. *TPhT* 675.
24. Pöggeler, p. 269.
25. *US* 96.
26. See the discussion of the derivative character of assertions in the preceding chapter.

realm of logic and "assertions" falls in the category of presentational thinking, while language in its true essence as primary articulation of the situational, historical understanding is something belonging to the way of being of man. From this standpoint, Heidegger could criticize theories which saw language merely as a tool of communication.[27]

The theme of language figures importantly in *Introduction to Metaphysics*. Devoted to the question "What is being?" the essay goes back to a fragment from Parmenides in which Heidegger finds the assertion that being is the same as that for which apprehending occurs. This means that "there is being only when there is appearing, entering into unconcealment, when there is disclosure."[28] Just as there can be no occurrence of being without apprehending, and no apprehending without being, so also there can be no being without language, and no language without being.

Suppose that man had no preknowledge of being, that no indeterminate meaning of being was present at all for man. Heidegger asks:

> Would there merely be a noun and a verb less in our language? No. *There would be no language at all.* No being, *as such,* would disclose itself in words, it would no longer be possible to invoke it and speak about it in words; for to speak of a being as such must include to understand it in advance as a being, that is, to understand its being.[29]

On the other hand, "if our essence did not include the power of language, all beings would be closed to us, that which we ourselves are no less than the being that we are not."[30] Without language man could not be, in any mode imaginable to us. Heidegger puts the matter bluntly: "For to be a man is to speak."[31] What an illusion, Heidegger remarks, to think that man *invented* language! Man does not invent language any more than he invents understanding, time, or being itself. ("How could man ever have invented the power which per-

---

27. SZ 162–66. Regarding a new kind of logic, see Hans Lipps, *Untersuchungen zu einer hermeneutischen Logik,* and Kitarō Nishida, *Intelligibility and the Philosophy of Nothingness.*
28. *IM* 139.
29. *Ibid.,* 82.
30. *Ibid.*
31. *Ibid.*

vades him, which alone enables him to be as a man?"[32]) Even the poetical act of naming is a response by man to the being of beings.

In writings after *Introduction to Metaphysics,* the emphasis on man as a respondent to the address or call of being increases. In the *Letter on Humanism,* for instance, Heidegger asserts that the "only affair of thinking is to bring ever and again to spoken form the arrival of being, which abides and in its abiding waits for man."[33] And of course being comes to light in language. The arrival of being in language is described in terms of the word *Geschick,* fate or destiny. "The fatefulness of the saying of being, as the fate of truth, is the first law of thinking."[34] The matter of history was not new, for in *Introduction to Metaphysics* Heidegger had presented language as the dynamic of man's being that enables him to become historical—indeed, to establish history. Apprehending and speaking were presented as specifically historical acts in which being comes into time and happens. The difference is principally one of emphasis: man does not so much contend with being as open himself to being, to the address by being. Questioning itself is not abandoned by Heidegger, however, for questioning is precisely the placing in question of presentational conceptions. Later titles, like *Was heisst Denken?* or Heidegger's wish to place both *das Wesen* and *der Sprache* in question marks as *Das Wesen? der Sprache?* show this. Questioning, in fact, remains a basic method of his thinking. The change in emphasis is only an effort to point more strongly to the primacy of being.

The implication of this for language is to reverse the customary direction of speaking, to say not that man speaks but that language itself speaks. This becomes most explicit in a collection of essays on language, *Unterwegs zur Sprache.* "Language is in its essence neither expression nor an activity of man. *Language* speaks."[35] Words sound in the stillness, and through them the realities of one's world, the conflict between earth and world, come to stand: "The sound in the silence is nothing human. On the contrary, the human is in its essence linguistic."[36] The human act of saying is what is specifically human.

32. *Ibid.,* 156.
33. *PL-BH* 118.
34. *Ibid.* I have changed the translation here slightly from the earlier rendering on p. 151.
35. *US* 19.
36. *Ibid.,* 30.

Yet the saying is in itself an act *by language*. What is brought to appearance in language is not something human but world, being itself.

In *Unterwegs zur Sprache,* Heidegger finds the very essence of language in speaking, and especially in saying *(das Sagen).* To say is to show.[37] Thus silence can sometimes say more than words. To saying belongs a capacity to listen, so that what is to be said can show itself; saying preserves what is heard.[38] In it, being shows itself in the form of occurrence. To put the matter in terms of expression and appearance: language is not an expression of man but an appearance of being. Thinking does not express man, it lets being happen as language event.[39] In this letting-happen lies the fate of man and also the fate of truth, and ultimately the fate of being.

Heidegger's turn toward the increasing emphasis on the linguisticality *(Sprachlichkeit)* of man's way of being, and his assertion that being leads man and calls him, so that ultimately it is not man but being that shows itself, are of course of incalculable significance for theory of understanding. It makes the very essence of language its hermeneutical function of bringing a thing to show itself. It means that the discipline of interpretation becomes an effort to take a decisive "step back" from mere analysis and explanation to the achievement of thinking dialogue with what appears in the text. To understand becomes a matter not only of questioning which is willing to be open and undogmatic but also of learning how to wait and how to find the place *(Ort)* out of which the being of the text will show itself. Interpretation becomes a helping of the language event itself to happen, for the hermeneutical function of the text itself is emphasized as the place where being shows itself. Language itself is in its essence hermeneutical, and hermeneutical in the highest degree in great poetry, for as Heidegger says in "On the Essence of Poetry," the poet is the messenger, the "hermeneut," between the gods and man.

Heidegger has identified the essence of being, thinking,

37. *Ibid.,* 258.
38. *Ibid.,* 255.
39. Thus the term *Sprachereignis* (language event) as the *Leitwort* of Ernst Fuchs's New Hermeneutic. See "Das Sprachereignis in der Verkündigung Jesu, in der Theologie des Paulus und im Ostergeschehen," *HPT* 281–305; and "The Essence of the Language-Event and Christology," *Studies of the Historical Jesus,* pp. 213–28.

man, poetry, and philosophy with the hermeneutical function of *saying*. Whether this is a tenable position need not be debated here. The fact remains that his own philosophy becomes centrally hermeneutical, and his major themes all seem to fall in the proper area of hermeneutics. Of course, he has changed the whole context of hermeneutics away from the older conception of it as the philological discipline of text interpretation. The subject-object schema, objectivity, norms of validation, the text as expression of life—all are foreign to Heidegger's approach. The definition of hermeneutics as dealing with the moment that meaning comes to light, which Ricoeur finds "too broad" an understanding since it does not necessarily include the act of interpreting a text, does bring a sweeping change in the topography of hermeneutics. And the very act of interpretation itself is redefined in an ontological setting.

EXPLICATION AND THE TOPOLOGY OF BEING

IT WOULD BE UNWISE and perhaps unfair to take Heidegger's own explications as paradigmatic for a theory of poetic exegesis in general, since his use of them lies in the context of his own inquiry into the nature of being and the nature of language. In a prefatory note to "On the Essence of Poetry," he specifically disclaims them as contributions to research in literary history or aesthetics.[40] Yet we may refer here for purposes of example to two places in which Heidegger turns to the question of explication, one in the early *Introduction to Metaphysics* and the other in *Unterwegs zur Sprache.*

In the latter part of *Introduction to Metaphysics*, Heidegger explicates the choral "Ode on Man" from Sophocles' *Antigone* in an effort to define more clearly the early Greek conception of man expressed in it. He states:

> Our interpretation falls into *three phases,* in each of which we shall consider the whole poem from a different point of view.
>
> In the first phase, we shall set forth the intrinsic meaning of the poem, that which sustains the edifice of words and rises above it.
>
> In the second phase, we pass through the whole sequence of

40. *EHD; EB* 232.

strophes and antistrophes and delimit the area that is opened up by the poem.

In the third phase, we attempt to take our stand in the center of the poem, with a view to judging who man is according to this poetic discourse.[41]

Clearly Heidegger is not taking a formalist approach, for such would be out of keeping with the intentions and question he is posing. Of interest is the fact that his procedure here anticipates his later "topological" approach in which the explication seeks to locate the "place" (*topos*) out of which the poem speaks, the location of the clearing within being that is lighted up by the passage. Thus the first phase does not begin serially but with an effort to find the meaning which sustains the whole edifice of words *and rises above it*. What is said stands within a meaning that is not totally explicit, the meaning that is below and above the text. This overarching meaning, this gestalt that is more than the sum of the parts, is the governing principle for the poem, clarifying its individual parts. It is the truth of the poem, the being that is coming to light—one might say the soul of the poem. Only in the light of this does Heidegger undertake the second phase, which is to pass from strophe to antistrophe and back, through the poem, to "delimit the area that is opened up by the poem."

"In the third phase, we attempt to take our stand in the center of the poem"—that is, at the crucial border between concealment and disclosure which was established in the poet's creative act of naming what man is, and to rethink in depth what is named. This means, of course, going beyond the poem to what was not said:

> If we content ourselves with what the poem directly says, the interpretation is at an end [with the second phase]. Actually it has just begun. The actual interpretation must show what does not stand in the words and is nevertheless *said*. To accomplish this the exegete *must use violence*. He must seek the essential where nothing more is to be found by the scientific interpretation that brands as unscientific everything that transcends its limits.[42]

The hermeneutical process in its essence comes not in the scientific explication of what is already formulated in the text;

41. *IM* 148.
42. *Ibid.*, 162.

it is rather the process of originative thinking by which meaning comes to light which was not explicitly present.

In *Unterwegs zur Sprache,* an essay titled "Die Sprache im Gedicht" prefaces a discussion of Trakl's poetry with some general remarks on poetic explication. Heidegger takes as his starting point a discussion of the German word meaning "discussion": *Erörterung.* Originally, the title of the essay had been "Georg Trakl: Eine Erörterung seines Gedichtes," and Heidegger seeks to define his own essay not as historical, biographical, sociological, or psychological, but as a consideration of the "place" (*Ort*) out of which Trakl is poetizing, the place that is lighted up by his poetry. For each great poet speaks out of a single overarching "poem" that is never spoken, and the task of a thinking dialogue with the poet must be to find the place in being that is the foundation of the poem: "Only out of the place of the [unspoken] poem does the individual poem shine and sound." [43]

Heidegger asserts that there is considerable danger that a thinking dialogue with a poem may "disturb the poem's saying, instead of letting it sing out of its own peace. . . . A discussion of the overarching poem can, above all, never be a substitute for the true hearing of poems, can never lead. A thinking discussion can at most render a hearing questionable, or in a favorable case make hearing more meaningful." [44] Has Heidegger here forsaken the earlier contention about doing violence to the text? One must look beneath the apparent change, and it would seem that, from the first, Heidegger wants to let the text speak with its own truth and voice. The issue of "doing violence" is principally a reply to critics who would restrict interpretation to the explicitness of the text. It reaffirms the need finally to transcend the text and re-ask the question with which the text is dealing.

Furthermore, the process of *"Erörterung"* at every step seems to go behind the text to the roots of each word, to a repetition of a line or lines over and over, with the explication hearing more and more from the line itself. These repetitions make clear that the function of explication is to *let the line speak,* not to try to say better what it says. The very idea of lighting up the "place" of the poem is an effort to "set the stage"

43. *US* 38.
44. *Ibid.,* 39.

for the poem, not to take its place on the stage. As in the New Criticism, the poem itself is supreme and not biographical background. The "background" for a poem is not the author's life but the subject matter of the poem. The New Critic and Heidegger would agree on the ontological autonomy of the poem and the heresy of paraphrase; the difference arises in that the New Critic has difficulty making his case for the "truth" of the poem within the context of his presuppositions. Too easily the text becomes an object and explication a conceptual exercise which works solely with the "given," accepting the restrictions of scientific objectivity; Heidegger's style of explication differs radically from any objective "analysis" of what is indisputably given. The points of essential kinship beneath external differences of style, however, suggest that Heidegger's hermeneutics might provide the basis for a revitalized form of New Criticism.

A HERMENEUTICAL CONCEPTION OF THE WORK OF ART

IN 1936 HEIDEGGER gave three lectures on art carrying the title "The Origin of the Work of Art." They were not published until 1950, when they appeared as the opening portion of *Holzwege* (*Paths in the Forest*). In them one finds Heidegger's most fully developed discussion of the nature of art. In essence, they transpose into the realm of art the essentially hermeneutical conceptions of truth and being, the conflict between positive formulations and a negative but creative ground, and language as speaking and saying, which have been discussed above. A great work of art *speaks,* and in doing so it brings a world to stand. This speaking, like all true saying, simultaneously reveals and conceals truth. "Beauty is a way that truth as unconcealment happens." [45] The poet names the holy and thus brings it to appearance in a form; Heidegger sees all art as intrinsically poetical, as a way of bringing the being of beings into unconcealment and of making truth into a concrete historical happening.

This aesthetic situation is described in terms of the intrinsic tension between earth, as the creative ground of things, and

45. *Ho* 44; *UK* 61.

"world." Earth represents for Heidegger the inexhaustible mother, the primordial source and foundation of everything. The work of art, as a happening in which truth comes into unconcealment, represents a capturing of this creative tension in a *form*. Thus it brings into the realm of beings as a whole and holds open to man the inner struggle between earth and world. A Greek temple, for instance, standing in the valley, makes an open space in being, creates its own living space. In the beauty of its form it lets its materials shine in their splendor. It has set the materials into such form as will "show" them forth and cause them to shine. The temple does not copy anything; it simply carves out of itself a world in which the presence of the gods is felt. Whereas the materiality of materials disappears in tools the more they fulfill their function as tools, the work of art opens up a world precisely through the showing of the materiality of the materials:

> The stone comes to move and rest, and so first really becomes *stone;* metal comes to shimmer and shine; colors come to radiate as colors; tones come truly to sound; and word *speaks*. All this comes forward in that the work puts itself back into the mass and weight of the stone, into the firmness and pliability of wood, the hardness and brilliance of metal, the sounding of tones and the naming power of a word.[46]

To say this is simply to observe that the work of art "lets earth be earth." [47] Earth is not merely something to walk on, any more than a tree is just something that stands in the way; earth is that which comes forth in the shining of metal and the sounding of tones—and then recedes. It is effortless and untiring. "On earth and in it historical man grounds his dwelling in the world." [48] In art the construction of a work out of earth creates a world; "the work grasps and holds earth itself in the openness of a world." [49] The building up of earth and the exhibition of world are, according to Heidegger, the two basic tendencies of the work of art.

The essence of art, then, lies not in mere craftsmanship but in disclosure. To be a work of art means to open up a world. To interpret a work of art means to move into the open space

46. *Ho* 35; *UK* 47.
47. *Ibid.*
48. *Ibid.*
49. *Ibid.*

which the work has brought to stand. The truth of art is not a matter of shallow agreement with something already given (i.e., the traditional view of truth as correctness); it brings the earth into the open in such a way that one can *see* it. The greatness of art, in other words, must be defined in terms of its hermeneutical function. What Heidegger has enunciated in the essay is a hermeneutical theory of art.

Heidegger's contribution to hermeneutical theory, then, is truly many-sided. In *Being and Time* he reconceived understanding itself in a radically new context, thus changing the basic character of any consequent theory of interpretation. He redefined the very word "hermeneutics," identifying it with phenomenology (also as he defined it) and with the primary function of words in bringing about understanding. In his later works he adopted as his typical method of philosophizing the exegesis of texts, suggesting that he is a "hermeneutical" philosopher in the more traditional sense of that term. But the deeper sense of the word for Heidegger is that of the mysterious process of disclosure whereby being comes into manifest existence. In terms of this essentially hermeneutical process, Heidegger approached language, works of art, philosophy, and existential understanding itself.

He moved decisively beyond Dilthey's apparently broad conception of hermeneutics as the methodological foundation of all humane disciplines; hermeneutics in Heidegger points to the event of understanding as such, not to historical methods of interpretation as over and against scientific methods. The historical-scientific dichotomy to which Dilthey devoted his whole lifetime is left behind in the assertion that all understanding is rooted in the historical character of existential understanding, and the ground is cleared for Gadamer's "philosophical" hermeneutics.

11 / Gadamer's Critique
of Modern Aesthetic
and Historical Consciousness

A DECISIVE EVENT in the development of modern hermeneutical theory occurred in 1960 with the publication of *Wahrheit und Methode: Grundzüge einer philosophischen Hermeneutik* (*Truth and Method: Elements of a Philosophical Hermeneutics*) by the Heidelberg philosopher Hans-Georg Gadamer. Within the covers of a single volume are presented a critical review of modern aesthetics and theory of historical understanding from a basically Heideggerian perspective, as well as a new philosophical hermeneutics based on the ontology of language.

In its rich philosophical thoroughness this work is to be compared only to the other two monumental treatments of hermeneutical theory written in this century, Joachim Wach's *Das Verstehen* and Emilio Betti's *Teoria generale della interpretazione*. Each of these three works set for itself a different purpose, and thus each made its own distinctive contribution. Wach's three-volume history of hermeneutics in the nineteenth century constitutes an indispensable reference for every serious student of hermeneutics. Yet it was written in the late 1920's and necessarily stands within the horizon of Dilthey's conception of hermeneutics.

Betti surveys the spectrum of different types of interpretation with a view to formulating an inclusive and systematic general theory and to developing a set of canons basic to all forms of interpretation which can serve as the basis for more valid interpretation. From the outset, this work takes as its goal a systematic *organon* of forms of interpretation rather than simply a history, and thus its length and copious documentation, as well as its systematic purpose, invaluably supplement Wach's earlier work. Yet Betti stands basically within the German idealistic tradition, philosophically speaking, and tends to accept in advance as axiomatic the very presuppositions which Heidegger calls radically into question. For Betti, Heidegger poses a threat to the very idea of objectively valid results in philology and historiography. After Betti, it remained, then, for Gadamer to perceive and develop the positive and fruitful consequences of phenomenology, and in particular Heidegger's thought, for hermeneutical theory. It was Gadamer who had to struggle with the philosophical problem of developing a new ontology of the event of understanding.

Thus with the appearance of *Truth and Method* hermeneutical theory enters an important new phase. Heidegger's radical reconception of understanding, which we have traced in the preceding chapter, is now in Gadamer brought to full systematic expression, and its implications for the way the aesthetic and historical are conceived come to light. The older conception of hermeneutics as the methodological basis specifically for the *Geisteswissenschaften* is left behind, and the status of method itself is called into question, for the title of Gadamer's book contains an irony: method is not the way to truth. On the contrary, truth eludes the methodical man. Understanding is not conceived as a subjective process of man over and against an object but the way of being of man himself; hermeneutics is not defined as a general help discipline for the humanities but as a philosophical effort to account for understanding as an ontological—the ontological—process in man. The result of these reinterpretations is a different kind of hermeneutical theory, Gadamer's "philosophical" hermeneutics.

It is vital at the outset to understand the distinction between Gadamer's philosophical hermeneutics and the kind of hermeneutics oriented to methods and methodology. Gadamer is not directly concerned with the practical problems of formulating right principles for interpretation; he wishes, rather, to bring the phenomenon of understanding itself to light. This does not mean that he denies the importance of formulating such principles; on the contrary, such principles are necessary in the interpretive disciplines. What it means is that Gadamer is working on a preliminary and more fundamental question: How is understanding possible, not only in the humanities but in the whole of man's experience of the world? This is a question which is presupposed in the disciplines of historical interpretation but which goes far beyond them. It is on this point that Gadamer explicitly links his definition of hermeneutics to Heidegger:

> Heidegger's temporal analysis of human existence has, I believe, persuasively demonstrated that understanding is not one among several attitudes of a human subject but the way of being of *Dasein* itself. In this sense I have used the term "hermeneutics" here [in *Wahrheit und Methode*]. It designates the basic movement of human existence, made up of its finitude and historicality, and therefore it encompasses the whole of his experience of the world. . . . The movement of understanding is encompassing and universal.[1]

The universality of hermeneutics does, of course, have consequences for efforts at methodology in the interpretive disciplines. For instance, the encompassing character of understanding raises the question of whether one can simply by fiat limit the purview of understanding or cut it down to one or the other aspect. Gadamer asserts that the experience of a work of art transcends every subjective horizon of interpretation, both that of the artist and that of the perceiver. For this reason, "the *mens auctoris* is no possible measure of the meaning [*Bedeutung*] of a work. Indeed, to speak about a work-in-itself, cut off from its ever renewed reality as it comes to stand in experience, is to take a very abstract view."[2] The decisive thing is neither the author's intention, nor the work as a thing in itself outside history, but the "what" that comes repeatedly to stand in historical encounters.

To grasp the consequences of Gadamer's more universal hermeneutics for the conception of method, it is necessary to go more deeply into the Heideggerian roots of Gadamer's thinking and the dialectical character of hermeneutics as Gadamer conceives it. Like Heidegger, Gadamer is a critic of the modern surrender to technological thinking, which is rooted in subjectism (*Subjektität*)—that is, in taking the human subjective consciousness, and the certainties of reason based on it, as the ultimate point of reference for human knowledge. The pre-Cartesian philosophers, for instance the ancient Greeks,

1. WM, Preface to the 2d ed., xvi.
2. *Ibid.*, xvii.

saw their thinking as a part of being itself; they did not take subjectivity as their starting point and then ground the objectivity of their knowledge on it. Theirs was a more dialectical approach that tried to allow itself to be guided by the nature of what was being understood. Knowledge was not something that they acquired as a possession but something in which they participated, allowing themselves to be directed and even possessed by their knowledge. In this way the Greeks achieved an approach to truth that went beyond the limitations of modern subject-object thinking rooted in subjectively certain knowledge.

Gadamer's approach, then, is closer to the dialectic of Socrates than to modern manipulative and technological thinking. Truth is not reached methodically but dialectically; the dialectical approach to truth is seen as the antithesis of method, indeed as a means of overcoming the tendency of method to prestructure the individual's way of seeing. Strictly speaking, method is incapable of revealing new truth; it only renders explicit the kind of truth already implicit in the method. The discovery of the method itself was not arrived at through method but dialectically, that is, through a questioning responsiveness to the matter being encountered. In method the inquiring subject leads and controls and manipulates; in dialectic the matter encountered poses the question to which he responds. One can only respond on the basis of his belonging to and in the matter. The interpretive situation is no longer that of a questioner and an object, with the questioner having to construct "methods" to bring the object within his grasp; on the contrary, the questioner suddenly finds himself the being who is interrogated by the "subject matter" (*Sache*). In such a situation the "subject-object schema" is only misleading, for the subject has now become the object. Indeed, method itself is generally seen within the context of the subject-object conception of the interpretive stance of man and is the foundation for modern manipulative and technological thinking.

It might be asked, Is not the Hegelian dialectic the very essence of subjectivist thinking, for does not the whole dialectical process lead to the self-objectification of consciousness? Self-consciousness is at the core of Hegelian thought, but Gadamer's dialectical hermeneutics does not follow the Hegelian concept of *Geist* to its ultimate grounding in subjectivity. It is grounded not in self-consciousness but in being, in the linguisticality of human being in the world, and therefore in the ontological character of linguistic happening. This is not a dialectic of refining opposed theses; it is a dialectic between one's own horizon and that of "tradition"—that which comes down to us, encounters us, and creates that moment of negativity which is the life of dialectic and the life of questioning.

Thus while Gadamer's dialectical hermeneutics has affinities with Hegel, it does not proceed from the subjectivism implicit in Hegel and indeed in all modern metaphysics prior to Heidegger. While it has similarities with dialectic in Plato, it does not presuppose Plato's doctrine of ideas or his conception of truth and language. It suggests, rather, a dialectic based on the structure of being as elucidated by the later Heidegger and on the prestructure of understanding as set forth in *Being and Time*. The objective of the dialectic is eminently phenomenological: to have the being or thing encountered reveal itself. Method involves a specific kind of questioning which lays open one side of a thing; a dialectical hermeneutics opens itself to be questioned by the being of the thing, so that the thing encountered can disclose itself in its being. This is possible, Gadamer contends, because of the linguisticality of human understanding and ultimately of being itself.

This direction of thought on the hermeneutical problem is to a great extent implicit in Heidegger. What is new is the speculative and dialectical—one might say the Hegelian—emphasis and the fully developed exposition of the implications of Heideggerian ontology for aesthetics and text interpretation. The reader is asked to remember in what follows that the basic Heideggerian conceptions of thinking, language, history, and human experience are carried over into Gadamer. This is most essential, for the argument in *Wahrheit und Methode* rests firmly on them, and the unconscious lapsing back into the conceptions presupposed in most contemporary English and American thinking about interpretation will create added difficulties in understanding. Furthermore, Gadamer's conceptions are interrelated, so that we can only gradually enter into the circle of his considerations. And finally, Gadamer's argument rests strongly on his detailed critical analyses of previous thinking about language, historical consciousness, and the aesthetic experience. So the obstacles to understanding Gadamer's thought are formidable. Nevertheless, an attempt will be made to suggest some of the main lines of how Gadamer develops Heidegger's theory of understanding into a formal critique of modern aesthetic and historical conceptions of interpretation.

THE CRITIQUE OF AESTHETIC CONSCIOUSNESS

ACCORDING TO GADAMER, the concept of "aesthetic consciousness," in distinction and isolation from "nonaesthetic" realms of experience, is relatively modern. In fact it is a consequence of the general subjectivizing of thought since Descartes, a tendency to ground all knowledge in subjective self-certainty. According to this conception the subject contemplating the aesthetic object is an empty consciousness receiving perceptions and somehow enjoying the immediacy of pure sensuous form. The "aesthetic experience" is thus isolated and discontinuous from other, more pragmatic realms; it is not measurable in terms of "content," since it is a response to form. It does not relate itself to the self-understanding of the subject, or to time; it is seen as an atemporal moment without reference to anything but itself.

The consequences of such a conception are many. In the first place, no adequate way is left to account for art except perceptual enjoyment. There can be no contentual measures for art, since art is not knowledge. Tortured distinctions are made between the "form" and the "content" of art and aesthetic pleasure is ascribed to the former. Art no longer has any clear place in the world, since neither it nor the artist himself belongs to the world in any specific way. Art is left without function and the artist without place in society. The evident "holiness" of art, which we sense in our outrage at any senseless destruction of a great work of art, is left without legitimation. And certainly the artist can hardly claim to be a prophet if all he is creating is a formal expression of feeling or aesthetic pleasure.

But such a conception of the aesthetic phenomenon is contradicted by our own experience of any great work of art. The experience of encountering a work of art opens up a world; it is not mere gaping in sensuous pleasure at the outsides of forms. As soon as we stop viewing a work as an object and see it as a world, when we see a world *through* it, then we realize that art is not sense perception but knowledge. When we meet art, the horizons of our own world and self-understanding are broadened so that we see the world "in a new light"—as if for the first time. Even common and ordinary objects of life appear in a new light when illuminated by art. Thus a work of art is not a world divorced from our own or it could not illuminate our own self-understanding even as we come to understand it. In an encounter with a work of art we do not go into a foreign universe, stepping outside of time and history; we do not separate ourselves from ourselves or from the nonaesthetic. Rather we become more fully present. As we take into ourselves the unity and selfhood of the other as world, we come to fulfill our own self-understanding; when we understand a great work of art, we bring what we have experienced and who we are into play. Our whole self-understanding is placed in the balance, is *risked*. It is not we who are interrogating an object; the work of art is putting a question to us, the question that called it into being. The experience of a work of art is encompassed and takes place in the unity and continuity of our own self-understanding.

But, it may be argued, when we behold a work of art, the world in which we are living our own life vanishes. The world of the work takes over and, for a brief moment, is a self-enclosed, self-sufficient "world." It requires no measure outside of itself, and it is certainly not to be measured as a copy of reality. How is this to be reconciled with the assertion that the work of art presents a world fully continuous with our own?

The justification must be ontological: when we see a great work of art and enter its world, we do not leave home so much as "come home." We say at once: truly it is so! The artist has said what *is*. The artist has captured reality in an image, a form; he has not conjured up an enchanted never-never-land but rather this very world of experience and self-understanding in which we live, move, and have our being. The transformation into form which is enacted by the artist is really a transformation into the truth of being. The legitimation of art is not that it gives aesthetic pleasure but that it reveals being. The understanding of art does not come through methodically cutting and dividing it as an object, or through separating form from content; it comes through openness to being, and to hearing the question put to us by the work.

Hence the work of art truly presents us with a world, which we are not to reduce to the measure of our own or to the measure of methodologies. Yet we only understand this new world because we are already participating in the structures of self-understanding which make it truth for us. This is the real basis for the same thing being understood as what was intended. The mediation of this self-understanding is form. The artist has the power to transform into an image or a form his experience of being. As form it becomes abiding and the encounter with it open to succeeding generations, repeatable. It has the character not simply of the *energy* of being but of a *work*. It has become truth that abides *(das bleibende Wahre).*[3]

The change that takes place in the materials by transformation into image *(Verwandlung ins Gebilde)* is not simple alteration but true transformation: "What was before is no longer, but that which now is, that which is presented in the play of art is truth which can now abide." [4] The fusion of the truth or being represented with the form is so complete that something new comes into being. There is a "total mediation" so that the interplay of elements in the form becomes its own world and no simple copy of anything. This apparent autonomy is not the aimless and isolated autonomy of "aesthetic consciousness" but the mediation of knowledge in the deeper sense of the term; the experience of beholding the work of art makes this knowledge shared knowledge.[5]

Gadamer's concept of total mediation has another side. It asserts the radical nondifferentiation of the aesthetic from other elements within the play of the work of art. We instinctively feel the general inappropriateness of referring to a ceremony or ritual as "beautiful"; aesthetic differentiation has no place in reference to a "good sermon," for it indicates that, even as one is listening to the sermon, he is separating content from form. Likewise the differentiation of aesthetic from nonaesthetic has no appropriateness for understanding our experience of a work of art. "The mediation of art must be thought of as a whole." [6] The aesthetic or formal side (Gadamer would reject the form-content dichotomy as a construction of reflexive thought) of the encounter with a work of art is so much a part of what is *said* in the work, the "thing meant," that aesthetic differentiation is artificial and invalid. Thus in contrast

3. *WM* 106.
4. *Ibid.*
5. *Ibid.*, 92.
6. *Ibid.*, 121.

to the "aesthetic difference" Gadamer asserts the principle of "aesthetic nondifferentiation" (*aesthetische Nichtunterscheidung*).[7]

What is central to the aesthetic experience of a work of art is neither content nor form but the thing meant, totally mediated into an image and form, a world with its own dynamics. In the aesthetic encounter with a work of art, then, one does not seek to separate the poetry from its raw materials, nor in experiencing a performance should one constantly seek to separate the thing meant from the performance. Both the raw materials and the performance realize in action what the thing meant actually demands, and they are so interpenetrated with it that separation is artificial and contrived. Gadamer asserts pointedly: "The double differentiation of poetry from its material and of poetry from its performance corresponds to a *double nondifferentiation* as the unity of truth which one recognizes in the play [*Spiel*] of art."[8] He goes on, in reference to drama: "It is a falling-away from the authentic experience of poetry when one adverts to its underlying story to see the play in the light of its derivation; and it is also a falling-out of the authentic experience of a play when the spectator thinks during the play of the underlying conception as such or of the performance as performance."[9]

Gadamer proposes something that represents an even further breakdown of the splendid isolation of the aesthetic. Over against the placelessness of art when seen in the light of "aesthetic consciousness," he suggests the idea of art as being decorative. Art is not placeless. It demands a place and creates from itself an open place. Works of art do not really belong in museums, collected together in a placeless place. The underlying problem is the concept of the art image as aesthetic rather than ontological in the encompassing sense. There is a definite need, says Gadamer, to change the conception of art which has prevailed in recent centuries and "the concept of representation with which modern galleries have made us familiar." We need, he says, to rehabilitate the decorative and occasional element in art, which was discredited by aesthetics based on "pure form" or "expression of experience."[10] Art is neither

7. *Ibid.*, 111-12.
8. *Ibid.*, 112; italics added.
9. *Ibid.*
10. *Ibid.*, 130.

placeless nor timeless. "The first item on the agenda is finding a way to win back a horizon that includes both art and history together."[11]

He suggests that two questions may point the way: (1) In what respect is an image distinguished from a copy of something? (2) How, from this point, does the relation of representation to its "world" arise?[12] Clearly art does "represent" something, the thing that called it into being; clearly, too, there is a world that opens up. The standpoint of an aesthetics that asserts the idea of the "purely aesthetic" will never uncover the answer to these questions, and an aesthetics based on experience in the older sense of the term is equally inadequate. Both proceed from the erroneous premise of referring the work of art back to the subject in a subject-object relation. Not until we have won a horizon of questioning which transcends the old model of the subject-object schema will we find a way through to understanding the function and purpose, the howness and what-ness, the temporality and place, of the work of art.

Game and the Way of Being
of a Work of Art

There are a number of significant elements in the phenomenon of "game" which shed light on the way of being of the work of art.[13] Gadamer is not here rehabilitating "play" theories of aesthetics based on aesthetic hedonism, however. Such theories see play as an activity of a human subject: art is a kind of playing that gives pleasure to the human subject who leaves the world to enjoy an aesthetic moment outside and above his mundane existence. The artist is conceived as that sensitive, overgrown child who derives sensuous pleasure from toying with forms, molding and manipulating materials into pleasing proportions. Gadamer sees in such aesthetic theories the modern error of referring everything to human subjectivity. By "game" Gadamer does not mean an attitude

11. *Ibid.*
12. *Ibid.*
13. *Ibid.*, 97–105. Although *Spiel* may be translated as "play," I have for the most part translated it as "game." Regarding other dimensions of the significance of *Spiel*, see Eugen Fink, *Spiel als Weltsymbol.*

or activity of a creating and enjoying human subject; he does not mean by it the "freedom" of human subjectivity which can engage in play. "Game" (or "play") refers instead to the way of being of the work of art itself. The object of Gadamer's discussion of the concept of game or play in relation to art is to free it from the traditional tendency to associate it with activity of a subject.

A game is "only a game" and not "serious"; as a game, however—starting with the game itself now—it has a holy kind of seriousness. Indeed, someone who does not take it seriously "spoils the game." The game has its own dynamics and goals independent of the consciousnesses of those playing.[14] It is not an object over against a subject; it is a self-defining movement of being into which we enter. The game, and not our participation in it, becomes the true "subject" of our discussion. Our participation in the game brings it into a presentation, but what is presented is not so much our inner subjectivities as the game: the game comes to stand, it takes place in and through us.[15]

From the subjectivist point of view, the game is an activity of a subject, a free activity into which one wills to enter and which is used for his own pleasure. But when we ask what the game itself is, and how it comes to pass, when we take the game and not human subjectivity as our starting point, then it takes on a different aspect. A game is only a game as it comes to pass, yet while it is being played it is master. The fascination of the game casts a spell over us and draws us into it; it is truly the master over the player.[16] The game has its own special spirit. The player chooses which game he will give himself to, but once he chooses he enters a closed world in which the game comes to take place in and through the players. In a sense the game has its own momentum and pushes itself forward; it wills to be played out.[17]

A game of bridge, a tennis match, children playing with each other—these games are not ordinarily presented to a viewer, they are played by and for the players themselves. Indeed, when a sport becomes primarily something for viewers,

14. *Ibid.*, 98.
15. *Ibid.*
16. *Ibid.*, 102.
17. In this sense it is like ritual, which has a power of its own and during its happening lifts one out of the ordinary progress of life.

it may become distorted and lose its character as a game. But what is the case with a work of art? Where would a drama be if the "fourth wall" did not open to the audience? When we encounter a work of art, are we participants or observers? Gadamer holds that we remain the audience and not the players in the play. But a distinction slips in here: a play is not a game, yet it *is* "played"—for an audience. More precisely, we say that a play is "presented," but we still do call it a "play" and its actors are "players." In German the words *Spiel* and *spielen* refer to a game and to playing: both are derived from the same verb, *spielen*. Thus in German the distinction between a game and a play is slurred over. On the other hand, in English we do well to remember the affinities between a game and a play. Both are self-contained, have their own rules, drive on to fulfillment, envelop the players in the service of a spirit larger than that of any one player.

But the differences between a play and a game are equally important, for the play achieves its meaning only as a presentation. Its real meaning is a matter of mediation. It does not exist primarily for the players but for the viewer. The play is as hermetically sealed and self-sufficient as any game, but *as* play it presents itself as *event* to the viewer. Gadamer states:

> We have seen that a game has its being not in the consciousness or actions of the players, but, on the contrary, it draws these into its own realm and fills them with its spirit. The player experiences the game as for him an overpowering reality. This applies even more where this reality is an "intended" reality—and this is the case where what is played appears as *presentation to a viewer*.[18]

Now the reason for the play is not simply to give the players the experience of playing and to catch them up into the "spirit of the game"; the reason for the play is to transmit the "overpowering reality" of what is "intended" in the play, the reality that has been transfused into form. What is the nature of the inner movement of this form? It is like a game—a special kind of game, where we are caught up as spectators. In the overpowering event of the game, the thing meant in the game (the structure and spirit of the game) is communicated. What is this "thing meant" in the case of a work of art? It is the "way things are," the "truth" of being, *die Sache selbst*. A work of

18. WM 104.

art is not a mere pleasure object; it is a presentation, transfused into an image, of a truth of being as event. "Not once is a poem grasped in its essential truth from the measure of aesthetic consciousness; rather, like all literary texts, it speaks to us in its contentual meaning." [19] We never ask about form first in a poem, nor is form what makes a poem a poem. We ask what the poem says, and we experience the meaning in and through the form, or we may say, in and through the game event of encountering the form, for form is event when we encounter it; we are seized and overpowered by the spirit of the poem.

In seeing the analogies between work of art and game, and indeed in taking the structure of game as the guiding model of a structure which has its own autonomy and yet which is open to the viewer, Gadamer has achieved several important goals. The work of art is viewed not as a static but as a dynamic thing. The standpoint of a subjectivity-centered aesthetic is transcended, and a structure is suggested which shows the inadequacy of the subject-object schema in reference to understanding a game, and by extension a work of art.

A basic strength of Gadamer's argument here is that he takes the experience of art as his starting point and evidence for substantiating his assertions. He shows that the "aesthetic consciousness" is not derived from the nature of the experience of art but is a reflexive construction based on subjectivist metaphysics. It is precisely the experience of art which shows that the work of art is no mere object that stands over against a self-sufficient subject. The work of art has its authentic being in the fact that, in becoming experience, it transforms the experiencer; the work of art works. The "subject" of the experience of art, the thing that endures through time, is not the subjectivity of the one who experiences the work; it is the work itself. This is precisely the point at which the mode of being of a game becomes important. The game, too, has its own nature independent of the consciousness of those who play it. Gadamer has found a model which not only demonstrates the bankruptcy of subjectivized aesthetics but one which can serve as a basis for substantiating the dialectical and ontological character of his own hermeneutics.

Is not this conception of the autonomy of the work of art, and the effort to see the dynamics of being of the work itself, basically similar in spirit to the New Criticism? Has Gadamer

19. *Ibid.*, 155.

only arrived at a position through elaborate analysis which the New Critics have held all along as an Aristotelian realism? There are similarities, so that the New Critic might find little to disagree with in the parallel that Gadamer has made. More significant is the fact that Gadamer's analogy offers a firm legitimation of the autonomy of the work of art without the isolation involved in accepting the myth of aesthetic differentiation. Hitherto the New Critics' defense of the autonomy of the literary work only served to undermine its relevance. Their splendid defenses of poetry merely reminded us that poetry and the poet no longer had a place in society and that their professorial defenders were futile angels flapping their luminous wings in a void (to paraphrase Arnold's famous reference to Shelley). Now, however, Gadamer's genuinely "objective" approach, which decisively frees interpretation from the myths of subjectivized aesthetics — most especially the subject-object and form-content dichotomies — still preserves the literary work in separation from the author's opinions and creative act, and from the tendency to take the reader's subjectivity as a starting point. The New Critics sometimes even speak of a "surrender" to the being of the work; in this they are truly in agreement with Gadamer.

Yet the New Critics remained entangled in the illusions of subjectivized aesthetics without knowing it. Gadamer's standpoint would have enabled them to see more clearly the nature of the continuity between the self-understanding attained from literature and the self-understanding in and through which we exist. In particular, the New Critics might have been able through him to grasp the historicality of literature. Too often followers of the New Criticism took form as the very starting point of their analyses, a procedure which immediately pushed them into all the errors that accompany aesthetic differentiation.

At the same time, too many interpreters of literature today still wince at the suggestion that literature is historical in character. Admittedly, a work of art is not the mere furniture of history writers, but it would be equally pernicious to gloss over the fact that the self-understanding of great spirits of the past is historically mediated to us through works of art. The differentiation of the formal aspects of literature as aesthetic from the nonformal tends to give the interpreter the feeling that he is no longer discussing the work as art when he tries to consider what the work *says*. To discuss the meaning of the

work for the present day would seem to have no justifiable place
in their philosophy of a literary work; indeed the tension between the past and present is often swallowed up in the timeless ahistoricality of formal analyses of poetry. Here again
modern literary criticism (including myth criticism) stands in
need of drastic clarification as to the historical and temporal
character of the literary work of art. This fact will be clearer
after Gadamer's critique of ordinary conceptions of history and
historicality has been presented.

The Critique of the Ordinary Understanding of History

GADAMER EXPLICITLY TAKES as the foundation
and starting point of his analysis of "historical consciousness"
Heidegger's analysis of the prestructure of understanding
and of the intrinsic historicality (*Geschichtlichkeit*) of human
existence. According to Heidegger's conception of the prestructure of understanding, we understand a given text, matter, or situation, not with an empty consciousness temporarily
filled with the present situation but rather because we hold
in our understanding, and bring into play a preliminary intention with regard to the situation, an already established way
of seeing, and certain ideational "preconceptions." This prestructure of understanding has already been mentioned in
the discussion of Heidegger's hermeneutics; now we need
merely note the consequences for historical consciousness.
The fundamental consequence can be stated quite simply at
the outset: There is no pure seeing and understanding of history without reference to the present. On the contrary, history
is seen and understood only and always through a consciousness standing in the present.

Nevertheless, the concept of historicality, even while affirm-
ing this, simultaneously affirms the operativeness of the past
in the present: The present is seen and understood only through
the intentions, ways of seeing, and preconceptions bequeathed
from the past. Gadamer's hermeneutics and his critique of
historical consciousness assert that the past is not like a pile of
facts which can be made an object of consciousness, but rather

is a stream in which we move and participate, in every act of understanding. Tradition, then, is not over against us but something in which we stand and through which we exist; for the most part it is so transparent a medium that it is invisible to us—as invisible as water to a fish.

Now the reader will perhaps recall this analogy from Heidegger's *Letter on Humanism*. He may even object that in the *Letter* the analogy is to being: being is the "element" in which we live. Actually, however, there is really no tension or contradiction involved, for language is the house of being and we live in and through language. Gadamer and Heidegger would agree, further, that language is the reservoir and communicating medium of the tradition; tradition hides itself in language, and language is a "medium" like water. For Heidegger and Gadamer, language, history, and being are all not only interrelated but interfused, so that the linguisticality of being is at the same time its ontology—its "coming into being"—and the medium of its historicality. Coming into being is a happening in and of history and is governed by the dynamics of historicality; it is a language event. But for purposes of analysis, let us defer consideration of linguisticality and look at the way in which the structure of historicality and preunderstanding affects the hermeneutical problem in relation to historical understanding.

The critique of "historical consciousness" in both Gadamer and Heidegger is primarily directed at the "historical school" in Germany, whose most famous representatives in the nineteenth century were J. G. Droysen and L. von Ranke. These represented an extension of "romantic hermeneutics." This hermeneutics should not be misconstrued, however, as romanticizing history in the style of Sir Walter Scott but, on the contrary, as the most strenuous effort at "objective" history. The task of the historian was not to inject his personal feelings into history but to enter completely the historical world of which he wished to give an account.

Dilthey had spent his life trying to establish a nonnaturalistic methodology for historical understanding and in his later phase to ground the humane studies in an historical and hermeneutical, not naturalistic, set of ideas and procedures. "Experience" and "life itself" were recurrent themes. Experience, when it was seen as a unit of meaning, became knowledge, and thus there was in "life itself" an "immanent reflexivity." [20] As Gadamer observes, "The relationship of life and knowing is a fundamental datum in Dilthey." [21] The understanding of history lies not in totally leaving one's own experience but in realizing that one is himself an historical being; ultimately it lies in one's common participation with other men in "life." It is this already-given understanding of life, says Dilthey, that enables one to understand "expressions of life" in great art and literature. And when one encounters and understands these expressions of life, he also comes to know himself: "Historical consciousness [for Dilthey] is a way of self recognition." [22]

Yet for Dilthey the expressions of life are really "objectifications" of life of which we can come to have "objective" knowledge. As much as Dilthey criticized the methods of natural science, he held to the ideal of achieving objective knowledge in the historical studies. The historical studies could be called "sciences," albeit "humane sciences" (*Geisteswissenschaften*). It is just here that Gadamer sees Dilthey entangled in the ideal of objectivity championed by the very historical school against which Dilthey had leveled so much criticism. Objective knowledge, objectively "valid" knowledge, suggests a standpoint above history from which history itself can be looked upon—such a standpoint is not available to man. Finite, historical man always sees and understands from his standpoint in time and place; he cannot, says Gadamer, stand above the relativity of history and procure "objectively valid knowledge." Such a standpoint presupposes an absolute philosophical knowledge—an invalid assumption. Dilthey is unconsciously borrowing a concept of inductive method from the sciences, but as Gadamer observes, "historical experience is not a procedure [*Verfahren*] and does not have the anonymity of a method. . . . [It has] a completely different kind of objectivity and is acquired in a completely different way." [23] Dilthey is a perfect example of the scientific compulsion to method-oriented thought effectively preventing a gifted and sincere searcher for historicality from

20. Cf. *ibid.*, 222.
21. *Ibid.*, 223.
22. *Ibid.*, 221.
23. *Ibid.*, 228.

finding it. We may see in him the archetype of our own present loss of authentic historicality in our tendency to use inductive methods to obtain "objectively valid" knowledge of literature.

Even before Heidegger and Gadamer, Husserl's phenomenological critique of objectivism on the basis of the intentionality of consciousness had spelled the end of old-style objectivism. As Husserl worked out his critique, it became increasingly clear that all the beings given in one's world stand within the intentional horizon of consciousness, within the "lifeworld." Over against the "objectively valid" and anonymous world seen by the scientist, Husserl opposed the intentional horizon in which one lives and moves, a horizon which is not anonymous but personal and shared with other experiencing beings; this he called the lifeworld. It is within the general concept of lifeworld that Heidegger was to begin his critique of historical consciousness.

But in Heidegger the human lifeworld is not just a fuller and more adequate way to describe the operations of a transcendental subjectivity located in and behind consciousness. The intentionality of consciousness is interpreted "historically" and becomes the basis for his critique of historical consciousness. Heidegger undertook simultaneously a critique of metaphysics in respect to the way its concept of subjectivity ultimately grounded all objectivity in a knowing human subject's self-certainty. Heidegger's *Being and Time,* while apparently applying Husserl's phenomenological method, constituted an effort to move away from transcendental subjectivity to a kind of objectivity which stands outside the subject-object distinction, an objectivity which takes the "facticity" of human existence as its ultimate point of reference. Thus there is in Heidegger a new kind of objectivity, opposed to the objectivity of the natural sciences, of Dilthey, of the historical school, of modern metaphysics, and ultimately of modern technological thinking with all its pragmatism. It is the objectivity of allowing the thing that appears to be as it really is for us.

The severe limits of objectivism become evident when one stops taking the "objective universe" (which its view of the world offers) as *the* world and uses the lifeworld as a starting point. One immediately sees that only a small fraction of his lifeworld can ever become something over against man as an object; indeed, as world it is the horizon within which other things are defined as objects while it remains world. One's lifeworld recedes from efforts to grasp it through any "method," and one generally stumbles on its nature by accident, principally through some kind of negativity or breakdown. The way of objectivity and methods will not disclose one's lifeworld to oneself. Yet in and through this lifeworld one makes judgments and reaches decisions; even the "objective world" is a structure within an experientially given lifeworld. How, then, can one get at the lifeworld? How can one persuade it to disclose itself? Heidegger suggests his phenomenological method as a way, which he also calls a "hermeneutic of facticity." This approach is based not on the way that the world belongs to a human subject but on the way in which the human subject belongs to the world. This belongingness occurs through the process of "understanding." So basic is the process that it is not so much one thing among others which one does but that process in which and through which one exists as a human being.

This interpretation of understanding is ontological, describing the process of being. Heidegger took this conception as his starting point for an analysis of being which would begin with the facticity of lifeworld, and specifically the facticity of human existence. His analysis showed existence to be a "thrown project"—oriented to the past in being "thrown" into time and the world in a certain way, and oriented to the future in reaching into the not-yet to seize as-yet unrealized possibilities. One significance of this is that since this description of understanding in *Dasein* is universal, it must apply to the process of understanding in all of the sciences.[24] Understanding as such is always functioning simultaneously in three modes of temporality: past, present, and future. For the understanding of history, this means that the past can never be seen as object in the past with an absolute separation from us in the present and future. The ideal of seeing the past in terms of itself turns out to be a dream running contrary to the nature of understanding itself, which is always in relation to our present and future. The intrinsic temporality of understanding itself in seeing the world always in terms of past, present, and future is what is called the historicality of understanding.

24. *Ibid.*, 249.

SOME HERMENEUTICAL CONSEQUENCES OF THE HISTORICALITY OF UNDERSTANDING

I / The Issue of Prejudgment .

The idea of freeing understanding and interpretation from the prejudices of the prevailing opinion of the time is quite common to us. It would be ridiculous, we commonly say, to judge the achievements of a past age by the standards of today. The objective of historical knowledge, then, can only be fulfilled through freedom from personal ideas and values on a subject and a perfectly "open mind" to the world of ideas and values of a past age. Dilthey's exploration of world views (*Weltanschauungen*) was predicated on an historical relativism which open-mindedly asserted that one historical age must not be judged in terms of another. Similarly, there are literary scholars who ask us to be open-minded about the theology of *Paradise Lost* because we have no right to judge a literary work by "today's standards." We read *Paradise Lost* as a "work of art," for the greatness of its style, the grandeur of its conception, its imaginative vigor—not because it is true. Such an argument separates beauty from truth, and ultimately we see the epic as a "noble monument to dead ideas." [25]

Ironically this false view of a literary text masquerades as the ultimate in open-mindedness, in spite of the fact that the present is presupposed as correct, as not to be put to the test, i.e., as absolute. Yet the present is to be suspended because the past cannot compete with it. Behind this open-minded suspension of prejudice is the unwillingness to risk our prejudgments; the past stands opposed to us as something almost irrelevant, an object of interest to antiquarians. Regrettably, literature professors generally may be classified as either formalist-aesthetes or antiquarians. The latter see the former as lacking in historical and philological depth, while the formalists criticize the philologist and historical scholars as not really seeing the literary work as "art." The position of the aesthetes rests on the untenable form-content separation in subjectivized aesthetics, for we have already seen that truth and beauty cannot be separated in the experience of a work of art. Now, it

25. As the critic Raleigh did in 1900.

follows from Heidegger's and Gadamer's conceptions of historical understanding that the antiquarians and philological devotees of the past as past have no firmer understanding of history than the aesthetes.

Actually the present cannot be left in order to go into the past; the "meaning" of a past work cannot be seen solely in terms of itself. On the contrary, the "meaning" of the past work is defined in terms of the questions put to it from the present. If we consider the structure of understanding carefully, we see that the questions we ask are ordered by the way we project ourselves in understanding into the future. In short, antiquarianism is a denial of true historicality, the historicality of all understanding of the past in which we stand in the present. What does this mean for the issue of prejudgment? It is a misconception bequeathed us from the Enlightenment. Gadamer even asserts that our prejudgments have their own importance in interpretation: "The self-interpretation [*Selbst-besinnung*] of the individual is only a flicker in the closed stream of historical life. For this reason the prejudgments of the individual are more than merely his judgments; they are the historical reality of his being." [26] In short, prejudgments are not something we must or can dispense with; they are the basis of our being able to understand history at all.

Hermeneutically, this principle can be stated as follows: There can be no "presuppositionless" interpretation.[27] A biblical, literary, or scientific text is not interpreted without preconceptions. Understanding, since it is an historically accumulated and historically operative basic structure, underlies even scientific interpretation; the meaning of a described experiment does not come from the interplay of the elements in the experiment but from the tradition of interpretation in which it stands and the future possibilities it opens up. The past-present-future temporality applies to both scientific and nonscientific understanding; it is universal. Inside or outside the sciences there can be no presuppositionless understanding. Where do we get our presuppositions? From the tradition in which we stand. This tradition does not stand over against our thinking as an object of thought but is the fabric of relations, the horizon, within which we do our thinking. Because

26. WM 261.
27. Cf. Rudolf Bultmann's "Is Presuppositionless Exegesis Possible?" (1957) in *Existence and Faith,* ed. Schubert M. Ogden, pp. 289-96.

it is not object and never fully objectifiable, the methods of an objectifying type of thought do not apply to it; rather there is a need for a thinking that can deal with the nonobjectifiable.[28] But we do not get our presuppositions wholly from tradition. We must remember that understanding is a dialectical process of interaction of the self-understanding of the person (his "horizon" or "world") with what is encountered. Self-understanding is not a free-floating consciousness, not a flickering translucence filled up with the present situation; it is an understanding that is already *placed* in history and tradition, and it can understand the past only by broadening its horizon to take in the thing encountered.

If there can be no presuppositionless understanding, if, in other words, what we call "reason" is a philosophical construction and no final court of appeal, then we must reexamine our relationship to our heritage. Tradition and authority need no longer be seen as the enemies of reason and rational freedom as they were in the Enlightenment and the Romantic period, and into our own day. Tradition furnishes the stream of conceptions within which we stand, and we must be prepared to distinguish between fruitful presuppositions and those that imprison and prevent us from thinking and seeing.[29] In any event, there is no intrinsic opposition between the claims of reason and those of tradition; reason stands always within tradition. Tradition even supplies reason with the aspect of reality and history with which it will work. Ultimately, Gadamer asserts, the consequences of recognizing that there can be no presuppositionless understanding are that we reject the Enlightenment interpretation of reason, and both authority and tradition win back a status they have not enjoyed since before the Enlightenment.

If there can be no presuppositionless interpretation, then the notion of one "right interpretation" as right in itself is a thoughtless ideal and an impossibility.[30] There is no interpretation without relationship to the present, and this is never permanent and fixed. A transmitted text, be it Bible or Shakespearean play, has to be understood in the hermeneutical situation in

28. Cf. Heidegger's unpublished letter to the 1964 Consultation on Hermeneutics at Drew University. See Heinrich Ott, "Das Problem des nicht-objektivierenden Denkens and Redens in der Theologie," *ZThK* LXI (1964), 327–52.
29. *WM* 263.
30. *Ibid.*, 375.

which it finds itself, i.e., in relation to the present. This does not mean that we thoughtlessly invoke external standards from the present into the past in order to find Shakespeare or the Bible irrelevant. On the contrary, this simply recognizes that "meaning" is not like a changeless property of an object but is always "for us." Nor does the insistence that a text be seen within the horizon of our historicality mean that the "meaning" is absolutely different for us from what it was for its earliest readers. It asserts that meaning is present-related, arising in the hermeneutical situation. Since a great work lays open a truth of being, we may assume that its *essential* truth corresponds to that which originally brought it into being—without asserting the idea of a truth-in-itself or a perennially right interpretation.

2 / *The Concept of Temporal Distance*

To Gadamer the tension between the present and the past is itself a central, and even in some ways fruitful, factor in hermeneutics: "A placement between strangeness and familiarity exists between the historically intended, distanced objectivity of the heritage and our belongingness to a tradition. *In this 'between' is the true place of hermeneutics*." [31] The mediation of hermeneutics, then, involves both that which was historically meant and tradition; yet this does not mean that the task of hermeneutics is to develop a methodical procedure for understanding, so much as to clarify the conditions under which understanding can take place. [32]

What is mediated by the text is not important to its interpreter primarily as the feeling or opinion of its author but rather in its own right as something intended. Nor is it interesting as "expression" per se, whether of "life" or of anything else; it is the subject itself which is interesting, one is interested in its truth for him. Logically, a work of art created today should then have the greatest meaning for us, its contemporaries, but we know from experience that only time will sort the significant from the insignificant. Why is this? Not because temporal distance has killed our personal interests in the subject, says Gadamer, but because it is the function of time to

31. *Ibid.*, 279.
32. *Ibid.*

eliminate what is inessential, allowing the true meaning that lies hidden in a thing to become clear. Thus temporal distance has both a negative and positive function: "It [temporal distance] not only allows certain prejudgments peculiar to the nature of the subject to die out but also causes those which lead to a true understanding to come forward." [33]

Thus we are confronted with the fruitfulness of separation in time, a phenomenon analogous to the concept of "aesthetic distance," in which the viewer must be a certain distance from the stage to see the unity that is meant and not be distracted by the face paint on the actors. In spite of the necessary sense of presentness, of the past becoming present, one finds it hermeneutically fruitful that time has passed. Only with the passage of time can we grasp "what it is that the text says"; only gradually does its true historical significance emerge and begin to address the present.

3 / *On Understanding the Author of a Text*

The task of hermeneutics is essentially to understand the text, not the author. Both the concept of temporal distance and the emphasis on meaning in historical understanding should make this self-evident. The text is understood not because a relation between persons is involved but because of the participation in the subject matter that the text communicates. Again, this participation emphasizes the fact that one does not so much go out of his own world as let the text address him in his present world; he lets it become present to him, contemporaneous (*gleichzeitig*).[34] Understanding is not a subjective process so much as a matter of placing oneself in a tradition and then in an "event" that transmits tradition to him.[35] Understanding is a participation in the stream of tradition, in a moment which mixes past and present. This conception of understanding is what must be brought to acceptance in hermeneutical theory, says Gadamer.[36] The subjectivity of neither the author nor the reader is the real reference point, but rather the historical meaning itself for us in the present.

33. *Ibid.*, 282.
34. *See ibid.*, 115 ff.
35. *Ibid.*, 275.
36. *Ibid.*

4 / *On Reconstruction of the Past*

Another consequence of the intrinsic historicality involved in understanding any ancient text is that one must reconsider the hermeneutical presupposition that reconstructing the world of the work of art is the primary task of understanding. Prior to Schleiermacher, reconstructing the historical background for a given text and determining the historical context in which it was placed were, together with grammatical interpretation, the fundamental concerns. Schleiermacher gave hermeneutics a more psychological and divinatory turn, but he still presupposed that the operation of reconstructing the historical context was basic to understanding any ancient text. The Scriptures are, after all, not an atemporal carrier of eternal ideas or a flight of poetical imagination without serious claim to truth; they are an historical creation in an historical language by an historical people.

Certainly reconstruction of the world out of which a work has come and reconstruction of the origin of the work of art are necessary for understanding, but Gadamer cautions against taking reconstruction as the basic or final operation in hermeneutics, or even as the key to understanding. Is what we work with in the process of reconstruction really what we label and search for as the "meaning" of the work? Is understanding rightly determined when we strive to see in it a second creation exactly like that of the original—a re-creation? Obviously not, for the meaning of a work depends on what questions we are asking in the present. "Restoration," says Gadamer, "if made central in hermeneutics, is no less absurd than all effort to restore and revive life gone forever." [37] Integration, not restoration, is the true task of hermeneutics.

5 / *The Significance of Application*

The structure of historicality in understanding suggests the importance of a factor long neglected in historical and literary hermeneutics—application, the function of interpretation in relating the meaning of the text to the present. For instance, the element of application is integral in both biblical and juridical hermeneutics, for in neither case is it sufficient to understand and explain the text in a general way; it has to be made

37. *Ibid.,* 159.

explicit in what way the text speaks to the present condition. In J. J. Rambach's *Institutiones hermeneuticae sacrae* of 1723, interpretation is said to involve three powers: *subtilitas intelligendi* (understanding), *subtilitas explicandi* (explication), and *subtilitas applicandi* (application).[38] These are not three separate "methods"; rather, *subtilitas* refers to a capacity or power that demands a special fineness of spirit. Together the three powers constitute the fulfillment of understanding.

In Schleiermacher and post-Romantic hermeneutics in general, there is asserted an inner unity of the first two elements; explaining is seen as the rendering explicit of understanding, and the emphasis on these two tends to leave no systematic place for the factor of application. Especially as Schleiermacher made hermeneutics a theory of understanding in dialogue, and as language and knowing came to the fore, there was little systematic place for application within the sphere of understanding as such. In fact, Schleiermacher places clear limitations even on the moment of explaining. He observes, "As soon as explication becomes more than the outside of understanding, it becomes the art of presentation. Only what Ernesti calls the *subtilitas intelligendi* genuinely belongs to hermeneutics." [39]

According to Gadamer's analysis, on the other hand, in understanding as such "something like an application of the text to be understood to the present situation always takes place." [40] To understand, in the sense of knowing and explaining, already involves within it something like an application or relation of the text to the present. Theological and juridical hermeneutics bring to attention this aspect of all understanding, and thus they constitute a better pattern for grasping the operations of understanding in history and literature than the philological tradition, which artificially omits the factor of application. Gadamer says:

> Juridical hermeneutics is in reality no "special case" but is suited to the task of giving back to historical hermeneutics its full breadth of problematic. It can reconstitute the old unity of the hermeneutical problem which was [in the eighteenth century] encountered in common by the jurist, the theologian, and the philologist.[41]

38. *Ibid.*, 291.
39. *H* 31.
40. *WM* 291.
41. *Ibid.*, 311.

Gadamer is suggesting here a striking idea: juridical and theological hermeneutics may serve as a model for literary interpretation.

Let us look into some of the creative possibilities of this idea. Both juridical and theological hermeneutics see the task of interpretation not merely as an antiquarian effort to enter another world but as an effort to span the distance between a text and the present situation. Whether it be handing down a judgment or preaching a sermon, interpretation must comprise not merely explaining what the text means in its own world but what it means in terms of our present moment. In other words, "Understanding the text is always already applying it." [42] Also, juridical and theological hermeneutics both tend to negate the idea that the text is understood on the basis of congeniality with its author—a Romantic illusion. We know that understanding can and does take place with or without congeniality with the author. Why is this? Because in fact we do not relate to the author but to the text.

In still another respect, juridical and theological hermeneutics constitute a helpful model for literary interpretation. In both legal and theological interpretation the interpreter does not so much apply a method as adjust and order his own thinking to that of the text. He is not so much appropriating a possession as being appropriated by the governing claim of the text. Interpreting the "will of the law" or the "will of God" are not forms of dominating the subject but of serving it. In no sense is this a procedure where one makes his own presuppositions immune to question and then conforms his understanding of the world and phenomena to methods built upon these presuppositions. On the contrary, the interpreter risks his own position to place it in the light of the governing claim of the text. Gadamer asserts, then, that even in historical interpretation understanding must perform the function of application "in that it expressly and consciously brings to acceptance the meaning of the text by bridging the temporal distance which separates the interpreter from the text; thus it overcomes [through application] the alienation of meaning which has befallen the text." [43]

In historical and literary hermeneutics the demand that one

42. *Ibid.*, 291.
43. *Ibid.*, 295.

serve the text, be governed by its claim, and simultaneously interpret it in the light of the present poses a real challenge. Such an approach would see the text in the light of the present, yet not overpower and dominate it with the present; the interpreter must be governed by the claim of the text, yet translate the meaning of the claim into the present. Gadamer does not mean that one should be uncritically given over to the claim of the text in denial of the present; rather, the claim of the text must be allowed to show itself as what it is. In the interaction and fusion of horizons the interpreter comes to hear the question which called the text itself into being. The dialectic of a questioning which is willing to place the claim of the present in the balance and risk it against tradition will be taken up later. It is clear at this point, however, that juridical and theological hermeneutics suggest an approach more in harmony with the universal, historical structure of understanding than has been in evidence recently in either historical or literary interpretation, and thus they could help literary and historical interpreters to regain a more adequate grasp of the hermeneutical problem.

The principle of application finds theological expression in the project of demythologizing. In Rudolf Bultmann's hermeneutics, for instance, it is a consequence of the tension between the text, standing in the past, and the need for present application. Demythologizing, it has been pointed out earlier, is not an Enlightenment-type effort to purge the Bible of myth by measuring everything in the light of the claims of reason; rather, it tries to locate the claim which the Bible has on us today. The claim is not a scientific truth claim but a call for personal decision. For this reason, to take a "scientific" attitude toward the Bible and treat it as an object which places no personal claim on us is effectively to silence the Bible; it must not simply be cross-examined, for when it speaks, one must himself become the "object" to which it is addressed. When a fixed and unquestioned standard is taken against which the biblical message is measured, the Bible is not being listened to; it is being tested out. But the Bible, according to Bultmann, is neither scientific treatise nor impersonal biography; it is proclamation, *kerygma*—a message.

In literary interpretation the effort at demythologizing is paralleled when we ask how we are to understand myth. What is speaking to us in and through it? The lead taken by Bultmannian theology in always emphasizing the relationship to the present and our analysis of historical understanding both warn against the illusion that the act of reading a literary work is merely going back and "reconstructing" a past world. The "meaning" of Milton, Shakespeare, Dante, Sophocles, or Homer is not solely in terms of the worlds erected in each great work; reading a work is an event, a happening that takes place in time, and the meaning of the work for us is a product of the integration of our own present horizon and that of the work. Something like demythologizing occurs in every authentic understanding of a literary work. An application to the present occurs in every act of understanding. The illusion that in reading a Shakespearean play we are "going back into the world of Shakespeare" and leaving our own horizon behind only shows that the aesthetic encounter has succeeded in rendering invisible the *subtilitas applicatio* factor. Yet it is important to remember that a Connecticut Yankee in Arthur's court will see things as a Connecticut Yankee and not in the same way as one of the Knights of the Round Table.

The situation involved in staging a Shakespearean or other older play likewise corroborates what we have said. The scenery provides elaborate help in going into the past, and costumes are occasionally made with meticulous loyalty to the period presented, yet the fact is that the play is staged in the present, now, before our eyes, in *our* understanding. The locus of happening in a play is in the collective mind of the audience. The actors know this and take it into account in playing their parts. Take, for instance, the problem of staging and playing the witches in *Macbeth*. Modern productions tend to deemphasize the supernatural element and play the women merely as old hags following the army of Macbeth. Their prophecies are presented as giving voice to speculations already present and spreading about trouble brewing. They create an atmosphere of foreboding. The "meaning" of the witches for us today is thus "interpreted" by the way they are played on the stage so as to bypass the possibly comic effect of an outmoded supernaturalism on contemporary audiences.

It is significant too that the dramatic illusion in plays is not dependent on scenery or costume, or even on the visible presence of the actors. The vocal presence, as in the case of phonograph recordings, is the really important element. The dramatic illusion is that the past is happening in the present, not in the historical past but in the experiential present. This phenomenon clarifies something significant about application in historical understanding: it is not a literal bringing of the past into externalities of the present; it is bringing what is essential in the past into our personal present, our self-understanding, or more accurately our experience of being.[44] We should not deceive ourselves; our understanding of a play—when we "know" what it "means"—is not a self-enclosed matter but a relating of the self-enclosed game that a play is to our present and to our future. Thus Gadamer's assertion: Understanding always includes application to the present.

CONSCIOUSNESS WHICH IS AUTHENTICALLY HISTORICAL

OVER AGAINST THE KIND OF HISTORICAL CONSCIOUSNESS he criticizes, Gadamer attempts to describe an authentic kind of awareness in which history is constantly at work. His term for this, the *wirkungsgeschichtliche Bewusstsein*, defies any adequate translation. A rather literal translation would be "consciousness in which history is ever at work," or "historically operative consciousness."[45] I shall generally use this latter term or the phrase "authentically historical consciousness," depending on the context. The authentically historical consciousness, Gadamer makes clear, is not the Hegelian historical consciousness that places awareness in the sphere of reflexivity and makes it the mediation of history and the present. It is certainly a speculative and dialectical awareness, but the dialectic is not the self-mediation of reason but the structure of experience itself.

Gadamer uses typologies of three kinds of I-thou relationships—not to be equated with Martin Buber's I-thou relationship[46]—to help situate and thus clarify the nature of the historically operative consciousness: (1) the thou as object

44. As we shall see, the "what" that we understand is not a personal "what" but an historical "what" in which we participate; to refer to "personal experience" is itself to fall into the fictions of the subjectivist fallacy.

45. I am indebted to Professor Theodore Kisiel for the suggestion of "historically operative consciousness."

46. Of interest is the earlier form of the "Ich-du Beziehung" in Ferdinand Ebner's "Das Wort und die geistigen Realitaten: Pneumatologische Fragmente," in his *Schriften*, I, 75-342.

within a field, (2) the thou as reflexive projection, and (3) the thou as tradition speaking.[47] Only the third is the hermeneutical relationship Gadamer has in mind as authentic historical awareness.

In the first I-thou relationship, the other person is seen as something specific within one's field of experience, most often something which can serve as a means of achieving one's goals. The other person is seen as an object in one's field of experience, and the thou is understood in terms of universals. Inherent in this approach to the thou is the teleology of all inductive thinking. Now if this model is applied to the hermeneutical relation to tradition, we easily lapse into "methods" and "objectivity." Tradition then becomes an object separate from us, swinging free and unaffected by us. We quickly deceive ourselves into thinking that, if only we can eliminate all subjective moments of relation to this tradition, we can have certain knowledge of what it contains. Such method-oriented "objectivity" often prevails in the natural sciences and also in the social sciences, except where phenomenology has made itself felt.[48] But it cannot serve the disciplines focused on human experience; it cannot be the foundation of a consciousness in which history is at work.[49]

A second way of experiencing and understanding the thou sees him as a person, but Gadamer shows that this "personal" relationship can still remain imprisoned in the I and actually is a relation between the I and a reflexively constituted thou.

> This I-thou relationship is not an immediate but a reflective relationship. . . . Thus there is always the possibility that each partner in the relationship will overplay the reflective activity of the other. He knows the claim of the other through his own reflection, and thus he understands the other better than the other himself does. But just this reflexivity empties the relationship of the immediacy which lays claim on one.[50]

Hermeneutically speaking, this second kind of relationship characterizes the historical consciousness against which Gadamer's critique is directed. This historical awareness knows the otherness of the other, not in a relatedness to the universal,

47. See WM 340-44.
48. See Stephen Strasser, *Phenomenology and the Human Sciences,* and Severyn Bruyn, *The Human Perspective in Sociology.*
49. WM 341.
50. *Ibid.*

which characterized the first I-thou relationship, but rather in its particularity. The otherness of the other and the pastness of the past are then only known in the same way as the I knows the thou – through reflection. In claiming to recognize the other in all his conditionedness, in claiming to be objective, the knower is really claiming to be master. But it is just this subtle kind of mastery through understanding which uses understanding merely to see history "out there" as a reflexively constituted thou; it objectifies it and effectively destroys its real claim to meaningfulness.[51]

The third kind of I-thou relationship is characterized by authentic openness to the thou. This is the relationship that does not project the meaning from the I but has an authentic openness which "lets something be said": "He who allows something to be said *to* him is in a fundamental way open."[52] Such a relationship is closer than the first two to what Buber has in mind as a true I-thou relationship. It is the kind of openness that wills to hear rather than to master, is willing to be modified by the other. It is the foundation of the historically operative consciousness, the *wirkungsgeschichtliche Bewusstsein.*

This consciousness consists of a relationship to history in which the text can never be fully and objectively "other," for understanding is not the passive "recognition" of the otherness of the past but rather a placing oneself so as to be laid claim to by the other. When an historical text is read as "merely historical," the present has already been dogmatized and placed outside of the question. Authentically historical consciousness, on the other hand, does not see the present as the apex of truth; it holds itself open for the claim which the truth in the work can address to it. "Hermeneutical consciousness finds its fulfillment not in methodical self-certainty but in the experiential readiness and openness that an 'experienced' person has in contrast to a dogmatic one. That is what characterizes historically operative awareness. . . . "[53] The "experienced" person does not so much have merely objectified *knowledge* as rather nonobjectifiable *experience* which has ripened him and made him open to tradition and the past. As we shall see in the next chapter, the concept of experience is very important for understanding Gadamer's hermeneutics.

51. *Ibid.,* 341-43.
52. *Ibid.,* 343.
53. *Ibid.,* 344.

12 / Gadamer's Dialectical Hermeneutics

THE STRUCTURE OF EXPERIENCE AND OF HERMENEUTICAL EXPERIENCE

GADAMER BEGINS HIS EXAMINATION of the hermeneutical experience by criticizing the prevailing concept of experience, which he finds too much oriented toward knowing as a perceptual act and knowledge as a body of conceptual data. In other words, we tend today to define experience in a way that is completely oriented toward scientific knowledge and heedless of the inner historicality of experience. In doing so, we unconsciously fulfill the goal of science, which is "so to objectify experience that no kind of historical moment clings to it." [1] Through rigorous methodical arrangement, the scientific experiment takes the object out of its historical moment and restructures it to suit the method. An analogous goal is sought, says Gadamer, in theology and philology with the "historical-critical method," which in some ways reflects the scientific rage to make everything objective and verifiable.[2] Insofar as this spirit prevails, only what is verifiable is real; no place is left for the nonobjectifiable and historical side of experience. Consequently, the very definition of "experience" excludes the data of these sciences from itself.

Over against the myth of purely conceptual and verifiable knowing, Gadamer places his carefully enunciated historical and dialectical concept of "experience," where knowing is not

1. *WM* 329.
2. *Ibid.*

simply a stream of perceptions but a happening, an event, an encounter. Although he does not share Hegel's presuppositions and conclusions, Gadamer finds in Hegel's dialectical account of experience the starting point for his own dialectical hermeneutic, and this may provide the starting point for our exposition of the concept.

Experience, as Hegel defines it, is a product of the encounter of consciousness with an object. Gadamer quotes Hegel as follows: "[There is a] movement in which awareness practices on both its knowing and its object; insofar as, for it, a new object is generated out of this, that is truly to be called 'experience.' "[3] According to Hegel, then, experience always has the structure of a reversal or restructuring of awareness; it is a dialectical kind of movement.

At the base of this tendency to reversal is an element of negativity: experience is first of all experience of "not-ness" — something is *not* as we had assumed. The object of one's experience is seen in a different light, is changed; and one is himself changed in knowing the object differently. The new object contains a truth above the old; the old "has served its time."[4] But for Hegel experience is the self-objectification of consciousness, so that experience is approached from the vantage point of knowledge which transcends it. Hegel is thus asserting a foundation in consciousness which Gadamer would contend is itself transcended by the objectivity of experience.

Experience, Gadamer asserts, has its dialectical fulfillment "not in a knowing but in an openness for experience, which is itself set in free play by experience."[5] Clearly, experience does not here mean some kind of informational knowledge preserved about this or that. As Gadamer uses the term, it is less technical and closer to ordinary usage. It refers to a nonobjectified and largely nonobjectifiable accumulation of "understanding" which we often call wisdom. For example, a man who has all his life dealt with people acquires a capacity for understanding them which we call "experience." While his experience is not objectifiable knowledge, it enters into his

3. "Die dialektische Bewegung, welche das Bewusstsein an ihm selbst, sowohl an seinem Wissen als an seinem Gegenstand ausübt, *insofern ihm der neue wahre Gegenstand* daraus *entspringt*, ist eigentlich dasjenige, was *Erfahrung* genannt wird" (*Ho* 115), in the essay "Hegels Begriff der Erfahrung," *WM* 336.
4. *WM* 337.
5. *Ibid.*, 338.

interpretive encounter with people. It is not a purely personal
capacity, however; it is a knowledge of the way things are, a
"knowledge of people" that cannot really be put into conceptual
terms.

Experience often suggests the pain of growth and new understanding. It has constantly to be acquired, and nobody can
save us from it. We would like to spare our children from unpleasant "experiences" we ourselves have had, but they cannot
be spared from experience itself, for experience is something
that belongs to the historical nature of man. "Experience,"
says Gadamer, "is a matter of multisided disillusionment based
on expectation; only in this way is experience acquired. The
fact that 'experience' is preeminently painful and unpleasant
does not really color experience black; it lets us see into the
inner nature of experience." [6] Negativity and disillusionment
are integral to experience, for there seems to be within the nature of man's historical existence a moment of negativity which
is revealed in the nature of experience. "Every experience runs
counter to expectation if it really deserves the name experience." [7]

Considering these facts, it is not surprising that Gadamer
refers to Greek tragedy and to the Aeschylean formula *pathei
mathos*, "through suffering learn." [8] This formula does not
mean that one acquires a scientific kind of knowledge, nor even
merely the kind of knowledge which will enable one to "know
better next time" in some similar situation; rather, through
suffering one learns the boundaries of human existence itself.
One learns to understand the finitude of man: "Experience
is experience of finitude." [9] Experience, in the true sense of
its inner meaning, teaches one inwardly to know that he is not
lord over time. It is the "experienced" man who knows the
limits of all anticipation, the insecurity of all human plans. Yet
this does not render him rigid and dogmatic but rather open
for new experience.

Since in experience one is reaching into the future in
expectation, and since past experience teaches the incom-
pleteness of all plans, there is clearly present here the structure
of historicality already stressed in our earlier discussion.

6. *Ibid.*
7. *Ibid.*
8. *Ibid.*, 339.
9. *Ibid.*

"True experience," Gadamer asserts, "is experience of one's own historicality."[10] In experience man's powers to do and his planning reason come up against their limits. Man, standing and acting in history, gains through experience the insight into the future within which expectation and plans are still open to him. The maturity in experience which places one in proper openness to the future and to the past is itself the essence of what Gadamer has in mind as historically operative consciousness.[11]

With these observations in mind, we may characterize "hermeneutical experience," which has to do with what one encounters as heritage. It is this heritage which, in the hermeneutical encounter, must come to be experienced. Whereas in general an experience is an event, one's heritage is "not simply an event which one recognizes through experience and comes to control; rather it is *language,* that is, it of itself speaks, like a thou."[12] The heritage is not something that one can control, nor is it an object over against one. One comes to understand it, even while standing in it, as an intrinsically linguistic experience. As one experiences the meaning of a text, he comes to understand a heritage which has briefly addressed him as something over against him, yet as something which is at the same time a part of that nonobjectifiable stream of experiences and history in which he stands.

The text which is met as a thou is not to be viewed, Gadamer asserts emphatically, as an "expression of life" (the Dilthey conception). The text has a specific content of meaning apart from all connection with a person saying it. Nor should the terms "I" and "thou" lead us to think in basically person-to-person terms, for the saying power resides not in the person saying it but in what is said. What Gadamer means by an I-thou relation to heritage is that in a text the heritage addresses and makes a claim on the reader, not as something with which he has nothing in common but in mutuality. The text must be allowed to speak, the reader being open to it as a subject in its own right rather than as an object. Precisely this authentic openness is what we have already described in connection with the I-thou structure of historically operative consciousness.

The I-thou structure suggests a relationship of dialogue or

10. *Ibid.,* 340.
11. *Ibid.*
12. *Ibid.*

dialectic. A question is addressed to the text, and, in a deeper
sense, the text addresses a question to its interpreter. The dialectical structure of experience generally, and of hermeneutical
experience in particular, reflects itself in the question-answer
structure of all true dialogue. Yet it is necessary to be wary of
conceiving the dialectic in person-to-person terms rather than
in terms of subject-matter. The significance of subject-matter
in dialogue will emerge in the ensuing analysis of questioning.

THE STRUCTURE OF QUESTIONING
IN HERMENEUTICS

THE DIALECTICAL CHARACTER OF EXPERIENCE is reflected in the movement and encounter with negativity found
in all true questioning. Gadamer goes so far as to say that "in
all experience, the structure of questioning is presupposed. The
realization that some matter is other than one had first thought
presupposes the process of passing through questioning." [13]
The openness of experience has the structure of a question: "Is
it thus or thus?" We have observed that experience fulfills itself in the realization of our finitude and historicality; so also
in questioning there is an ultimate wall of negativity, always
the knowledge of not knowing. This suggests the famous
Socratic *docta ignorantia* that reveals the true negativity underlying all questioning.

To question genuinely, says Gadamer, means to "place in
the open" because the answer is not yet determined. Consequently a rhetorical question is not a true question, for there is
no genuine questioning when the thing spoken of is never
really "questioned." "In order to be able to question one must
will to *know,* and that means, however, to know that you do not
know." [14] When one knows he does not know, and when he does
not therefore through method assume that he only needs to
understand more thoroughly *in the way he already understands*, then he acquires that structure of openness characterizing authentic questioning. Socrates sets the pattern with
his playful exchanges of question and answer, knowing and
not knowing, which probe the subject-matter itself for an appropriate access to its true nature.

13. *Ibid.,* 344.
14. *Ibid.,* 345.

The openness of questioning, however, is not absolute, because a question always has a certain direction. The sense of the question already contains the direction in which the answer to *that* question must come, if it is to be meaningful and appropriate. With the placing of the question, what is questioned is put in a certain light. This already "breaks open" the being of what is questioned. The logic which unfolds this already opened-up being already essentially implies an answer, for any answer has meaning only in terms of the question. Real questioning, then, presupposes openness—i.e., the answer is unknown—and at the same time it necessarily specifies boundaries.

This phenomenon raises the problem of procuring the right question. The vantage point from which the question is asked may be wrong. If so, it yields no true knowledge; thus "A wrong question can have no answer, neither false nor true but only wrong, for the answer does not lie in the direction in which the question was asked." [15] According to Gadamer, there is only one way to find the right question and that is through immersion in the subject itself. A true dialogue is the opposite of an argument, for an argument holds to its opening response to the question: "A dialogue does not try to argue down the other person, but one tests his assertions in the light of the subject itself." [16] A dialogue on love, ethics, justice, or any other subject in Plato moves in unforeseen directions because the partners are guided by a common immersion in the matter under discussion. To test the assertions of the other person, one does not try to weaken them but rather to strengthen them, that is, to find their true strength in the subject itself. This is one reason, says Gadamer, that the Platonic dialogues are of highest contemporary significance.

In hermeneutical dialogue, then, the general subject in which one is immersed—both the interpreter and the text—is the tradition, the heritage. One's partner in the dialogue, however, is the text, already in the stark fixedness of written form. Thus there is a need to find a way through to the give-and-take of dialogue: this is the task of hermeneutics. Somehow the fixed formulation must be placed back in the movement of conversation, a movement in which the text questions the in-

15. *Ibid.*, 346. Zygmunt Adamczewski discussed this topic in a paper presented at the annual meeting of the Society for Phenomenology and Existential Philosophy, October 27, 1967, Purdue University.
16. *WM* 349.

terpreter and he questions it. The task of hermeneutics is "to bring the text out of the alienation in which it finds itself [as fixed, written form], back into the living present of dialogue, whose primordial fulfillment is question and answer." [17]

When a transmitted text becomes an object for interpretation, it places a question to the interpreter which he is trying to answer through interpretation. Authentic interpretation will relate itself to the question "placed" by the text. (The text has a place and a subject.) To understand the text means to understand this question. To interpret a text, the first requirement is to understand the horizon of meaning or of questioning within which the direction of meaning of the text is determined. [18]

Yet the text itself is an assertion. In a sense it is itself the answer to a question—not the question we put to it, but the question the "subject" of the text puts to it. Now if one understands the text in terms of the question it answers, it is clear that one must go questioningly behind the text in order to interpret it. One must also ask what is not said: "Going back behind what is said, one has necessarily gone outside what is said. One understands the text in its meaning only insofar as he attains a question horizon which necessarily also encompasses other possible answers." [19] The meaning of any sentence is relative to the question for which it is an answer; that is, it necessarily goes beyond what is explicitly said. For the humanistic interpretation of texts, this is decisive. One must not be satisfied with merely rendering more explicit what is already explicit in the text; the text must be placed within the horizon of the question that called it into being. R. G. Collingwood, operating on this principle in historical interpretation, says that to understand an historical event, one must reconstruct the question for which the historical actions of persons were the answer. [20] Collingwood, claims Gadamer, is one of the few modern thinkers to try to formulate a logic of question and answer, and even this effort is not systematically and exhaustively carried through.

However, reconstruction of the question to which a text or an historical act is the answer can never be thought of as a self-enclosed task. As Gadamer's critique of historical con-

17. *Ibid.*, 350.
18. *Ibid.*, 351–52.
19. *Ibid.*, 352.
20. See R. G. Collingwood, *Autobiography.*

sciousness indicates, the horizon of meaning within which a text or historical act stands is questioningly approached from within one's own horizon; and one does not leave his own horizon behind when he interprets, but broadens it so as to fuse it with that of the act or text. Nor is this a matter of finding the intentions of the actor in history or the writer of the text. The heritage itself speaks in the text. The dialectic of question and answer works out a fusion of horizons. What makes this possible? The fact that both are, in a sense, universal and grounded in being. So the encounter with the horizon of the transmitted text in reality lights up one's own horizon and leads to self-disclosure and self-understanding; the encounter becomes a moment of ontological disclosure. It is an event in which something emerges from negativity—the negativity of realizing that there is something one did not know, that things were not as one had assumed.

The disclosure, in other words, comes as the kind of event whose structure is the structure of experience and the structure of question and answer; it is a dialectical matter. And what is the medium in and through which this ontological disclosure can take place in the dialectical event of experience as questioning and answer? What is the medium that is of such a universality that horizons can interfuse? What is the medium in which the cumulative experience of a whole historical people is hidden and stored? What is the medium that is inseparable from experience itself, inseparable from being? The answer must be: language.

THE NATURE OF LANGUAGE

1 / *The Noninstrumental Character of Language*

Fundamental to Gadamer's conception of language is the rejection of the "sign" theory of the nature of language. Over against the emphasis on form and instrumental functions of language, Gadamer points to the character of living language and our participation in it. The transformation of word into sign, Gadamer contends, lies at the base of science, with its ideal of exact designation and unambiguous concepts. So familiar and self-evident has the conception of words as signs become that "it requires a feat of mental gymnastics to remember that outside the scientific ideal of unambiguous designation, the life of language itself goes its way unaffected." [21] To see words as signs is to rob them of their primordial power and make them mere instruments or designators. "Everywhere that word is seen in its mere sign function, the primordial relationship of speaking and thinking is turned into an instrumental relationship." [22] The word becomes the tool of thinking and stands over against thinking and the thing designated. No demonstrable organic relationship is seen between the word and what it designates; it is merely a sign. Thinking seems to be separate from words and uses words to point to things.

When did the sign theory of language arise in Western thought? Gadamer traces the conception to the idea of the *logos* in Greek thought. He asserts:

> If the realm of the noetic in the multiplicity of its elements is represented by the realm of the *logos,* then the word, like the number, becomes a mere sign of a well-defined and therefore preknown being. Questioning is thereby in principle reversed; now one does not go from the matter involved to ask about the being of words as mediators; rather, we *start* with the medium—the words—and ask what and how the sign transmits something to him who uses it. In the very nature of the "sign" is the fact that it has its being and its only real property in the function of being applied.[23]

It disappears into its function of designating; it is no longer seen to be important in itself as word but only as sign. Its power to reveal being is not referred to; rather the *logos* supplies the signs with a ready-made and preknown reality to which they refer, and the real problem is only on the side of the subject who uses them. Words are viewed as tools of man for communicating his thought. Language is ultimately seen as an instrument of subjectivity fully separated from the being of the thing that is thought.

Closely related to this idea is the concept, familiar to us in the philosophy of Ernst Cassirer, of language as symbolic form. Again, the instrumental function of language is the starting point and basis, although in a way which transcends the function of mere sign. Gadamer would contend that Cassirer,

21. *WM* 410.
22. *Ibid.*
23. *Ibid.,* 390.

modern linguistics, and modern philosophy of language generally, err in taking the *form* of language as their basic and central focus. Is the concept of form adequate to the phenomenon of language? Is language as language symbolic form, and does the concept of form really do justice to what may be called the linguisticality of human experience? Or is it a static concept which robs the word of its character as event, its power to speak, its status as far more than a mere tool of subjectivity?

If language is neither sign nor symbolic form created by man, what is it? In the first place, words are not something that belong to man, but to the situation. One searches for words, the words that belong to the situation. What is brought to words when one says "The tree is green" is not so much human reflexivity as the subject-matter itself. What is important here is not the form of the assertion or the fact that the assertion is being put forward by a human subjectivity. The important fact is that the tree is being disclosed in a certain light. The maker of this assertion did not invent any of the words; he learned them. The process of learning the language came only gradually, through immersion in the stream of the heritage. He did not make a word and "endow" it with a meaning; the imagining of such a procedure is a pure construction of linguistic theory. Gadamer asserts:

> The linguistic *word* is not a "sign" which one lays hold of; it is also no existing thing that one shapes and endows with a meaning, making a sign to render some other thing visible. Both possibilities are wrong; rather, the ideality of the meaning lies *in the word itself. Word is always already meaningful.*[24]

The nature of experience is not a nonlinguistic datum for which one subsequently, through a reflective act, finds words; experience, thinking, and understanding are linguistic through and through, and in formulating an assertion one only uses the words already belonging to the situation. The devising of words to describe experience is no random act but a conforming to the demands of the experience.

The formation of words, then, is not a product of reflection but of experience. It is not an expression of spirit or mind but of situation and being: "Thinking that seeks an expression is not relating itself to 'mind' but to fact, to matter." [25] To make

24. *Ibid.*, 394; italics added.
25. *Ibid.*, 403.

clear the close relationship of word, thinking, and saying, Gadamer refers to the doctrine of the Incarnation: "The inner unity of thinking and saying which corresponds to the trinitarian mystery of the Incarnation [the Word was still Word even before it became flesh] includes the idea that the inner word of the spirit is *not formed through a reflexive act.*" [26] Someone who "expresses himself" is really expressing that which he is thinking. Certainly the word emerges from a process of mental activity; what Gadamer asserts is that it is not a self-externalization of reflection itself. The starting and ending point in the formation of words is not reflection but the matter that is coming to expression in words.

To see language and words as the tools of human reflection and subjectivity is to allow the tail to wag the dog. To take form as the starting point in language is to make essentially the same error as to take form as the starting point in aesthetics. The event character of the phenomenon and its temporality are lost, and, most importantly, one falls into the error of designating the human subject, instead of the nature of the thing coming to expression, as the fixed point of reference. In the case of language, its saying power, not its form, is the central and decisive fact. Form cannot be separated from content, but when we think of language in instrumental terms, we automatically do so. Languages, says Gadamer, should not be typed according to form but according to what the language transmits to us historically. Language cannot be divorced from thought.

The unity of language and thought itself, the nonreflexivity of the formation of words, both refute the idea of language as sign. Language is an encompassing phenomenon, like understanding itself. It can never be grasped as "fact" or fully objectified; like understanding, language encompasses everything that *can* become object for us. The early Greeks, Gadamer notes, had no word or concept for language itself; like being and understanding, language is medium, not tool. He summarizes his thinking on form, the inseparableness of thought, language, and understanding, and the desirable invisibility of language as follows:

> The language that is living in speech, language which encompasses all understanding and all interpreters of texts, is so fused with the process of thought [and therefore interpretation] that we have far

26. *Ibid.*

too little in hand when we turn away from what languages hand down to us in content and wish to think of language as form. Unconsciousness of language has not ceased to be the authentic way of being for language.[27]

LANGUAGE AND THE DISCLOSURE OF THE WORLD

IF THE FUNCTION OF LANGUAGE is not that of pointing at things, and if the direction of language is not *from* subjectivity *through* the sign tool *to* the designated thing, then one needs a concept of language and its function which moves in the other direction—from the thing, or situation, through language to subjectivity. For this purpose, Gadamer chooses the concept of disclosure or representation. Language discloses our world—not our environmental scientific world or universe, but our lifeworld. To understand Gadamer's concept of language, we must first recall what he means by world, for language creates the possibility that man can have world.

World is not the same as environment, for only man has a world. "To have a world one must be able to hold open a space before him in which the world can open up to him as it is. To have a world is at the same time to have language." [28] Gadamer asserts that animals, for instance, do not have world and they do not have language. Certainly they have a way of understanding each other, but this is not language except to a scientist with a purely instrumental view of language as sign. But language as the power of laying open a space in which world can disclose itself—this animals do not have. Animals, for instance, could not use their communicative apparatus to reach an "understanding" about a situation or circumstance, as such, in the past or future; only language in its real power to establish a world can do this.

It is an error to think of this "world" as basically a possession or property of subjectivity; this is the mistake typical of modern subjectivity-oriented thinking. Rather, world and language both are transpersonal matters, and language is made to fit the world, and therefore it is ordered to the world rather than to our subjectivity. In this sense (but not in the scientific sense) language is objective:

27. *Ibid.*, 382.
28. *Ibid.*, 419.

Out of the commensurateness of language to world follows its
peculiar objectivity [*Sachlichkeit*]. A situation or matter that be-
haves so and so—therein lies the recognition of self-sufficient otherness that presupposes its own distance between the matter and the
speaker. On the basis of this distance, something like "situation"
can come to definition and ultimately be capable of becoming the
content of a statement that another can understand.[29]

World is not impersonal, nor does it circle an isolated individual, figuratively speaking, like a giant balloon projected by
mind and perceptions. World is more aptly seen as *between*
persons. It is the shared understanding between persons, and
the medium of this understanding; and what makes it possible
is language. Language, as a realm of interaction, is not really a
constructed "tool" for understanding. In this regard man lives
in something like the community of understanding existing
among animals. But with man this is a linguistic understanding, and therefore what is between people is world. Linguistic
understanding, Gadamer tells us, "takes that in which it takes
place [i.e., world] as process and puts it between the parties,
like a disputed object. World is a common ground recognized
by everybody, binding on all who communicate in it."[30]

Since the open space in which man exists is the realm of
shared understanding created by language as world, man
clearly exists *in* language. "Language is not just a fixture which
man finds in his world; rather, in and through it comes the possibility of having world at all."[31] This is to say that language
and world transcend all possibility of being fully made into an
object. One does not, in some kind of knowing or reflection,
transcend language or the world; rather, "the linguistic experience of the world is an absolute."[32] This experience of
world as already resident in language transcends all relativi-
ties and relationships in which beings might show themselves;
every object of knowledge is encompassed within the world
horizon of language. We may call this the linguisticality of
human experience of the world.

This conception tremendously broadens the horizon within
which we see the hermeneutical experience. What is understood through language is not only a particular experience but
the world within which it is disclosed. The power of language

29. *Ibid.*, 421.
30. *Ibid.*, 422.
31. *Ibid.*, 419.
32. *Ibid.*, 426.

to disclose transcends even time and place, and an ancient text from a people long extinct can render present with the most amazing exactness the interpersonal linguistic world that existed among those people. Thus our own language worlds have a certain universality in this power to understand other traditions and places. Gadamer notes:

> Our own language world, this world in which we live, is not a tight enclosure that hinders the knowing of things as they are; rather, it encompasses basically everything which our insight is able to broaden and lift up. Certainly one tradition sees the world differently from another. Historical worlds in the course of history have differed from each other and from today. At the same time, however, the world is always a human, and this means a linguistically created, world which is presented in whatever heritage it may be.[33]

Such is the saying power of language that it creates the world within which everything may be disclosed; such is its comprehensiveness that we can understand the most diverse worlds that have come to expression in language; such is its disclosing power that even a relatively short text can lay open a world different from our own yet one which we are able to understand.

LINGUISTICALITY AND THE HERMENEUTICAL EXPERIENCE

THE HERMENEUTICAL EXPERIENCE, as already noted, is an encounter between heritage in the form of a transmitted text and the horizon of the interpreter. Linguisticality provides the common ground in which and on which they can meet. Language is the medium in which the tradition conceals itself and is transmitted. Experience is not so much something that comes prior to language, but rather experience itself occurs in and through language. Linguisticality is something that permeates the way of being-in-the-world of historical man. As we have observed, man has "world" and lives in a world because of language.

Just as one says that he "belongs" to a certain group, one also belongs to a certain time and place in history, and to a certain country. One does not assert that the group belongs to him,

33. *Ibid.*, 423.

or that history is a personal possession of his subjectivity, nor does he in any way control his country to the same extent that it controls and orders his life. He belongs to them, not they to him; he participates *in* them. In the same way, we belong to language and history; we participate in them. We do not possess and control language so much as we learn it and conform to its ways. The power of language to order and conform thought is not a matter of the rigidity in language or its inadequacy; the power is grounded in the situation or case it communicates. It is to the situation or case that we must conform our thinking. Language is thus not a prison but an open space in being that allows infinite expansion, depending on one's openness to tradition.

This phenomenon of belonging (*Zugehörigkeit*) is of greatest significance to the hermeneutical experience, for it is the ground for the possibility of encountering one's heritage in the text. Because of our belongingness to language and because of the belongingness of the text to language, a common horizon becomes possible. The emergence of a common horizon is what Gadamer calls fusion of horizons as it occurs for the historically operative consciousness. Linguisticality, then, becomes the basis for authentic historical consciousness. The belongingness to, or participation in, language as the medium of our experience of the world—indeed, the ground of the possibility that we can have world as that open space in which the being of things can be disclosed—is the real ground of the hermeneutical experience.

Methodologically, this means that one does not seek to become master of what is in the text but to become the "servant" of the text; one doesn't so much try to observe and see what is in the text as to follow, participate in, and "hear" what is said by the text. Gadamer plays on the relationship between listening and belonging and serving which the word "belongingness" (*Zugehörigkeit*) suggests. (*Hören* means to hearken, hear, or listen; *gehören* means to belong to; *gehörig* means proper to, or appropriate.) Hearing, asserts Gadamer, is a far greater power than seeing: "There is nothing that is not made accessible to hearing through language."[34] Why is this? Because through hearing, through language, one gains access to the *logos*, to the world to which we belong. It is precisely this deeper dimension, this ontological dimension accessible

34. *Ibid.*, 438.

through language, that gives the hermeneutical experience its significance for the present life of the interpreter.[35] The peculiar objectivity of language, which is able to reveal things as they are, grounds language in a universal linguistic ontology. The deeper dimensions of language, from which it derives its power to reveal things in their being, give that fundament of ontological universality which makes the hermeneutical experience one of immediately meaningful ontological disclosure. This is the reason that the tradition can address us, not casually or decoratively, but in a way that affects and means something directly to us.[36]

The method appropriate to the hermeneutical situation involving the interpreter and the text, then, is one that places him in an attitude of openness to be addressed by the tradition. The attitude is one of expectancy, of waiting for something to happen. He recognizes that he is not a knower seeking his object and taking possession of it—in this case, by coming to know "how it really was" or what the text "really meant," by trying to shake off his prejudices and see with a purely "open" mind. Rather, the methodical discipline is one designed to restrain his own will to master. He is not so much a knower as an experiencer; the encounter is not a conceptual grasping of something but an event in which a world opens itself up to him. Insofar as each interpreter stands in a new horizon, the event that comes to language in the hermeneutical experience is something new that emerges, something that did not exist before. In this event, grounded in linguisticality and made possible by the dialectical encounter with the meaning of the transmitted text, the hermeneutical experience finds its fulfillment.

THE SPECULATIVE STRUCTURE OF LANGUAGE AND OF THE NATURE OF POETRY

FOR GADAMER, language itself has an intrinsically speculative structure. It is not fixed and dogmatically certain, but because it is always in process as event of disclosure, it is ever moving, shifting, fulfilling its mission of bringing a thing to understanding. The movement of living language is constantly resisting the fixity of bald and final statements. The

35. *Ibid.*
36. *Ibid.*

conscientious secretary who keeps the minutes of a meeting is systematically reducing the events to statements—statements which try to capture the distilled meaning of what has occurred. But these statements, just because they are statements, tend to distort what was really said and with methodical exactness cover over the horizon of meaning within which the statements were placed.

True saying, the kind of saying that occurs in everyday life between people who understand each other, allows the unsaid so to accompany the said that the two together comprise a unity; this is the unity of making oneself understood through saying instead of through the said. He who speaks in this manner, Gadamer says,

> may use only the most common and ordinary words and yet is able just through them to bring to language what is unsaid, the unsaid that needs to be said and here *is* said. He who speaks is proceeding *speculatively* in that his words are not copying anything "real" but are actually expressing a relation to the whole of being and letting it come to expression.[37]

Everything that is said is really ordered by a larger direction of meaning in the ungraspable. This ungraspableness makes the speculative structure of language evident. Even the purest restating of the sense of something requires the backdrop of what is never fully objectifiable.

This phenomenon is encountered in a greatly heightened form in poetic utterance, where we are confronted with an assertion, a statement. One legitimately asks that the poetic statement itself be self-sufficient and not depend on special occasional knowledge for its understanding. The poetic statement gives the appearance of being a stark and bald statement rightly dissolved from all subjective opinion and experience of the poet. But is it? Emphatically not, Gadamer tells us. The words of poetry have the same quality as the saying that happens in daily life between people who understand each other. "The words are speculative . . . in the same way as the speaking in daily living: in speaking the speaker brings, as we said before, a relation to being into language." [38] More explicitly: "The poetical assertion as such is speculative insofar as the

37. *Ibid.*, 444–45.
38. *Ibid.*, 445.

linguistic happening of the poetic word on its side expresses its special relation to being." [39]

This last statement brings something new into the discussion: the poetical word is speculative not only in the sense that it requires the backdrop of the unsaid in order that the explicitly said will also say what in the unsaid needs to come to be understood. The poetical word also has its own relation to being and brings something new into the realm of the said. Why? Because the poet is the speculative experiencer par excellence; he opens up, through his own openness to being, new possibilities in being. The poet, as Hölderlin has told us, first consciously frees himself of the ordinary, customary, and well-worn words and usages. As he looks around himself, he beholds the world as if for the first time, new and unrecognized. His knowing, his perspective, art, and nature – all are suspended in indeterminateness. This is the suspension of the conventional patterns of being and thought which enables the great poet to hammer out new ways of thinking and feeling. "The poetical assertion is speculative," then, as Gadamer tells us, "insofar as it does not copy the world now in being, does not simply mirror the view of things in the existing order, but rather presents to us the new view of a new world in the imaginative medium of poetical invention." [40]

We speak here not of the speculative character of the hermeneutical experience, but of the writing of poetry. Yet the hermeneutical question immediately arises: How, if one is keeping to conventional patterns of thought, will he be able to understand the poetical utterance specifically designed to open up a new relationship to being? Obviously, the interpreter must himself share something of the openness to new possibilities that the poet possessed. Yet here we recall that there is no standing place for the interpreter outside of history; a subject can never be seen from the vantage point of eternity. Every appropriation of the tradition, Gadamer tells us, is itself the experiencing of a view of the subject-matter itself. It is guided by the subject-matter that is communicated, but this is the paradox of interpretation, that the subject-matter is the same and in each interpretation different. "All interpretation is in truth speculative. Hermeneutics has, therefore, to see

39. *Ibid.*
40. *Ibid.*, 446.

through all dogmatic belief in an infinite meaning in itself, just as critical philosophy has seen through the dogmatism of experience." [41] The interpretation of a text, then, is not passive openness but dialectical interaction with the text; it is not bald reenactment but a new creation, a new event in understanding.[42]

Speculativity, then, involves that movement, suspension, and openness which wills to let new possible relationships in being speak to us and address our understanding. For the poet, it is openness to being coming to language; for the interpreter, it is openness to place one's horizon in the balance and be willing to subject it to modification, in the light of the new understanding of being that may emerge from an encounter with the meaning of the text. Ultimately, speculativity is grounded in a creative negativity, in the nature of being, which forms the background of every positive assertion. A speculative hermeneutics is alive to the significance of this negativity as the source of every new disclosure of being and as a continuing antidote to dogmatism.

THE UNIVERSALITY OF HERMENEUTICS

AT THE CLOSE OF *Wahrheit und Methode*, Gadamer makes the assertion for which he has painstakingly laid the foundation: the development of the hermeneutical problem from before Schleiermacher through Dilthey and into Husserl and Heidegger is not merely an interesting exercise in the methical self-examination of philology as "hermeneutics"; it leads to a systematic position for philosophical inquiry itself. It is not simply an effort to find a manner of questioning proper to the historical and literary understanding of texts; it asserts that human understanding *as such* is historical, linguistic, and dialectical. In the development of a questioning position designed to move beyond the confines of the subject-object schema, Gadamer's hermeneutics suggests a new kind of objectivity (*Sachlichkeit*) grounded in the fact that what is disclosed constitutes not a projection of subjectivity but something which acts on our understanding in presenting itself.

41. *Ibid.*, 448.
42. *Ibid.*

The principle of resisting the fixed givenness of statement is applicable not merely to the hermeneutical experience, but to experience generally. The idea that the dialectic presents us with a possibility of moving away from seeing experience as an activity of the subject and toward seeing it as an act of the subject-matter or situation itself—that is, that this dialectic makes it possible to see experience speculatively, as a movement that grasps the speaker—is of more than merely methodological significance. In a meaningful paragraph at the close of his book, Gadamer summarizes his argument and the way it leads up to the assertion of a more comprehensive hermeneutics:

> We perceive now that this speculative movement [of going from being as a whole and being led by things rather than subjectivity] was what we had in view when we were led by our analysis of hermeneutical experience to a critique of aesthetic as well as historical consciousness. The being of a work of art was no being-in-itself from which the repetition or contingency of its appearances could be distinguished; only in a secondary thematizing of one against the other can we differentiate "aesthetic" from "nonaesthetic." The same thing applies with respect to our historical or philological encounter with our heritage: what seemed to stand out over against us—the meaning of an event or the sense of a text—was no firm and self-enclosed object for us merely to identify and describe. For the historical consciousness includes in itself actually a mediation of past and present. Now, in that we recognized in language the universal medium for this mediation, we broadened the vantage of our questioning [*unsere Fragestellung*] from its starting point—i.e., the critique of aesthetic and historical consciousness—to comprise a universal direction for questioning. For the human relation to his world is simply and from the ground up linguistic and therefore understandable. Hermeneutics is, as we saw, a universal way of being of philosophy and not just the methodological basis for the humane disciplines.[43]

Continuing, Gadamer says that because he takes linguisticality and ontology for his foundation, he does not necessarily fall into Hegelian metaphysics. For him, language is not the instrument of subjectivity, nor does language fulfill itself in the self-contemplation of an infinite intellect; language is instead finite and historical, a repository and a carrier of the experience of being which had come to language in the past.

43. *Ibid.*, 450-51.

Language must lead one in understanding the text; the task of hermeneutics is to take seriously the linguisticality of language and experience and to develop a truly historical hermeneutics.

Both history and the work of art confront one, address one, present themselves. Speculativity lies in their very nature, and also in the nature of all beings one encounters: everything, insofar as it tries to make itself "understood," divides itself from itself, the said from the unsaid, the past from the present; self-presentation and becoming understood are not special characteristics of history and art and literature but are universal. This is the speculativity which Gadamer sees as a universal characteristic of being itself: "The speculative conception of being which lies at the base of hermeneutics is of the same universal compass as reason and language." [44] Speculativity, if deeply understood, is not only the key to understanding Gadamer's hermeneutics but the true ground of his claims for its universality.

When it is understood what speculativity means to Gadamer, it becomes somewhat more meaningful to label his hermeneutics a speculative hermeneutics than, as has been done here, a dialectical hermeneutics. But since the term has a special sense in Gadamer, and a title is the introduction and not really the conclusion of a chapter, a more immediately intelligible term was chosen to help lead into the area of thinking within which it is possible to conceive of speculativity in relation to hermeneutics.

CONCLUSION

IN *Wahrheit und Methode*, Gadamer brings hermeneutics to a new level of comprehensiveness. Dilthey and Betti had both argued for a comprehensive general hermeneutics — for the *Geisteswissenschaften*. What about the natural sciences? Do they require a different understanding? The general conclusion has been that the interpretation of an historically transmitted text requires an act of historical understanding quite distinct from the understanding practiced by a natural scientist. Gadamer leaves this distinction behind, for he no longer conceives of hermeneutics as restricted either to a text or to the *Geisteswissenschaften*.

44. *Ibid.*, 452.

Understanding, says Gadamer, is always an historical, dialectical, linguistic event—in the sciences, in the humanities, in the kitchen. Hermeneutics is the ontology and phenomenology of understanding. Understanding is conceived not in the traditional way as an act of human subjectivity but as the basic way of *Dasein's* being in the world. The keys to understanding are not manipulation and control but participation and openness, not knowledge but experience, not methodology but dialectic. For him, the purpose of hermeneutics is not to put forward rules for "objectively valid" understanding but to conceive understanding itself as comprehensively as possible. In comparison with his critics Betti and Hirsch, Gadamer is concerned not so much with understanding more correctly (and thus with providing norms for valid interpretation) as with understanding more deeply, more truly.

Gadamer has gone deeply into Heidegger's original comprehensive definition of understanding, following Heidegger's later writings by developing an ontological and linguistic emphasis. In doing so, and in trying to work out a systematic hermeneutics, he has come closer to that great moving force in German philosophy, Hegel. Thus the references to dialectic and to speculativity suggest Hegel at once, and the parallel of Gadamer's phenomenology of understanding to Hegel's phenomenology of *Geist* inevitably arises. A number of the distinctions between Hegel's and Gadamer's phenomenologies have been mentioned earlier, especially with regard to subjectivity as a starting point, yet the parallels in the treatment of the objectivity of subject-matter (*Sachlichkeit*) in Gadamer and the objectivity of *Geist* in Hegel deserve further explication.

It may be said, then, that insofar as Gadamer moves away from Heidegger, he tends toward a rapprochement with Hegel. But is this a liability or a positive asset? Heidegger himself would possibly regard any such move with the greatest suspicion; he would wonder whether his radical vision of facticity as the starting point of philosophizing would be lost. On the other hand, Gadamer argues persuasively that the inner movement of Heidegger's own thinking throughout is dialectical.[45]

45. Cf. Gadamer, "Anmerkungen zu dem Thema 'Hegel und Heidegger,' " *Natur und Geschichte: Festschrift für Karl Löwith*, pp. 123-31. Also on Hegel and Heidegger, see Thomas Langan, "Heidegger beyond Hegel: A Reflexion on 'The Onto-theo-logical Constitution of Metaphysics,' " paper read to the Heidegger Circle, University of Pittsburgh, April 27, 1968.

Thus Gadamer's dialectical hermeneutics is simply an extension of an inherent tendency in Heidegger's thought itself.
He has taken Heidegger's theory of understanding, ontology,
and critique of modern humanist subjectism and technology
and evolved without radical contradiction of Heidegger a hermeneutics that is language-centered, ontological, dialectical,
and speculative.

The Hegelianism of Gadamer's basically Heideggerian
hermeneutics is probably an improvement over Heidegger's
conception. This becomes clear when one notes the tendency
in later Heidegger to describe understanding exclusively with
a vocabulary of passive terms: understanding is no longer
viewed as an act of man but as an event in man. There emerges
a danger that man will be seen as a passive speck in the stream
of language and tradition. Gadamer does not go to the other
extreme of taking man's subjectivity as the starting point for
all thinking about understanding, but he does take a position
that allows a greater degree of dynamic interaction when he
speaks of "experience" and of "fusion of horizons." In this
regard, it is interesting how much less a recent criticism by
Jean-Marie Domenach of the structuralism of Lévi-Strauss
and Michel Foucault applies to Gadamer than to Heidegger:

> A convergent undertaking [in philosophy today] seeks to reverse
> the order of terms under which philosophy has lived up to the pres-
> ent, and to negate the autonomous activity of consciousness. I don't
> think, *I am thought;* I don't speak, *I am spoken;* I don't deal with
> something, *I am dealt with.* It is from language that everything
> comes and to language that everything returns. The System, which
> is seized in the midst of itself, is proclaimed the master of man. . . .
> The System, a thinking that is cold, impersonal, erected at the ex-
> pense of all subjectivity, individual or collective, negates at last
> the very possibility of a subject capable of expression and inde-
> pendent action.[46]

It must be said at once that the disembodied objectivity of a
pure system that leaves man out of account stands at once
worlds apart from any phenomenological approach, which
takes as its foundation the lifeworld. Thus it would be absurd
to equate either Heidegger or Gadamer with objective struc-
turalists. Yet it is of interest that, precisely in the measure that
Gadamer is dialectical and speaks of the dialectical character

46. "Le Système et la personne," *Esprit* (May 1967), pp. 772–73.

of experience as basic in his hermeneutics, he allows for conceiving understanding as a personal act and not simply an event that "takes place."

It is difficult to resist asking what kind of ethics and doctrine of man are presupposed in Heidegger. Is man simply to live in a kind of responsive surrender to the call of being? And it would be of interest to put the same question to Gadamer. How does the operation of language in understanding take into account the functions of will and desire in man? Gadamer would probably reply first that his analysis in *Wahrheit und Methode* was of the event of understanding itself, not of the motivations for it or the personal affect surrounding it. Furthermore, he would say that he was not proposing an ethics or doctrine of man but trying in all honesty to describe understanding as an ontological structure or dynamic process. This may be so, but it would be very enlightening to know how Gadamer would answer this question. I believe that here again the dialectical character of Gadamer's hermeneutics as over against that of Heidegger would more adequately provide for the contribution made by the person doing the understanding to the hermeneutical experience. This would valuably supplement and extend the final portion of the book dealing with the hermeneutical experience.

Wahrheit und Methode, then, opens up a whole new horizon of considerations in hermeneutical theory, perhaps heralding the beginning of a fruitful new stage in modern thinking about interpretation. While Heidegger's hermeneutics already conceives of the event of understanding ontologically, Gadamer develops the ontology of understanding into a dialectical hermeneutics that calls into question the most fundamental axioms of modern aesthetics and historical interpretation. And it could provide the philosophical foundation for a radical critique of the conceptions of interpretation prevailing in literary criticism today.

PART III

A Hermeneutical Manifesto
to American Literary Interpretation

Preamble

THE TIME HAS COME to question the heavily armed vision in American literary interpretation.[1] The fruitful impetus given to it by the New Criticism could not continue forever; today there is a broad spectrum of content-oriented and formalist approaches, preeminently myth criticism.[2] Yet in spite of the rich variety of activity in criticism and the arsenal of weapons for literary analysis, there is general obscurity and confusion about what literary interpretation does. This calls for a radical re-asking of the question: What is interpretation?

What American criticism needs today is not more tools for "getting at" a literary work but a rigorous reexamination of the presuppositions upon which its conception of interpretation is based. Philosophically, the heyday of realism is receding into the past, and the phenomenological revolution is making its critique of realism and of idealism felt. Consequently, the reexamination of the question of interpretation cannot proceed naively on the basis of common-sense notions, or presuppose at the outset a realism that belongs to the past. On the contrary, literary theory must boldly explore the phenomenological critique of realism in Edmund Husserl, Martin Heidegger, and Hans-Georg Gadamer. Hermeneutics in Gadamer furnishes the fruitful conjunction of phenomenology and theory of understanding; it constitutes the basis for a creative reexamination of literary interpretation theory.

1. See Stanley Edgar Hyman, *The Armed Vision*.
2. See John B. Vickery, ed., *Myth and Literature*, and Northrop Frye, *Anatomy of Criticism*. For a short overview of the various approaches, see Walter Sutton's valuable survey, *Modern American Criticism*.

[221]

To clarify the critique of prevailing conceptions of literary interpretation which is implicit in phenomenological hermeneutics, and to set forth in a preliminary way the character of a theory of literary understanding based on it, the following manifesto is addressed to American interpreters of literature.

13 / Toward Reopening the Question: What is Interpretation?

WHAT DOES UNDERSTANDING A TEXT MEAN?

AMERICAN LITERARY INTERPRETERS and theorists have fallen into a crassly naturalistic and technological way of seeing their task. They cannot within their present perspective even meaningfully ask themselves the very question they most need to pose: What happens when one "understands" a literary text? Such a question is either treated in an abstract, logical, and technological way, or pushed aside as irrelevant, since it would seem to deal not with the object of analysis but with the subjective experience of it.

But what is assumed? That one can speak of an object of analysis in terms of its form and "objective meaning" in such a way that the work seems to exist independently of our experience of it! Gradually there comes to be no correlation between the analysis of the object and our own experience of it in understanding. The abstract analysis of form and of logical contradictions comes to be the hallmark of subtle interpretation, and ultimately the dynamics of experiencing the work are unconsciously bypassed, or dropped as leading to "fallacy." Yet such objectivity assumes a rational rather than experiential access to the work; it takes interpretation out of its living context and purges it of its historical character.

It should be said at the outset that the subject-object model of interpretation is a realist fiction. It is not derived from the experience of understanding but is a model constructed reflexively and projected back onto the interpretive situation.

[223]

There is no such thing as a nonpositional subject, and therefore there is also no such thing as a nonpositional understanding. Understanding is always positional; it stands at a given point in history. There is no privileged access to a work of literature, no access that stands outside of history and outside one's own horizon of understanding. Some interpreters apparently wish that this were so, but wishing will not make it so. To bring up the historicality and positionality of understanding is not to drag in an irrelevant and subjective element (the use of the word "subjective" in this context rests on untenable conceptions of objectivity); it is a fact about the interpretive situation which our disregard will not change. To ignore it is to weaken one's conception of interpretation, for it has led in some extreme formalist critics to the assumption that literature is not essentially historical in nature, and that understanding literature is not a deeply historical act.

The indictment of the future of contemporary formalism will be for its lack of real historical consciousness. By historical consciousness I do not mean merely sensing the "historical element" in a literary work, but rather a genuine comprehension of the way that history is constantly at work in understanding, and a consciousness of the creative tension between the horizon of the work and that of one's own present time.

THE CONSEQUENCES OF THE SUBJECT-OBJECT SCHEMA

To ASK MEANINGFULLY about what happens when one understands a literary work means transcending the prevailing definition of the interpretive situation in terms of the subject-object schema. Let us look at some of the general consequences of assuming the subject-object model of the interpretive encounter. Within this framework, when the interpreter confronts a literary work, consciousness is encountering an "object." The status of the object is *as* object for a subject, so that ultimately its status, like that of the whole world, is traceable back to subjectivity and the reflexive operations of the mind. "Scientific objectivity," for instance, stands within this interpretive framework and asserts that it wants to acquire only clean, clear ideas about these "objects." Numbers are the cleanest, clearest, and abstractest of ideas, so they are especially prized. Then comes everything that is measurable, repeatable, or visualizable as schema. Knowledge and experience that are not reducible to the forms of a primarily ideational (visualizing) thinking tend to be regarded as unreal or unimportant.

In such a framework for viewing interpretation, the power and ubiquity of language and history in one's existing are unperceived. Language is seen as an object to communicate "meaning." Man is considered a symbol-making animal, with language his master system of symbols. But all this is rooted in the erroneous metaphysics of the modern perspective since Descartes. The reason we today see language as a set of man-made signs and history as merely past events is that we take without question a nonhistorical human subjectivity as the origin and reference point for everything. Thus despite the word "objectivity," the center from which our bearings are taken is subjectivity. But if everything goes back to subjectivity and there is no reference point outside it, human will-to-power becomes the mainspring of human activity. This shallow subjectivism is the chief ground for the modern frenzy for technological knowledge; when human subjectivity is the final court of appeals, there is nothing left for man but to control the "objects" in his world ever more completely.

Despite the protestations in modern criticism on behalf of the humane, the mode and focus of modern literary interpretation have become technological, a matter of mastering the object of analysis. The New Criticism constitutes in some ways an exception to this, with its references to "surrendering" to a being of a work, with its wholesome effort to avoid the heresy of paraphrase in favor of the direct experience of the work, and its intention to speak about the form and content of the work rather than becoming lost in a mire of extrinsic information about it. This movement has restored tremendous vitality and meaningfulness to the study of literature and rescued it from dry historicism and philology. Yet the philosophical base of New Criticism was always shaky and uncertain, vacillating between realism and idealism.[3] What it needed was a greater philosophical clarity as to the character of interpretation; too often its contextualism did not concentrate on the perception of the work as the true locus of the "work" and fell into an

3. See Murray Krieger, *The New Apologists for Poetry.*

Aristotelian realism, organicism, or formalism. Such a formalism, unclear about its ground in experience rather than in the "form" of the work as an object, too often fell victim to an atemporal and ahistorical conception of interpretation, and interpretations often seemed to be in terms of static knowledge rather than vital experience.

Such a conception of interpretation tends to equate conceptual mastery with understanding. The work when conceived as an object (instead of a work) becomes simply an entity about which knowledge is acquired through spatializing ideation, dissection, and analysis. Such an approach represents the transposition into criticism of a technological approach to the world, an approach which looks only for such knowledge of an object as will give mastery and control over it. With this comes a profound misconception of literary understanding, for the critic sees his task as trying to say how a work is constructed, how it evolves, and ultimately whether it is a success (generally in terms of achieving logical contradictions and irony). Thus the interpreter does not see his task as removing hindrances to understanding so that an event of understanding can take place in its fullness and the work can speak with truth and power, but rather as bringing the work under control through conceptual mastery. Would such a critic, if he had a profound religious experience, speak objectively and conceptually about it in terms of its "structure and pattern"? Of course not (unless he were the abstractest of men), for the decisive thing is not pattern but what happened. The hubris of trying to be the absolute master of a religious experience is apparent; the hubris of trying to be the master in the literary encounter is less apparent but no less real.

A further flaw in modern-style objectivity is that to see a work as "object" rather than as "work" places the reader at a distance from the text; the purpose of literary interpretation, however, is to overcome the reader's estrangement from the text. It is not enough to know a work in the way a psychoanalyst knows his patient's problems; literary interpretation should enable the language event to seize and overpower and transform the interpreter himself. A work does not speak by being cut to pieces in order for the analytical reader to see how and why it is made as it is; one must enable a work to speak by knowing how to listen, both to what is spoken in the words and what is left unsaid but still present behind the words. To put the matter in the familiar terminology of Martin Buber's I-thou relationship, it is helpful to see the work not as an it that is at my disposal but as a thou who addresses me, and to remember that meaning is not an objective, eternal idea but something that arises in relationship. A wrong relationship will produce a distorted and incomplete meaning.

Methodical questioning runs the risk of closing to the interpreter the possibility of being led by the work itself.[4] A method will pose a list of questions, thus structuring in advance the encounter one will have with the work. These dangers of method or methodical analysis need not, of course, foreclose its use altogether nor lead to the rejection, root and branch, of all methods of conceptual analysis. Nor is it suggested that one should purposely take a simple-minded attitude toward reading a literary text and abandon with a sigh of relief the rigors of conceptual thought. It means, rather, that the interpreter needs to realize in a more comprehensive way the limitations of method, and the way that conceptual analysis can all too easily serve as a substitute for experiential understanding, especially when one has no adequate concept of literary understanding itself.

Toward a More Comprehensive Conception of Understanding

It is the service of Martin Heidegger in *Being and Time* to have opened up the ontological character of understanding in a way that moves radically beyond the older conception of it within the subject-object schema.[5] According to Heidegger, understanding is not some faculty among others that man possesses; understanding is his fundamental mode of existing in the world. Through understanding we are able to have a sense of the way we are placed, we grasp meaning through language, and something like world can come to be the horizon in which we exist. If we start with subjectivity, then understanding will seem to be a faculty of man; if we start with the facticity (*Faktizität*) of the world, however, understanding becomes the way in which the facticity of the

4. See *WM* 435 ff.
5. See also Heidegger, "Wissenschaft und Besinnung" and "Überwindung der Metaphysik," *VA* 45-99.

world is presented to man. Heidegger takes this latter approach, and therefore understanding is seen as grounded not in the autonomous reflexive activity of man but in the act of the world, the facticity of the world, on man. Understanding is then the medium by which the world comes to stand before a man; understanding is the medium of ontological disclosure.

Understanding is not a tool for something else—like consciousness—but rather the medium in which and through which one exists. It can never be objectified, for it is within understanding that all objectification takes place. An existing human being cannot survey understanding from without; understanding is always the position from which all that is seen is seen. Now understanding, just because it stands under everything, is not an empty and amorphous mass, a flickering translucence totally filled with the sensations of the present moment. On the contrary, understanding is always necessarily "in terms of" the character of the seeing that is handed down, of our understanding of the present situation, and of a sense of what the future can or will hold. Thus this ground upon which we stand in understanding has a fairly definite topography, and every act of interpretation stands within its horizon. The repository of the past and the medium of our way of seeing is language. Language is equally as primordial as understanding, for understanding is linguistic; it is through language that something like a world can arise for us. This world is a shared world; it is the realm of openness created by shared understanding in the form of language. The realm of openness created by shared understanding through language has, as has just been noted, a certain definiteness. It is finite and changes with the passage of time. This means *it is historically formed, and that every act of understanding contains the acting of history in and through understanding.*

It may be said, then, that understanding is linguistic, historical, and ontological. Because Heidegger's analysis takes the facticity of understanding as its starting point, it asserts that what comes to stand in understanding is not something subjective but something which encounters man from the outside and discloses itself to understanding as world. Understanding is thus not a projection of the reflexive consciousness but the medium by which a situation or matter is disclosed as it is. Understanding does not impose its categories on the world,

Heidegger asserts; the subject-matter of world imposes itself on understanding, and understanding conforms to it. But was it not just asserted that all understanding is in terms of the topography of understanding built up in time and mediated in language? If so, then is not the subject projecting this understanding on what comes to meet him in the situation and not purely receiving it from the outside as it actually is? No, again. What discloses itself is the being of the object *as it is disclosed to understanding.* To speak of the being of a thing as it "actually is" is to indulge in metaphysical speculation: as it is for whom? There is no human perspective from which one can say what a being "actually is." On the other hand, what the subject seems to "project" in understanding is nothing personal or reflexive, although it is admittedly nonobjective and largely nonobjectifiable. The subject understands through the shared world of understanding already given in and through his language and the historical positionality in which his understanding stands. To call this subjective or to trace it back to the individual consciousness is untenable, since the individual did not create the shared understanding and language but only participates in them. They are, in a word, objectively real; at the same time they are not traced back to an empty reflexive consciousness or to a transcendental ego. Shared understanding, historicality, and language become the ground from which a position can be derived that goes beyond the scientism and subject-centeredness of the subject-object schema within which we, today, tend unconsciously to operate, and which prevailing aesthetic and literary theory presupposes.

With the new position opened up by Heidegger's conception of understanding as the organ of ontological disclosure, it becomes possible to speak of the objectivity of language in the sense that language is what it is and we conform to it. Take, for example, a case in which one is searching for words to convey a situation to another person. He will try one word and then another and then perhaps find a third which is satisfactory. Do we have a right to speak of the reflexive consciousness "expressing" itself here? Not necessarily, for what is coming to expression is the being of the situation, the way in which it discloses itself to us. If the situation did not itself hold the possibility to be seen in this way, it could not come to expression. Were the first and second words he found unsatisfactory for any other reason than that the matter itself demanded the third word? This is the sense in which we can speak of the objectivity of language.

The erroneous theory of language as basically an "instrument of communication" again reveals the way in which a conception has been distorted by subject-object thinking, the scientific predilection for ideation, and the will-to-power technological vision of man as master of the universe and manipulator of tools. Language is not man's means of putting wordless thoughts and wordless experience into a form to which he has assigned a meaning; thinking, understanding, and experience are all completely linguistic, for it is through language that one has the world of understanding in and through which objects take their place in his experience. Nor is language something that can be invented; only in the most artificial situation is any word "assigned" a meaning. Rather, it always has a general meaning already, one chosen to express a situation. Although sometimes a word may be used daringly in an unusual way to express something unusual about the situation, is it not what is unusual in the situation, not the user, that has given the word the new significance?

Thus we do not originate meanings. When a scientist coins a new word, he generally takes an already existing word and gives it a restricted meaning. This, however, is not so much creating a new word as paring down and partially destroying the primal saying power of the original word – the power which actually brought it into being – in the interest of creating a specific and narrow concept. Very seldom is a word coined by randomly putting together sounds, and then it is usually ugly and hopelessly vague. The creating of artificial languages on an experimental basis does not refute our position here, since these languages derive their real and only power by reference to a living language. The image of man "creating a language" and using it as a tool, then, is a naive fiction of science-oriented imaginations, a fiction denied by the patent fact that we do not in fact invent our language, nor do we assign the meanings that the words have, nor can we solely through subjective willing make words say something other than what they in fact do say. This is the objectivity of language. And of course the structure of understanding as being always and fully linguistic makes the "sign theory" of language, based as it

is on a total misconception of consciousness and on an ignorance of how understanding operates, obviously a mere theoretical construction based on erroneous realist presuppositions.

Gadamer makes clear in *Wahrheit und Methode* that language is the medium in and through which one has a "world";
it makes an open place in being through the disclosure of
being.[6] This disclosure is not personal and private but a shared
understanding which language enables us to have in the first
place, as well as enabling us to communicate it. One does not
invent and manipulate language to suit himself; he participates in language and allows a situation to come to stand in
language. Language, like understanding, can never be simply
an object in the world, since it pervades the world as the medium
in and through which one sees every object. Only a profound
misconception of understanding as being nonlinguistic, then,
can lead to the belief that language is merely a set of objects
in the world, which can be manipulated and modified at one's
personal whim.

DEFINING UNDERSTANDING IN TERMS OF EXPERIENCE[7]

NOWHERE MORE THAN IN literary interpretation
does the poverty of seeing understanding in terms of conceptual knowing become so apparent. It leads to extensive
analyses which contribute little to enabling one to experience
in a compelling way the saying power of the work. All analysis
must be measured in the light of whether it deepens the language event of understanding; some analysis can even be
harmful by causing one to ask meaningless questions and thus
leading to a shallow conceptual event of understanding.

To understand a work is to experience it. Experience is not
some subschema within the framework of the subject-object
dichotomy; it is not some nonhistorical, nontemporal, abstract
knowing outside time and space where an empty, placeless

6. See esp. Pt. III, "Ontologische Wendung der Hermeneutik am Leitfaden
der Sprache," *WM* 361-465.
7. See "Der Begriff der Erfahrung und das Wesen der hermeneutischen
Erfahrung," *ibid.*, 329-44.

consciousness receives a configuration of sensations or perceptions. Experience is something that happens in living, historical human beings. Let us for a moment desert the abstractness of the scientific model of our knowing of the world and ask what happens in experience, what is meant in the ordinary usage of the word "experience."

One learns through experience, it is said, and only secondarily through precept. Hidden in this expression is an element of negativity, for the experience referred to is primarily negative and painful experience in which one learns what he did not know before and did not expect. In experience, then, there is a shattering of expectations, and one emerges as a sadder and wiser person. We would like to save our children from painful experiences, especially those experiences we have had ourselves, yet from experience itself nothing can save them.

Inquiring from outside experience as to its structure, what is noticed immediately is the temporal character of its relation to expectations developed in the past, held in the present, and extending into the future. Experience, as has been observed, contradicts expectations, and thus it is the great teacher, for which there is no substitute. Like language, experience can never be an object for us, yet it participates invisibly in every event of understanding. A man who is "experienced" in judging people (or simply in living) cannot really put his experience into the form of precept. He might write a book on "how to judge character on sight," but he would convey empty knowledge and not his own power to judge.

The truly experienced person, one who has wisdom and not just knowledge, has learned the limitations, the finitude, of all expectations. Experience teaches him not so much a storehouse of facts that will enable him to solve the same problem better next time but how to expect the unexpected, to be open to new experience. It teaches him, in short, the poverty of knowledge in comparison with experience.

For literary interpretation, the lesson we learn from the structure of experience is to remain sensitive to the fact that its dimensions transcend every conceptualization; the richness of the experience of understanding a text and the richness of the text's experience are not to be mistranslated into the shallow categories of knowledge. And it suggests, in view of the limitations of conceptual knowledge, a stance of dialectical openness to the text.

THE DIALECTIC OF QUESTION AND ANSWER IN THE HERMENEUTICAL EXPERIENCE

THE ENCOUNTER with an historically transmitted work has the structure not of simple knowing but of experience—it may be called the hermeneutical experience.[8] It has not only the encompassing, nonobjectifiable character of experience, as described above, but also its dynamic dialecticality. The creative negativity of true questioning, which is essentially the negativity in experience that teaches and transforms, is the heart of the hermeneutical experience. For to experience is to understand not better but differently; experience does not tell one what he expected, but tends to transcend and negate expectations. A "deep" experience teaches us not to understand better what is already partially understood so much as that we were understanding wrongly.

But we cannot understand "differently" if we ask all the questions. A question, after all, posits a preliminary way of seeing; just as understanding is not placeless and empty, so questioning is not without its own horizon of expectations. The point is that our own presuppositions must not be taken as absolute (for these are the foundation of our expectations) but as something subject to change. Analysis and methodical questioning, however, tend not to call into question their own guiding presuppositions but rather to operate within a system, so that the answer is always potentially present and expected within the system. Thus they are not so much forms of true questioning as of testing. But experience does not follow the model of solving a problem within a system; it is the means of reaching outside the system, a means of creative transcendence and a striking down of the system. When any truly great work of art or literature is encountered, it transforms one's understanding; it is a fresh way of seeing life. It is for this "freshness" that a work is read, but just this freshness is what escapes analytical seeing (which might also be called "analytical blindness"). The element of creative negativity is absent from most methods, for the truly creative moment lay in the creation of the method itself—a moment not methodically arrived at, in most cases. Creative negativity, then, may be called the life and ground of true dialectical questioning.

8. *Ibid.*

What is needed in literary interpretation is a dialectical questioning which does not simply interrogate the text but allows the thing said in the text to interrogate back, to call the interpreter's own horizon into question and to work a fundamental transformation of one's understanding of the subject. This does not mean a denial of the interpreter's horizon, nor does it mean making one's own horizon absolute, as is implicit in most analysis and method; it means a creative fusion of horizons. It is but partially true that one can understand only within one's own horizon and through it. If this were so, no significant alteration of horizons could occur. Rather, in true experience there is a partial negation of one's own horizon, and through this a more encompassing understanding emerges. The dialectical approach of Socrates may serve as a model for all truly dialectical questioning, for in his vacillation between knowing and not knowing, in the playful probing of the subject from different angles, lies the willingness to risk everything and to be instructed by the subject-matter itself. Beneath the artful shiftiness of Socrates is the serious intention to let the subject under discussion lead the way. He circles the subject, flexible, open, undogmatic, always trying new approaches. Instead of trying to weaken his opponent's arguments, he tries to find their true strength, so that his own understanding may be transformed. The literary interpreter today needs to cultivate this kind of openness to what is being "said" in a literary text. In dialogue with the text, the questioning and being placed in question must go both ways.

On Being Able to Hear What the Text Did Not Say

It takes a great listener to hear what is actually said, a greater one to hear what was not said but what comes to light in the speaking. To focus purely on the positivity of what a text explicitly says is to do an injustice to the hermeneutical task. It is necessary to go behind the text to find what the text did not, and perhaps could not, say.[9]

Just as every question contains a preliminary assertion, so every assertion may be seen as the answer to a question. A

9. See *KPM* 181; English trans., 206.

literary text is such an assertion. The assertion must not be seen as some independent and discrete entity but as the response to a question, as something whose meaning stands within a certain horizon of thinking. Thus to interpret the work means to step into the question horizon within which the text moves. But this means also that the interpreter moves into a horizon within which other answers are possible. It is in terms of these other answers—in the temporal context of the work and also in the present day—that one must understand what the text is saying. What is said can be understood, in other words, only in terms of what is *not* said.

The reconstruction of the question that called the text into being is not a matter of simple historical reconstruction, of mere "restoration"; such taxonomy would be no less absurd than any effort to bring back what is gone forever. Nor is it a matter of simply finding out the author's intentions, although this may be relevant; for what is speaking in the text is the subject-matter about which it was written, the question that called it into being and to which it is an answer. Yet the interpreter too approaches the text questioningly, and the text must light up the horizon of the interpreter or the process of understanding it is an empty and abstract exercise. Here the historical task arises of hearing in the text what it says today— to hear, in other words, what it did not and could not say. Queasiness about "doing violence to the text" must not become an excuse for turning away from the hermeneutical task of hearing deeply into the "what" behind the explicitness of the text.

ON THE SIGNIFICANCE OF APPLICATION
TO THE PRESENT

JUST AS INTERPRETATIONS which deal only with the explicit meaning of a text fail to do justice to the hermeneutical task, so also theories of interpretation which satisfy themselves solely in terms of the past horizon of meaning are misconceptions of what interpretation demands. Such theories see interpretation basically as reconstruction and restoration of the past, following in the path of nineteenth-century apostles of objectivity (Leopold von Ranke, for example) who imagined historical understanding to be a matter of merely reconstructing a past age. But this rests on a misconception of the dialectic of understanding. One addresses a question to the text, a question standing within one's own horizon; to assert otherwise is to assume absurdly that one engages in historical research with no purpose. One has a reason for wanting to understand, and that reason is really a question put to the text. In every interpretation, then, something like an application to the present takes place.[10]

Literary interpretation, therefore, does well not to take its lead methodologically from the objectivist perspectives of philology and historical research but to study the problems that confront theological and juridical theory of interpretation. For both juridical and theological hermeneutics are obliged to see understanding not simply as an antiquarian effort to enter another world for its own sake but as an effort to bridge the distance between the text and the present situation. Whether it be handing down judgment or preaching a sermon, the moment of interpretation is not merely explaining what the text means in its own world but what it means to us. Juridical and theological hermeneutics both tend to reject the idea that one "understands" a text because of some intrinsic congeniality with its author; one can interpret a biblical or legal text and even personally disapprove of its author. A text is understood not on the basis of congeniality but because the subject-matter of the text is something shared. The ground of this sharing is not strictly personal, it is language. One exists in and through language, and interprets his very being through language; even when he has to bridge the gap of two different languages, he is still interpreting within a linguistic world where being comes to stand in language.

Literary interpreters can learn from juridical and theological interpretation in another respect. In both, the objective is to let the text lead the understanding and open up the subject. The interpreter is not so much applying a method to the text as an observed object, but rather trying to adjust his own thinking to the text. He is not appropriating another possession for his closet of knowledge, but being appropriated himself by the governing claim of the text. In other words, interpreting either the will of the law or of God is not a form of dominating the subject of the text but of serving it.

Both the interpreter of law and the interpreter of the Bible must have an acute sense of the tension between the past and

10. See WM 290–95, 312–16, 322, 381.

the present. Both must sense what is applicable and meaningful and what is secondary and inapplicable. To do so is really to go behind the text to the question which brought it into being; to do so is to ask what the text did not or could not say. Since the creative bridging of the tension between the horizon of the text and that of the interpreter is the task of interpretation, the basic importance of an authentic historical consciousness can hardly be disputed. Literary interpreters in America need to be reminded that literary interpretation, because it bridges temporal distance, is an intrinsically historical act and requires an understanding of the nature of historical encounter, for hermeneutical experience is historical encounter.

ON THE CATEGORY OF THE AESTHETIC, AND ATTENDANT MISCONCEPTIONS

THE IDEA, which has come down to us from the Enlightenment, of "the aesthetic" or of a purely "aesthetic" element in a work of art is a reflexive fiction.[11] The aesthetic dimension of a literary work, in particular, cannot be considered apart from its meaning, i.e., the meaning of its words and therefore its "historical" meaning. The use of such words as "pleasure" and "delight" in reference to a literary work should not be construed as a reaction to the "purely formal" side of a work, to its construction and the craftsmanship of its composition. On the contrary, an authentic reaction to a great poem or work of literature is to what it says; the "way in which it is said" is in fact not separable from "what it says." To believe that such separation is possible is an error of modern subjectivized aesthetics since Kant,[12] which wrongly speaks of the encounter with a work of art only from the side of the perceiving subject.

Aristotle, in the *Ethics,* gave a better perspective on pleasure when he defined it as a by-product of the proper functioning of an organ. He pointed out that a life directed specifically toward the acquisition of pleasure was untenable; one should aim at virtue, and pleasure will come as a by-product of virtuous activity. Likewise in literature, the pleasure of reading is the

11. *Ibid.,* 77–96, esp. 83.
12. *Ibid.,* 39–52.

pleasure of understanding in and through form; it is not a
response to form as such. The separation of form from what
is said is a reflexive act, a conceptual construction based not
on a dichotomization occurring in experience but rather on a
philosophically untenable conception of experience that separates thinking and truth from feeling and "perceptual pleasure"
in form—as if a configuration of sensations were pleasurable
in themselves as sensations. Try the experiment, for instance,
of asking someone who does not speak German to listen to a
poem by Goethe and say whether it is ugly or beautiful.

The content-form separation is simply another highly misleading fiction of the modern subjectivized approach to art.
What is central to the aesthetic experience of a work of art is
neither content nor form but the thing meant, totally mediated
into an image and form, into a world with its own dynamics.
In the aesthetic encounter with poetry, one does not separate
out the raw materials; in witnessing a musical or dramatic
performance, one is truest to the experience of the work as
art when he does not reflexively differentiate between work
and performance. To differentiate between the materials, the
work, and the performance of it represents a falling away from
the aesthetic experience. During a performance one is seized by
what is being spoken in the work. To turn aside from this to
see the performance as performance or the material aspects
of the work as materials is to make trivial the aesthetic moment
of encounter with the work. When one turns aside in either of
these directions, the work of art is no longer a subject speaking
but an object being judged and evaluated by the reflexive
processes of thought. Thus to focus on form as form apart from
the "speaking" of the work is not really to find its "purely
aesthetic" side but to move away from the aesthetic moment
itself. Aesthetic pleasure is not a sensuous response to form
but to the total movement of meaning in the form of a work
of art. To state the matter more explicitly: aesthetic pleasure
is a by-product of one's encounter with the fresh truth of being
set forth in the world of a work of art.

To render this sudden reference to "truth" in art intelligible,
and at the same time to show more conclusively why the idea
of form as "pure sensuous form" apart from meaning is a
fabrication of reflective thinking, let us clarify what makes
an art work "art." It is not craftsmanship or the appeal of a
pure formal harmony as an end in itself; a work of art has its

being as art in setting forth a world into material form. This is not to deny the formal side of art; on the contrary, form is central to art, but in a way that "formalists" often do not realize. It is not a pleasure in form setting forth a world differentiated from the form, which makes the work of art really art. The world known through form in art is so set into the materials that the "thought" cannot be differentiated from it, nor indeed the "aesthetic" differentiated from the "nonaesthetic" elements.[13] As Heidegger makes clear in *Der Ursprung des Kunstwerkes,* a Greek temple creates an "open space in being" so that one can stand in the light of this clearing.[14] To put the matter in Heidegger's ontological terms, it is so with every great work of art: it creates, through its form, a world in which being comes to stand. Being is encountered in understanding not as a discrete entity but as a part of a unity, in relation to the horizon of understanding or what may be called "world." Phenomenologically speaking, then, form cannot be seen as the expression of an idea prior to the form; form and idea come to stand together in an indivisible unity as world, and apart from world neither has any true existence. World is the unity that appears in the work of art, and the work of art is art only as it causes a world to stand.

Art, then, is ultimately not a matter of knowing through sense perceptions but of understanding. When one encounters a great work of art, he finds the horizons of his own world, his way of seeing his world, his self-understanding, broadened; he sees "in a different light," sometimes as for the first time, but always in a more "experienced" way. This shows that the world in the work of art is not a world divorced from one's own; it is contiguous with it and illuminates self-understanding even as one comes to understand it. In the encounter with a great work, one does not go into a foreign universe and step outside time and history; one does not finally separate aesthetic understanding from one's total understanding so as to leave the "nonaesthetic" behind and go into the "aesthetic" realm. Rather, one becomes more fully *present* to himself; when one understands a great work of literary art, he brings everything he has and is with him. To understand it and to fuse its world in its fullness to one's own means to place one's self-understanding in the balance. Gone is the myth that the

13. *Ibid.,* 88.
14. *Ho* 7–68; *UK* 7–101.

interpreter is interrogating a mere object possessed of sensuously pleasurable harmonies; the work of art is putting a question to him, the question that called it into being. Because the experience of a work of art is encompassed and takes place in the unity and continuity of self-understanding, it is tested not by the norms of formal harmony but by truth. Art reveals being, discloses "the way things are"—truth.

This is the reason that when one enters the world of a great work of art, one does not leave the norms of his own self-understanding unrisked and safe at home; he "comes home." He says in a burst of ontological recognition: Truly it is so! The artist has said what *is*. The artist has not conjured up an enchanted never-never-land, but rather has broken through to a deeper level of the world of experience and self-understanding in which one lives. The universality of art, then, is an ontological universality; all great art reveals being. The transformation into form which is enacted by the artist is not an expression of his subjectivity; it is not "feeling" transmuted into "form." The transformation is really truth, the truth of being, transmuted totally into the unity of the work of art. The legitimation of art is not that it gives aesthetic pleasure but that it reveals being.

The time has come to renounce the splendid isolation that has been artificially granted the "aesthetic phenomenon" by identifying it with pure sensuous form in art and by making form-content distinctions which have no part in the phenomenology of the aesthetic encounter. These distinctions have not served the cause of art but have in the last century and a half proved inimical to it. We have found, with the isolation of the aesthetic, the absurdity of "art for art's sake," the loss of any legitimation for the claim that art presents us with truth, the loss of historical consciousness in the understanding of art, the loss of the place of the artist in society, and further, the loss of the place of art itself in society. In literature, we are confronted with the situation that if poetry is for pleasure and delight, many students decide that they prefer other pleasures. And among pleasures there is no disputing, as among tastes—unless there is a standard outside of pleasure by which the pleasure itself is measured. But our subject-centered aesthetics can find no objective legitimation of art. The time has come to reject the unconscious taking of human subjectivity as our reference point (which all thinking within the subject-object schema presupposes), to stop asking how art affects us, and to start with the way of being of the work of art. The way of being of a work of art is disclosure—disclosure of a world, an event in which being comes to stand. The legitimation of art is that it discloses being to our self-understanding so that our own world, the horizon within which we live and move and have our whole existence, is broadened and given greater definition. Beauty *is* truth, the truth of being which discloses itself to us in art.[15]

We now see that the experience of encountering a work of art is an opening up of a world; this is especially true of a work of art in language. But it was necessary here to advert to the aesthetic phenomenon in nonlinguistic art to render explicit the grounds of rejecting the "pure aesthetic" in isolation from the total impact of a work of art, and to clarify the ontological content of art, i.e., its "truth" value.

To this conception of the inseparable place of the aesthetic within the total experience of what a work of art says, we now may add all we have said about questioning, experience, understanding, language, and historical consciousness for a unified conception of the hermeneutical experience. Within this conception, we may see what is involved in literary interpretation. To recapitulate what has been set forth here, and partially to build on it, I have formulated a series of thirty assertions or theses relating to literary interpretation, or the hermeneutical experience. These are set forth in the next chapter.

15. The reason the meaning of the assertion that "beauty is truth" remains obscure and even completely hidden from us lies partly in the fact that, as Heidegger has shown, we hold to a subjectivity-centered (ironically) "objective" definition of truth as correspondence or agreement—i.e., truth is defined merely as a verifiable statement.

14 / Thirty Theses
on Interpretation

ON THE HERMENEUTICAL EXPERIENCE

1. *The hermeneutical experience* (the encounter with a literary work of art) *is intrinsically historical.* Because of our prevailing misconceptions of history, understanding, language, and the ontological status of the literary work, however, it is difficult even to comprehend what this means. This failure is a clear symptom of the prevailing lack of historical consciousness.

2. *The hermeneutical experience is intrinsically linguistic.* It is not possible to understand the full importance of this until language is conceived within the horizon of "linguisticality," that is, not as the tool of a manipulating consciousness but as the medium through which a world comes to stand before us and in us.

3. *The hermeneutical experience is dialectical.* The fruits of this fact can only be reaped when experience is conceived of not as consciousness perceiving objects, but as understanding encountering a negativity which broadens and illuminates self-understanding.

4. *The hermeneutical experience is ontological.* The meaning of this will not emerge until the ontological function of understanding and language has come into view; both are ontological, for they disclose the being of things. But they do not disclose being as an object over against subjectivity; rather, they light up the being in which we are already standing. Nor is the being that is disclosed merely the being of an object but our own being, that is, "what it means to *be*."

5. *The hermeneutical experience is an event—a "language event."* Literature is robbed of its true dynamism and power to speak when it is conceived of in the static categories of conceptual knowing. As experience of an event and not as mere conceptual knowing, the encounter with the being of a work is not static and ideational, outside of all time and temporality; it is truth that happens, emerges from concealment, and yet eludes every effort to reduce it to concepts and objectivity.

6. *The hermeneutical experience is "objective."* This statement will be understood in the wrong sense so long as the old and presently prevailing definition of objectivity, the "scientific" definition, is not rejected. According to this conception, deriving from the Enlightenment struggle against superstition, bigotry, and naive acceptance of tradition, objectivity is the means by which clean, clear, conceptual knowledge unalloyed by subjective preconceptions is obtained by accepting nothing that the "natural light" of reason cannot "verify" through experiment. The verifying reason becomes the final court of appeals, and all truth finds its validation in the reflexive operations of the mind, that is, in subjectivity. This "subjective" form of objectivity is not meant here in the statement that the hermeneutical experience is "objective"; what is meant is not a scientific but a truly "historical" objectivity. This objectivity refers to the fact that the being which appears in language and which comes to stand in a literary work is not the product of a reflective activity of the mind. What appears is not, on the other hand, a discrete entity which is imagined to give off a meaning somehow outside of time and history. Rather, in meeting the resistances of the world which he does not really shape, form, and control, one moves within and conforms himself to the forms that have been handed down to him historically, that is, within a tradition of ways of understanding and seeing the world.

The proper word for man's relationship to language, history, and world is not "using" them but "participating" in them; one does not personally shape language, history, or his "world"; one conforms his linguistic activity to them. Language is not one's tool, really, but the way being can come to appear. When one wishes to convey the being of a situation, he does not devise language to fit it, so much as find the language demanded by the situation. Thus what comes to expression in the language is not really one's "reflexivity" but the situation itself; words do not primarily function to refer to this subjectivity but on the contrary to the situation. The ground of objectivity lies not in the subjectivity of a speaker but in the reality which comes to expression in and through language. It is in this objectivity that the hermeneutical experience must find its ground.

7. *The hermeneutical experience should be led by the text.* The text is not fully analogous to a partner in dialogue because it must be helped to speak, which need brings about the difficulties peculiar to genuine hermeneutical experience: the need to feel the objective claim of the text in its full otherness without, at the same time, making it a mere object for our subjectivity. We must see the task of interpretation not primarily as analysis — for this immediately renders the text an object — but as "understanding." Understanding is most open when it is conceived of as something capable of being seized by being rather than as a self-sufficient grasping consciousness. An interpretive "act" must not be a forceable seizure, a "rape" of the text, but a loving union that brings to stand the full potentialities of interpreter and text, the partners in the hermeneutical dialogue.

The surrender of the interpreter to the text, therefore, cannot be an absolute surrender but is, like the femininity referred to in the *Tao Tê Ching,*[1] an overcoming from beneath. The hermeneutical encounter is not a denial or negation of one's own horizon (for one must see through it and can never see at all without it) but a willingness to risk it in a free opening of oneself. Paul Tillich defines love as the overcoming of separation;[2] the union of text and interpreter overcomes the historical estrangement of the text, a union made possible by a common ground in being (that is, in language and history). In the fusion of horizons which is the core of the hermeneutical experience, some elements of one's own horizon are negated and others affirmed; some elements in the horizon of the text recede and others come forward (e.g., demythologizing). In this sense, then, every true hermeneutical experience is a new creation, a new disclosure of being; it stands in a firm relationship to the present, and historically could not have happened before. Such is man's "participation" in the ever new and fresh ways that being can come to stand.

8. *The hermeneutical experience understands what is*

1. See Arthur Waley, *The Way and Its Power: A Study of the "Tao Tê Ching" and Its Place in Chinese Thought,* esp. poems 6 and 28.
2. See his *Love, Power, and Justice.*

said in the light of the present. Another way to say this is that every true interpretation involves an "application" to the present. It is not enough to say what a poem means grammatically in the light of the context of its own historical horizon. Interpretation is not a taxonomical task of philological reconstruction and restoration (if this were possible). Interpretation calls upon the interpreter to render explicit a work's meaning today; interpretation calls upon one to bridge the historical distance between his horizon and that of the text. In both theological and legal interpretation, the moment of application is explicitly necessary and even central. Literary interpretation could learn from a study of the struggle within theology and law to overcome the challenge of historical estrangement; theology and law could furnish helpful models of the hermeneutical situation which might lead literary interpretation back to the historical consciousness it has lost.

9. *The hermeneutical experience is a disclosure of truth.* The interpreter today cannot, without a new ground in objectivity (described above) and a new definition of truth, see the nature of what is meant here by disclosure of truth. Truth must not be conceived as a correspondence of statement to "fact"; truth is the dynamic emergence of being into the light of manifestness.[3] Truth is never total or unambiguous; the emergence into "unconcealment" is rather the simultaneous covering up of truth in its inexhaustible fullness. Truth is grounded in negativity; this is the reason that the discovery of truth proceeds best within a dialectic in which the power of negativity can operate. The emergence of truth in hermeneutical experience comes in that encounter with negativity which is intrinsic to experience; in this case the experience comes as "aesthetic moment" or "language event." Truth is not conceptual, not fact — it happens.

10. *Aesthetics must be swallowed up in hermeneutics.* The "aesthetic moment" must be defined not in terms of sensuous pleasure in form but in what makes a work of art truly "art" — the fact that in a definite form a world is abidingly able to come to stand, to open up a space in being, to enable the truth of being to become manifest. The so-called aesthetic moment does not have an existence (phenomenologically speaking) apart from the dynamics of the hermeneutical experience; to

3. See *PL* in *PL-BH.*

try to separate the aesthetic element from the hermeneutical experience creates fundamental misconceptions and artificial problems. Every distinction between the "aesthetic" and the "nonaesthetic" rests on invalid form-content separations and represents a falling-away from the true experiential character of the aesthetic moment. The aesthetic moment cannot be understood apart from the total interpretive encounter.

ON TRANSCENDING THE SUBJECT-OBJECT SCHEMA

11. The leading challenge to literary interpretation in America today is to transcend the subject-object schema (through which the work tends to be placed at a distance from the interpreter as an object of analysis). Phenomenology opens the way to meet this challenge. The German hermeneutics of Heidegger and Gadamer is one avenue for doing this. Another way is shown in French phenomenological literary criticism (Sartre, Blanchot, Richard, Bachelard)[4] and contemporary French phenomenological philosophy (Ricoeur, Dufrenne, Gusdorf, Merleau-Ponty[5]). Many avenues are open.

ON THE AUTONOMY AND OBJECTIVE STATUS OF THE WORK OF ART

12. The New Criticism is essentially right about the autonomy of the literary work of art; to look in a work for the subjectivity of the author is rightly held as a fallacy (the intentional fallacy), and the testimony of the author as to his own intentions is correctly regarded as inadmissible evidence. For instance, one is not centrally interested in Milton's own intentions or feelings about the archangel who plummets headlong, flaming, from the ethereal sky; rather, a way of seeing Satan here comes to stand in the text. One's interest is in the "thing said" itself, not in Milton's intentions or personality. In the text a "reality" is brought to stand. In the Garden of Eden scenes in *Paradise Lost*, a reality is brought to stand; one is not deeply

4. See Neal Oxenhandler, "Ontological Criticism in America and France," *MLR* LV (1960), 17–23.
5. Works by these authors are available in translation from Northwestern University Press.

interested in whether Milton actually had these feelings, nor does one really care whether Adam and Eve "actually" had them, for in them something deeper and more universal is coming to expression: the possibilities resident in being, lighted up now for a moment in their truth, not in a scientific truth, but in a truth, nevertheless.

ON METHOD AND METHODS

13. Method is an effort to measure and control from the side of the interpreter; it is the opposite of letting the phenomenon lead. The openness of "experience"—which alters the interpreter himself from the side of the text—is antithetical to method. Thus method is in reality a form of dogmatism, separating the interpreter from the work, standing between it and him, and barring him from experiencing the work in its fullness. Analytical seeing is blindness to experience; it is analytical blindness.

14. The modern technological way of thinking and the will-to-power that lies at its root lead one to think in terms of "mastery of the subject" and "attacking" the matter. In literature this technological focus is seen in the seeking out of such knowledge of the "object"—the text—as will give knowledge or control of it. Such rape theories of interpretation, if we may call them so, take such an ego-centered, dogmatic, closed approach to the work that it becomes frigid. An argument for the "pleasures" of literature is little advanced by cold analyses of structure and pattern.

15. *Form should never be the starting point of a literary interpretation,* nor should the moment of form be separated out and labeled as the truly "aesthetic" element. On the contrary, the belief that form is separable from content and/or from the total meaningful unity of the work is a misconception based on wrong philosophical premises; there is no pure aesthetic, just as there is no art for art's sake. The separation of idea or theme from its material form is also a purely reflexive activity, for it has no ground in one's experiential encounter with the work itself. Therefore, to assert that the aesthetic element of a work belongs to its form apart from the non-aesthetic elements is invalid; any separation of aesthetic and nonaesthetic becomes a word game based on erroneous defini-

tions, for the aesthetic moment is a unity in which a world comes to stand. The meaning or idea content of this world cannot be separated from the sensuous form of the work, and it is not, in fact, separated from it in the moment of aesthetic encounter. Since the separation of form from content is invalid aesthetically, and since it is a product of reflexive thinking after the experience itself, to start with considerations of form means that even at the outset literary interpretation has fallen away from the unity and fullness of the aesthetic moment.

16. The beginning point for literary interpretation must be the language event of experiencing the work itself—i.e., what the work "says." The saying power of a literary work, not its form, is the ground of our meaningful encounter with it, and is not something separate from the form but rather speaks in and through the form. The inner unity of form and what is said is the basis of the inner unity of truth and aesthetic experience. The saying done by a literary work is a disclosure of being; its shining-forth is the power of the truth of being; the artist has the power to use the inner light of the materials (e.g., the texture of sound, the hardness of metal and its shininess, and the powers of color) to bring the truth of being to stand. Language has the power to say, to bring a world to stand. This is what Heidegger means when he says, with Hölderlin, that man dwells "poetically" on this earth.[6]

17. True love of literature is not and has never been a delight in pure form. Love of literature is a responsiveness to the saying power of literature. Just as decking out a poodle to furnish "aesthetic delight" may be an act of egotism unconnected with any deeper love for the animal himself, so also the view of literature as mere play or as entertainment shows no true understanding of literature. The domineering tendency in an instant demand for conceptual mastery is not love either, but a mothering and a smothering.

18. It is not the interpreter who grasps the meaning of the text; the meaning of the text seizes him. When we watch a play or a game or read a novel, we do not stand above it as subject contemplating an object; we are caught up in the inner movement of the thing that is unfolding—we are seized. This is a hermeneutical phenomenon which is largely ignored by a technological approach to literature; one wrongly interprets the hermeneutical situation if one sees himself as the master and

6. See "Hölderlin und das Wesen der Dichtung" in *EHD; EB* 270-91.

manipulator of the situation. On the contrary, one is a partici-
pator and not even quite fully that, since one cannot step into
the situation to change it but is powerless to alter the fixity of
the text.

19. Some approaches to art emphasize the craftsmanship,
but it takes great craftsmanship to make a shoe, to carpenter, or
to make any utensil. A work of art is not a utensil. The enjoyment of art is not simply sensuous delight in form; a work of art
is not some cheap pleasure object. Craftsmanship is involved,
yes; sensuous pleasure is involved; but to take these as the
starting point or the central aspect of art is naive reductionism.
Art is art when it brings a world to stand before one; and great
art has such a fullness of the truth of being that one finds his
own horizon negated (in part), and a freshness of understanding occurs that can only be understood in terms of the category
"experience." Encountering a great work of art is always an
experience, in the deepest sense of the word.

20. Reading a work, then, is not a gaining of conceptual
knowledge through observation or reflection; it is an
"experience," a breaking down and breaking open of one's old
way of seeing. It is not the interpreter who has manipulated the
work, for the work remains fixed; rather, the work has im-
pressed itself on him and he is so changed he can never regain
the innocence lost through experience.

21. Present methods of trying to "understand" a literary
work tend to operate with conceptual definitions of understanding that are not true to the hermeneutical experience. Too often
they take set formulae and hold them in mind in advance: they
anticipate irony and paradox, or recurrent images, or archetypal
situations. They do not so much listen to the work as cross-
examine it. The interpretation of literature should not have the
character of an Aristotelian formal analysis, its categories all
marked out in advance; the process of coming to understand a
literary work is more like a Socratic dialogue of dialectical
circling and advancing into the subject itself through question
and answer. There is a great difference between a question
asked by the analyst who is merely looking for an answer and
sure of his own position, and the real query that arises from self-
questioning, from admission of one's own uncertainty. This
questioning says: Is it not so that . . . ? This latter is no longer a
mere questioning of the "object," but of the "subject" (to put
the matter in subject-object terminology).

22. A method receives its validation only if it works. Now if the way of being of a work of art—as event that discloses a world—recedes and escapes from present methods, then even on scientific grounds of their incommensurability with the nature of the phenomenon the results of the method have questionable value. Even on scientific grounds, they lose their validity.

23. To understand a text is not simply to bombard it with questions but to understand the question it puts to the reader. It is to understand the question behind the text, the question that called the text into being. Literary interpretation needs to develop the dynamics and art of hearing, of listening. It needs to develop an openness for creative negativity, for learning something it could not anticipate or foresee.

THE NEED FOR HISTORICAL CONSCIOUSNESS IN LITERARY INTERPRETATION

24. A critical problem in American literary interpretation today is a lack of historical consciousness and, consequently, an inability to see the essential historicality of literature. A sizable fraction of the teachers of literature in America, probably the majority, may be classified either as "formalists" or "antiquarians." The former take their lead unconsciously from the errors of subjectivized aesthetics and believe that the essence of the aesthetic moment of encounter is fundamentally a matter of form. For this reason the encounter with the literary work is seen in static, atemporal categories, and the "historical" character of literature is lost. The antiquarians are not taken in by the effort to transform the interpretation of literature into formal analysis, but they take as their aim to understand the work in terms of itself and its time, so that a scholar of eighteenth-century literature sees his task as that of living in the eighteenth century as fully as possible. He imagines that that century may even be more interesting than the present, for coffee houses and the atmosphere they symbolize are less in evidence today. Neither the antiquarian interest in exploring the past, however, nor the reduction of literature to its formal dynamics shows any authentic historical awareness. On the

contrary, they are symptoms of the modern lack of understanding of what history is.

25. *Literature is intrinsically historical.* To understand a work of literature, one does not primarily use formal or scientific categories; rather, in the prestructure of one's understanding, he must refer to his historically formed vision of himself and his world. The shape of one's intentions, preconceptions, and way of seeing—this is bequeathed from the past. So one moves and exists in the historically formed world of his understanding; when a work of literature is encountered, it presents another "world." This world is not absolutely discontinuous with that of the reader; on the contrary, to experience it in sincerity is to find one's own self-understanding deepened. It supplements and augments one's own historically formed understanding; to read a great work of literature is a truly "historical" experience.

"Experience" is a significant word, for experience is itself historical in character. It is the way in which one's understanding of "world" is shaped. Just as experiences in daily life teach something one may have forgotten or did not know before, so the encounter with a literary work is truly "experience" and becomes a part of one's own history, a part of the stream of tradition-bequeathed understanding in which he lives and moves.

26. *The task of interpretation, then, is that of bridging historical distance.* When interpreting a text from a past age, the interpreter does not empty his mind or leave the present absolutely; he takes it with him and uses it to understand in the dialectical encounter of his horizon with that of the literary work. The idea of historical reconstruction, or knowing the past solely in terms of itself, is a romantic myth, an impossibility like the idea of "presuppositionless interpretation." There is no such thing. Literary interpretation must, like theological and legal interpretation, relate to the present or die. That in literature which cannot be related to us standing in the present is dead. The task of interpretation may in some cases be to take what seems to be dead and to show its relation to the present, i.e., the present horizon of expectations and the present world of self-understanding. Demythologizing (which is not the dissolving of myth but the realization that we must see what it is in myth that is meaningful) should, in principle, be the task of literary interpretation. Only when interpreters today acquire an

historical consciousness, and therefore a grasp of the historical problems in interpreting literature, will they see the significance of demythologizing for literature.

27. Historical understanding and historical consciousness must, for us today, come in the form of the phenomenologist's critique of scientific seeing. The basis for this critique is the analysis of preunderstanding, which reveals the historicality of our understanding and world. And a leading result will be the discovery of temporality. Understanding literature or any work of art stands within the modes of temporality. That is, one encounters the work in the present, but also on the basis of recollection (one's historically formed understanding) and anticipation (the way in which one's understanding projects a future). Understanding is not a static knowing outside of time; it stands in a specific place in time and space—in history. Its interpretation will take on a different character as it makes its appearance to the reader now, in this hour, in this place.

28. Understanding a work of literature, then, is not to be grasped in the spatial, static, nontemporal categories of conceptual knowledge, for it has the character of event (i.e., history). The meaning of a literary work is dynamic, temporal, personal. In conceptual knowing, only a part of one's mind is really involved, but in understanding literature one's self-understanding must come into play. The work addresses one as a person, or the encounter with it has been to no avail. Literature, in short, is not conceptual knowledge but experience.

29. Science and conceptual knowing go together; experience and history go together. Literary interpretation must come to know itself as belonging with the latter. This does not mean that one rejects conceptual knowing but that one must transcend and encompass it.

30. The task of interpretation today, then, is to break out of scientific objectivity and the scientist's way of seeing and to recover a sense of the historicality of existing. So overcome with the perspective of technological thinking are we that only in scattered moments does our historicality come into view at all.

We come up against the historical character of interpretation when we recognize that no interpretation is "once and for all" the "right interpretation"; each age reinterprets Plato, Dante, Shakespeare, Milton, and the other great lights in our heritage. We glimpse this fact in our tentativeness before art and literature that is contemporary. We cannot know the "verdict of history" on John Barth, John Updike, and James Baldwin, despite our reviews and brave talk. In fact the verdict on Hemingway, Faulkner, and T. S. Eliot is far from final. We become aware of historicality when we ask for something beyond the bogus objectivity of the theoretical and scientific, the visualizable and the mathematical—indeed, all the static, mechanical, purely ideational things that stand outside of history and do not involve our self-understanding to grasp them. We are reaching for the historical in the plea for "personal knowledge," [7] in the impatience with science's frantic search for origins, causal grounds, neurological antecedents, and in the plea for a return to the richness and complexity of concrete awareness in interpreting literature.[8] We glimpse the historicality of existence when we juxtapose the clean, clear world of scientific concepts with the world of conflict, ambiguity, and suffering in which we live our daily lives, for "lived experience" is historical in its structure. Language is historical—the repository of our whole culture's way of seeing. In short, interpretation itself is historical, and if we try to make it something else, something less, we have impoverished interpretation—and ourselves.

7. Michael Polanyi, *Personal Knowledge.*
8. Maurice Natanson, "Phenomenology and the Theory of Literature," in *Literature, Philosophy, and the Social Sciences,* pp. 79–100.

Bibliography

THE PRESENT BIBLIOGRAPHY is divided into three sections. Section A contains articles and books by and about the four major hermeneutical theorists discussed in this book, and some works in general hermeneutical theory, many of which were cited in footnotes. Section B contains articles and books in the area of theological hermeneutics, and some works by Ebeling, Fuchs, Robinson, and others who are identified with the New Hermeneutic. Section C contains articles and books cited in the text which did not fall into the first two categories, but more particularly it lists titles the writer has encountered which seem to offer significant ideas for theorizing about the general nature of interpretation.

No attempt has been made here to encompass the many secondary works available on the four theorists. Bibliophiles are directed to Tice's recent bibliography on Schleiermacher literature; a helpful list of secondary works on Dilthey can be found in Müller-Vollmer; and on Heidegger, see Lübbe, Schneeburger, and Macomber. Fortunately many of Gadamer's scattered articles and papers have just been published in his *Kleine Schriften;* this made it unnecessary to list them here, although some of those not appearing in the *KS* have been listed here to give some idea of Gadamer's other publications. A lengthy and systematic bibliography of hermeneutics will appear in late 1968, by Norbert Henrichs.

The third section is intended simply to be suggestive of the diversity of fields that relate to hermeneutical theory and whose significance, as was suggested in Chapter 5, has yet to be explored. For most of the German titles in philosophy of language I am indebted to the collection of works in the library of the Institute for Hermeneutics in Zurich where the bulk of the research for the present book was done.

A. Hermeneutical Theory and Theorists

Apel, Karl Otto. "Szientifik, Hermeneutik, Ideologie-Kritik: Entwurf einer Wissenschaftslehre in erkenntnisanthropologischer Sicht," *M&W*, I (1968), 37-63.

Betti, Emilio. *Die Hermeneutik als allgemeine Methodik der Geisteswissenschaften.* Philosophie und Geschichte series, Pamphlet Nos. 78-79. Tübingen: J. C. B. Mohr, 1962. 64 pp.

————. *Teoria generale della interpretazione.* 2 vols. Milan: Dott. A. Giuffrè, 1955. 634 pp., 348 pp. Translated into German by its author as *Allgemeine Auslegungslehre als Methodik der Geisteswissenschaften.* Tübingen: J. C. B. Mohr, 1967. 771 pp.

————. *Zur Grundlegung einer allgemeinen Auslegungslehre.* Tübingen: J. C. B. Mohr, 1954. 89 pp. Reprinted from *Festschrift für Ernst Rabel.* Tübingen: J. C. B. Mohr, 1954. II, 79-168.

Bollnow, Otto Friedrich. *Dilthey: Eine Einführung in seine Philosophie.* 2d ed. Stuttgart: Kohlhammer, 1955. 224 pp.

————. *Das Verstehen: Drei Aufsätze zur Theorie der Geisteswissenschaften.* Mainz: Kirchheim, 1949. 112 pp.

Castelli, Enrico, ed. *Herméneutique et tradition.* Papers from the International Colloquium at Rome, January 10-16, 1963. Paris: Vrin, 1963.

Dilthey, Wilhelm. *Briefwechsel zwischen Wilhelm Dilthey und dem Grafen Paul Yorck von Wartenburg: 1877-1897.* Halle-an-der-Salle: Niemeyer, 1923. 280 pp.

————. *Das Erlebnis und die Dichtung.* 13th ed. Stuttgart: B. G. Teubner, 1957. 482 pp.

————. *Das Leben Schleiermachers.* Vol. I. Ed. Hermann Mulert. Berlin: Reimer, 1870. 688 pp. Reprinted Berlin: W. de Gruyter, 1922. 879 pp. To be reissued as Vol. XIII of *GS.*

————. *Das Leben Schleiermachers.* Vol. II. Ed. Martin Redeker. Göttingen: Vandenhoeck & Ruprecht, 1967. 811 pp. Vol. XIV of *GS* (1967).

————. *Gesammelte Schriften.* 14 vols. Göttingen: Vandenhoeck & Ruprecht, 1913-1967. Vols. I-XII reissued Stuttgart: B. G. Teubner, 1958.

Diwald, Hellmut. *Wilhelm Dilthey: Erkenntnistheorie und Philosophie der Geschichte.* Göttingen: Musterschmidt, 1963. 262 pp.

Gadamer, Hans-Georg. "Anmerkungen zu dem Thema 'Hegel und Heidegger,'" in *Natur und Geschichte: Festschrift für Karl Löwith zum 70. Geburtstag.* Stuttgart: Kohlhammer, 1967. 470 pp.

————. "Hegel und die antike Dialektik," *Hegel-Studien*, I (1961), 173-99.

————. "Hermeneutik und Historismus," *PhR*, IX (1962), 241-76. Republished as an appendix to the 2d ed. of *WM.*

————. *Kleine Schriften*. Vol. I: *Philosophie/Hermeneutik*. Vol. II: *Interpretationen*. Tübingen: J. C. B. Mohr, 1967. 230 pp., 234 pp. Vol. III forthcoming.

————. "Die phänomenologische Bewegung," *PhR*, XI (1963), 1-45.

————. *Plato und die Dichter*. Frankfurt: Klostermann, 1934. 36 pp.

————. *Platos dialektische Ethik: Phänomenologische Interpretationen zur "Philebos."* Habilitation Lectures. Leipzig: Meiner, 1931. 178 pp.

————. *Le Problème de la conscience historique*. Lectures presented in Louvain, 1959. Louvain: Publications universitaires de Louvain, 1963. 89 pp.

————. "The Problem of Language in Schleiermacher's Hermeneutics," an unpublished lecture presented at Vanderbilt Divinity School, Nashville, Tennessee, February 29, 1968, at a Consultation commemorating the second centennial of Schleiermacher's birth. While in America during March, 1968, Gadamer lectured at a number of universities, including Northwestern, Johns Hopkins, Texas, Yale, and Harvard. The lectures either repeated the Schleiermacher paper, or were on one of two other topics: "Image and Word," and "The Concept of the Divine in Pre-Socratic Philosophy." These three lectures will probably be appearing individually in American journals, thus making some of Gadamer's recent writing available in English. An article, "Notes on Planning for the Future," was published in *Daedalus*, XCV (1966), 572-89; it is not directed specifically to hermeneutics.

————. *Volk und Geschichte im Denken Herders*. Lecture given in Paris on May 29, 1941. Frankfurt: Klostermann, 1942. 24 pp.

————. *Wahrheit und Methode: Grundzüge einer philosophischen Hermeneutik*. Tübingen: J. C. B. Mohr, 1960. 476 pp. 2d ed., 1965, 512 pp., contains a new preface and the article "Hermeneutik und Historismus" as an appendix. Italian and French translations are in preparation. English translation forthcoming from Sheed and Ward, London.

————, and H. KUHN, eds. *Philosophische Rundschau: Eine vierteljahresschrift für philosophische Kritik*. Tübingen: J. C. B. Mohr. Founded in 1953 by the editors and still under their direction. See individual issues for many reviews and articles by Gadamer.

Die Gegenwart der Griechen im neueren Denken: Festschrift für Hans-Georg Gadamer zum 60. Geburtstag. Ed. DIETER HENRICH, WALTHER SCHULTZ, and KARL-HEINZ VOLKMANN-SCHLUCK. Tübingen: J. C. B. Mohr, 1960. 316 pp.

HEIDEGGER, MARTIN. *Erläuterungen zu Hölderlins Dichtung*. 2d ed. Frankfurt: Klostermann, 1951. 144 pp. Partially translated in *EB*.

————. *Existence and Being*. Ed. and with an extensive analytical introduction by WERNER BROCK. Chicago: Regnery, 1949; paperback, 1961. 369 pp.

———. *Gelassenheit.* Pfullingen: Neske, 1959. 73 pp. English translation by JOHN M. ANDERSON and HANS FREUND, *Discourse on Thinking.* New York: Harper, 1966. 90 pp.

———. *Holzwege.* 4th ed. Frankfurt: Klostermann, 1963. 345 pp. First essay, *UK,* translated; see entry below.

———. *Identität und Differenz.* Pfullingen: Neske, 1957. 76 pp.

———. *An Introduction to Metaphysics.* Trans. RALPH MANHEIM. New Haven: Yale University Press, 1959. 214 pp.

———. *Kant und das Problem der Metaphysik.* Frankfurt: Klostermann, 1951. 222 pp. English translation by JAMES S. CHURCHILL, *Kant and the Problem of Metaphysics.* Bloomington: Indiana University Press, 1962. 255 pp.

———. *Platons Lehre von der Wahrheit: Mit einem Brief über den "Humanismus."* Bern: Francke, 1947. 119 pp. Translations of both essays are in WILLIAM BARRETT and H. D. AIKEN, eds., *Philosophy in the Twentieth Century.* 4 vols. New York: Random House, 1962. III, 251–70, 270–302.

———. *Sein und Zeit.* Halle: Niemeyer, 1927. Citations are from the 7th ed., unchanged. Tübingen: Niemeyer, 1963. 437 pp. English translation by JOHN MACQUARRIE and EDWARD ROBINSON, *Being and Time.* London: SCM Press, 1962. 589 pp.

———. *Unterwegs zur Sprache.* Pfullingen: Neske, 1959. 270 pp. Translation forthcoming from Harper.

———. *Der Ursprung des Kunstwerkes.* Einführung von Hans-Georg Gadamer. Stuttgart: Reclam, 1965. 126 pp. Translation of this essay from *Ho* by ALBERT HOFSTADTER, in *Philosophies of Art and Beauty,* ed. A. HOFSTADTER and RICHARD KUHNS. New York: Random House, 1964. 701 pp.

———. *Vom Wesen des Grundes.* 5th ed. Frankfurt: Klostermann, 1965. 54 pp. Bilingual ed., English translation by T. MALICK, *The Essence of Reasons.* Evanston: Northwestern University Press, 1969.

———. *Vom Wesen der Wahrheit.* 5th ed. Frankfurt: Klostermann, 1967. 27 pp.

———. *Vorträge und Aufsätze.* Pfullingen: Neske, 1954. 284 pp.

HENRICHS, NORBERT. *Bibliographie der Hermeneutik und ihrer Anwendungsbereiche zeit Schleiermacher.* Kleine Bibliographien aus dem Philosophischen Institut der Universität Düsseldorf. Düsseldorf: Philosophia-Verlag, 1968. 250 pp.

"Hermeneutics," *OED,* V (1933), 243.

HERRMANN, FRIEDRICH WILHELM VON. *Die Selbstinterpretation Martin Heideggers.* Meisenheim: Anton Hain, 1964. 278 pp.

HIRSCH, E. D., JR. *Validity in Interpretation.* New Haven: Yale University Press, 1967. 274 pp.

HODGES, H. A. *The Philosophy of Wilhelm Dilthey.* London: Routledge & Kegan Paul, 1952. 368 pp. (This work should not be confused with the earlier and much shorter *Introduction to the Philosophy of Wilhelm Dilthey* by the same author and publisher.)

HOPPER, STANLEY ROMAINE, and DAVID L. MILLER, eds. *Interpretation: The Poetry of Meaning.* New York: Harcourt, Brace & World, 1967. 137 pp. See esp. HEINRICH OTT, "Hermeneutics and Personhood," pp. 14–33.

KIMMERLE, HEINZ. "Hermeneutische Theorie oder ontologische Hermeneutik," *ZThK,* LIX (1962), 114–30. Translated in *HH,* 107–21.
———. "Metahermeneutik, Application, hermeneutische Sprachbildung," *ZThK,* LXI (1964), 221–35.

KOCKELMANS, JOSEPH J. *Martin Heidegger: A First Introduction to His Philosophy.* Pittsburgh: Duquesne University Press, 1965. 182 pp.

LANGAN, THOMAS. *The Meaning of Heidegger: A Critical Study of an Existentialist Phenomenology.* New York: Columbia University Press, 1959. 247 pp.

LARENZ, KARL. *Methodenlehre der Rechtswissenschaft.* Berlin: Springer, 1960. 381 pp.

LIPPS, HANS. *Untersuchungen zu einer hermeneutischen Logik.* Frankfurt: Klostermann, 1959. 144 pp.

LOHMANN, JOHANNES. "Gadamers *Wahrheit und Methode," Gnomon,* XXXVII (1965), 709–18. A review; for a list of other reviews ι ᶜ*WM,* see *WM,* 2d ed., p. xiii.

LONERGAN, BERNARD J. F. *Insight: A Study of Human Understanding.* London: Longmans, 1964. 785 pp.

LÜBBE, HERMAN. "Bibliographie der Heidegger-Literatur 1917–1955," *Zeitschrift für Philosophische Forschung,* XI (1957), 401–52.

MACOMBER, W. B. *The Anatomy of Disillusion: Martin Heidegger's Notion of Truth.* Evanston: Northwestern University Press, 1967. 227 pp.

MAYR, FRANZ. "Philosophie im Wandel der Sprache: Zur Frage der 'Hermeneutik,'" *ZThK,* LXI (1964), 439–91.

MEIER, GEORG FRIEDRICH. *Versuch einer allgemeinen Auslegungskunst.* Düsseldorf: Stern-Verlag, 1965. 136 pp. Photomechanical reproduction of the 1757 edition.

MÜLLER-VOLLMER, KURT. *Towards a Phenomenological Theory of Literature: A Study of Wilhelm Dilthey's "Poetik."* Stanford [University] Studies in Germanics and Slavics. The Hague: Mouton, 1963. 217 pp. Available in U.S. through Humanities Press.

NOLLER, GERHARD. *Sein und Existenz: Die Ueberwindung des Subjekt-Objektschemas in der Philosophie Heideggers und in der*

Theologie der Entmythologisierung. Munich: Kaiser, 1962. 167 pp.

PANNENBERG, WOLFHART. "Hermeneutik und Universalgeschichte," *ZThK,* LX (1963), 90–121. Translated in *HH* 122–52.

PÖGGELER, OTTO. *Der Denkweg Martin Heideggers.* Pfullingen: Neske, 1963. 318 pp.

RICHARDSON, W. J. *Martin Heidegger: Through Phenomenology to Thought.* The Hague: Nijhoff, 1964. 764 pp.

RICOEUR, PAUL. *De l'interprétation: essai sur Freud.* Paris: Editions du Seuil, 1965. 533 pp.

———. "Existence et herméneutique," *Dialogue,* IV (1965–66), 1–25.

ROTHACKER, ERICH. *Die dogmatische Denkform in den Geisteswissenschaften und das Problem des Historismus.* Mainz: Verlag der Akademie der Wissenschaften und der Literatur, 1954. 55 pp.

———. *Einleitung in die Geisteswissenschaften.* 2d ed. Tübingen: J. C. B. Mohr, 1930. 288 pp. Originally published in 1919.

———. *Logik und Systematik der Geisteswissenschaften.* Bonn: H. Bouvier, 1948. 172 pp.

SCHLEIERMACHER, FR. D. E. *Hermeneutik.* Ed. and with an introduction by HEINZ KIMMERLE. Heidelberg: Carl Winter, Universitätsverlag, 1959. 166 pp.

———. *Hermeneutik und Kritik: mit besonderer Beziehung auf das Neue Testament.* Ed. FRIEDRICH LUCKE. Vol. VII of the First Division of his *Sämmtliche Werke.* Berlin: Reimer, 1838.

SCHNEEBERGER, GUIDO. *Ergänzungen zu einer Heidegger-Bibliographie.* Bern: Hochfeldstrasse 88 (privately published by author), 1960. 27 pp.

SCHULTZ, WERNER. "Die unendliche Bewegung in der Hermeneutik Schleiermachers und ihre Auswirkung auf die hermeneutische Situation der Gegenwart," *ZthK,* LXV (1968), 23–52.

SEIDEL, GEORGE JOSEPH. *Martin Heidegger and the Presocratics: An Introduction to His Thought.* Lincoln: University of Nebraska Press, 1964. 169 pp.

SINN, DIETER. "Heidegger's Spätphilosophie," *PhR,* XIV (1967), 81–182.

THULSTRUP, NIELS. "An Observation Concerning Past and Present Hermeneutics," *OL,* XXII (1967), 24–44.

TICE, TERRENCE N. *Schleiermacher Bibliography: With Brief Introductions, Annotations, and Index.* Princeton Pamphlets, No. 12. Princeton: Princeton Theological Seminary, 1966. 168 pp.

VERSÉNYI, LASZLO. *Heidegger, Being, and Truth.* New Haven: Yale University Press, 1965. 201 pp.

WACH, JOACHIM. *Das Verstehen: Grundzüge einer Geschichte der hermeneutischen Theorie im 19. Jahrhundert.* 3 vols. Tübingen: J. C. B. Mohr, 1926–1933. Vol. I: *Die grossen Systeme,* 1926. 266 pp. Vol. II: *Die theologische Hermeneutik von Schleiermacher bis*

Hoffmann, 1929. 379 pp. Vol. III: *Das Verstehen in der Historik von Ranke bis zum Positivismus*, 1933. 350 pp. Reprinted, 1 vol., Hildesheim: Georg Olms, 1965.

WOLF, FRIEDRICH AUGUST. "Darstellung der Altertumswissenschaft nach Begriff, Umfang, Zweck und Wert," in *Museum der Altertumswissenschaft*, ed. F. A. WOLF and PH. BUTTMANN, Vol. I. Berlin: Reimer, 1807. 584 pp.

————. *Vorlesung über die Enzyklopädie der Altertumswissenschaft.* Vorlesungen über die Altertumswissenschaft series, ed. J. D. GÜRTLER, Vol. I. Leipzig: Lehnhold, 1831. 498 pp.

B. THEOLOGICAL HERMENEUTICS

BARR, JAMES. *Old and New in Interpretation.* New York: Harper, 1966. 215 pp.

BARTHEL, PIERRE. *Interprétation du langage mythique et théologie biblique: étude de quelques étapes de l'evolution du problème de l'interprétation des représentation d'origine et de structure mythique de la foi chrétienne.* Leiden: Brill, 1963. 399 pp.

BARTSCH, HANS WERNER, ed. *Kerygma and Myth.* Trans. REGINALD H. FULLER. 2 vols. 2d ed. London: Billing, 1964. 228 pp., 358 pp.

BEHM, JOHANNES. *Ermēneuo, ermēneia* ... Article in the *TDNT*, trans. GEOFFREY W. BROMILEY. Grand Rapids, Mich.: Eerdmans, 1964. Originally in the *Theologisches Wörterbuch zum Neuen Testament*, 1935.

BLACKMAN, E. C. *Biblical Interpretation.* Philadelphia: Westminster Press, 1957. 212 pp.

BRAATEN, CARL E. *History and Hermeneutics.* New Directions in Theology Today series, ed. WILLIAM HORDERN, Vol. II. Philadelphia: Westminster Press, 1966. 205 pp.

BROWN, JAMES. *Kierkegaard, Heidegger, Buber, and Barth: Subject and Object in Modern Theology.* New York: Collier Books, 1962. 192 pp.

BULTMÄNN, RUDOLF. *Glauben und Verstehen: Gesammelte Aufsätze.* 4 vols. Tübingen: J. C. B. Mohr, 1952-1965. 336 pp., 293 pp., 212 pp., 198 pp. Vol. II translated by J. C. G. GREIG as *Essays: Philosophical and Theological.* New York: Macmillan, 1955. 337 pp. Other essays appear in *Existence and Faith: Shorter Writings of Rudolf Bultmann*, ed. and trans. SCHUBERT M. OGDEN. London: Hodder and Stoughton, 1961. 320 pp.

————. *History and Eschatology.* Edinburgh: The University Press; New York: Harper, 1957. 155 pp.

————. *The History of the Synoptic Tradition.* Trans. JOHN MARSH. Oxford: Blackwell, 1963. 456 pp.

————. *Jesus.* Berlin: Deutsche Bibliothek, 1926. 204 pp. Reprinted

Tübingen: J. C. B. Mohr, 1958. English translation by Louise Pettibone Smith and Erminie Huntress Lantero, *Jesus and the Word.* New York: Scribner's, 1958. 226 pp.

——. *Jesus Christ and Mythology.* New York: Scribner's, 1958. 96 pp.

——. *Theology of the New Testament.* Trans. Kendrick Grobel. 2 vols. London: Lowe & Brydone, 1959. 395 pp., 278 pp.

Castelli, Enrico, ed. *Demitizzazione e immagine.* Padua: A. Milani, 1962. 351 pp. Papers from the International Colloquium at Rome, January, 1962, by Ricoeur, Ott, Bartsch, Mathieu, and others.

——, ed. *Il Problema della demitizzazione.* Padua: A. Milani, 1961. 334 pp. Papers from the International Colloquium at Rome, January, 1961, by Bultmann, Danièlou, Ricoeur, Gadamer, Bartsch, Anz, Marlé, and others. A list of titles from other years may be obtained from the publisher.

Dobschütz, E. "Interpretation," *ERE*, VII (1914), 390–95.

Doty, William G. *A New Utterance: Studies in New Testament Hermeneutics.* New York: Herder & Herder, forthcoming in late 1969.

Ebeling, Gerhard. *Evangelische Evangelienauslegung: Eine Untersuchung zu Luthers Hermeneutik.* Munich: Kaiser, 1942. Reissued Darmstadt: Wissenschaftliche Buchgesellschaft, 1962. 520 pp.

——. *God and Word.* Trans. James W. Leitch. The Earl Lectures at Pacific School of Religion, 1966. Philadelphia: Fortress Press, 1967. 49 pp.

——. "Hermeneutik," *RGG*, III (1959), 242–64.

——. *Kirchengeschichte als Geschichte der Auslegung der Heiligen Schrift.* Tübingen: J. C. B. Mohr, 1947. 28 pp. Reprinted as the first essay in *Wort Gottes und Tradition.*

——. *The Nature of Faith.* Trans. Ronald Gregor Smith. Philadelphia: Fortress Press, 1961. 191 pp.

——. *The Problem of Historicity in the Church and Its Proclamation.* Trans. Grover Foley. Philadelphia: Fortress Press, 1967. 120 pp. Originally published in German in 1954.

——. *Theologie und Verkündigung: Ein Gespräch mit Rudolf Bultmann.* Tübingen: J. C. B. Mohr, 1962. 146 pp. English translation by John Riches, *Theology and Proclamation.* Philadelphia: Fortress Press, 1966. 187 pp.

——. *Word and Faith.* Trans. James W. Leitch. Philadelphia: Fortress Press, 1963. 442 pp.

——. *Wort Gottes und Tradition: Studien zu einer Hermeneutik der Konfessionen.* Göttingen: Vandenhoeck & Ruprecht, 1964. 235 pp.

Ebner, Ferdinand. *Schriften.* 3 vols. Munich: Kösel, 1963, 1965. 1086 pp., 1190 pp., 808 pp.

Ernesti, Johann August. *Institutio interpretis Novi Testamenti.*

4th ed. with observations by CHRISTOPHER FR. AMMON. Leipzig: Weidmann, 1792. (1st ed., 1761.) English translation by MOSES STUART, *Elements of Interpretation.* 3d ed.; Andover: M. Newman, 1827. 124 pp. 4th ed.; New York: Dayton and Saxton, 1842. Another English translation is by CHARLES H. TERROT, *Principles of Biblical Interpretation.* 2 vols. Edinburgh: T. Clark, 1832-33.

FARRAR, FREDERIC W. *History of Interpretation.* Grand Rapids, Mich.: Baker Book House, 1961. 553 pp. Originally published in 1884.

FORSTMAN, H. JACKSON. "Language and God: Gerhard Ebeling's Analysis of Theology," *Interpretation,* XXII (1968), 187-200.

FRÖR, KURT. *Biblische Hermeneutik: Zur Schriftauslegung in Predigt und Unterricht.* Munich: Kaiser, 1961. 396 pp. 3d ed., rev., appeared as *Wege zur Schriftauslegung: Biblische Hermeneutik für Unterricht und Predigt.* Düsseldorf: Patmos, 1967. 414 pp. English translation forthcoming, James Thin, Edinburgh.

FUCHS, ERNST. "Existentiale Interpretation von Römer 7, 7-12 und 21-23," *ZThK,* LIX (1962), 285-314.

———. *Glaube und Erfahrung: Zum christologischen Problem im Neuen Testament.* Tubingen: J. C. B. Mohr, 1965. 523 pp.

———. *Hermeneutik.* Stuttgart: R. Müllerschön, 1963. 271 pp. Originally published in 1954.

———. *Marburger Hermeneutik.* Tübingen: J. C. B. Mohr, 1968. 277 pp.

———. *Studies of the Historical Jesus.* Trans. ANDREW SCOBIE. London: SCM Press, 1964. 239 pp.

———. *Zum hermeneutischen Problem in der Theologie.* Tübingen: J. C. B. Mohr, 1959. 365 pp.

FUNK, ROBERT W. *Language, Hermeneutic, and Word of God.* New York: Harper, 1966. 317 pp. (Another book by Professor Funk on language and hermeneutics is in preparation.)

———, and GERHARD EBELING, eds. *The Bultmann School of Biblical Interpretation: New Directions?* Journal of Theology and the Church series, Vol. I. New York: Harper, 1965. 183 pp.

———, eds. *History and Hermeneutic.* Journal of Theology and the Church series, Vol. IV. New York: Harper, 1967. 162 pp.

GRANT, ROBERT M. *A Short History of the Interpretation of the Bible.* Rev. ed. New York: Macmillan, 1963. 224 pp.

HEINRICI, GEORG. "Hermeneutik," *RPTK,* VII (1899), 719.

HERZOG, FREDERICK W. *Understanding God.* New York: Scribner's, 1966. 191 pp.

KRAUS, HANS-JOACHIM. *Geschichte der historisch-kritischen Erforschung des Alten Testaments von der Reformation bis zur Gegenwart.* Neukirchen: Verlag der Buchhandlung der Erziehungsvereins, 1956. 478 pp.

LESSING, GOTTHOLD E. *Lessing's Theological Writings: Selections.*

Trans. and with an introductory essay by HENRY CHADWICK. Stanford: Stanford University Press, 1957. 110 pp.

LORENZMEIER, THEODOR. *Exegese und Hermeneutik: Eine vergleichende Darstellung der Theologie Rudolf Bultmanns, Herbert Brauns, und Gerhard Ebelings.* Hamburg: Furche, 1968. 232 pp.

MACQUARRIE, JOHN. *An Existentialist Theology: A Comparison of Heidegger and Bultmann.* London: SCM Press, 1955. 252 pp.

———. *The Scope of Demythologizing: Bultmann and His Critics.* London: SCM Press, 1960. 255 pp.

MARLÉ, RENE. *Introduction to Hermeneutics.* Trans. from the French *L'herméneutique* by E. FROMENT and R. ALBRECHT. New York: Herder & Herder [1967]. 128 pp.

MICHALSON, CARL. *The Rationality of Faith: An Historical Critique of Theological Reason.* New York: Scribner's, 1964. 160 pp.

MÜLLER-SCHWEFE, HANS-RUDOLF. *Die Sprache und das Wort: Grundlagen der Verkündigung.* Hamburg: Furche, 1961. 268 pp. The book consists of four parts: "Die Struktur der Sprache," "Sprache und Existenz," "Sprache und Geschichte," and "Die Sprache und das Wort Gottes."

NEILL, STEPHEN. *The Interpretation of the New Testament: 1861–1961.* London: Oxford University Press, 1964. 358 pp.

NIEBUHR, RICHARD R. *Schleiermacher on Christ and Religion: A New Introduction.* New York: Scribner's, 1964. 267 pp.

OGDEN, SCHUBERT M. *Christ Without Myth.* New York: Harper, 1961. 189 pp.

———. *The Reality of God and Other Essays.* New York: Harper, 1966. 237 pp.

OTT, HEINRICH. *Denken und Sein: Der Weg Martin Heideggers und der Weg der Theologie.* Zollikon: Evangelischer Verlag, 1959. 226 pp.

———. "Das Problem des nicht-objektivierenden Denkens und Redens in der Theologie," *ZThK,* LXI (1964), 327–52.

RAMSEY, IAN. *Religious Language: An Empirical Placing of Theological Phrases.* New York: Macmillan, 1957. 191 pp.

ROBINSON, JAMES M. *A New Quest of the Historical Jesus.* London: SCM Press, 1959. 128 pp.

———. "Theology as Translation," *Theology Today,* XX (1964), 518–27.

———. "World in Modern Theology and in New Testament Theology," in *Soli Deo Gloria: New Testament Studies in Honor of William Childs Robinson.* Richmond, Va.: John Knox Press, 1968, Chap. 7.

———, and JOHN B. COBB, JR., eds. *The Later Heidegger and Theology.* New Frontiers in Theology series, Vol. I. New York: Harper, 1963. 212 pp.

———, eds. *The New Hermeneutic.* New Frontiers in Theology series,

Vol. II. New York: Harper, 1964. 243 pp. See the valuable Introduction, pp. 1-77.

——, eds. *Theology as History*. New Frontiers in Theology series, Vol. III. New York: Harper, 1967. 276 pp.

SCHULTZ, WERNER. "Die unendliche Bewegung in der Hermeneutik Schleiermachers und ihre Auswirkung auf die hermeneutische Situation der Gegenwart," *ZThK*, LXV (1968), 23-52.

SMALLEY, B. *The Study of the Bible in the Middle Ages*. 2d ed. Oxford: Blackwell, 1952. 406 pp.

SMART, JAMES D. *The Interpretation of Scripture*. Philadelphia: Westminster Press, 1961. 317 pp.

SPIEGLER, GERHARD. *The Eternal Covenant: Schleiermacher's Experiment in Cultural Theology*. New York: Harper, 1967. 205 pp.

SPINOZA, BENEDICT DE. *A Theologico-Political Treatise*. Trans. R. H. M. ELWES. Classics of the St. John's Program series. Ann Arbor, Mich.: Edwards Brothers, 1942. 278 pp.

STEIGER, LOTHAR. *Die Hermeneutik als dogmatisches Problem*. Gütersloh: Gerd Mohn, 1961. 200 pp.

WOOD, JAMES D. *The Interpretation of the Bible: A Historical Introduction*. Naperville, Ill.: Alec R. Allenson, 1958. 179 pp.

C. OTHER WORKS CITED OR POTENTIALLY SIGNIFICANT TO HERMENEUTICAL THEORY

ADORNO, THEODOR W. *Zur Metakritik der Erkenntnistheorie: Studien über Husserl und die phänomenologischen Antinomien*. Stuttgart: Kohlhammer, 1956. 251 pp.

ALBRECHT, ERHARD. *Beiträge zur Erkenntnistheorie und das Verhältnis von Sprache und Denken*. Halle: Niemeyer, 1959. 570 pp.

AMMANN, HERMANN. *Die menschliche Rede: Sprachphilosophische Untersuchungen, Teil I und II*. Darmstadt: Wissenschaftliche Buchgesellschaft, 1962. 337 pp.

ARENS, HANS. *Sprachwissenschaft: Der Gang ihrer Entwicklung von der Antike bis zur Gegenwart*. Munich: Verlag Karl Alber, 1955. 568 pp. A methodical and well-documented history of linguistics from Plato and Aristotle to the mid-twentieth century, including coverage of American, French, Russian, and other developments in the twentieth century. Extensive bibliography.

ARISTOTLE. *The Basic Works*. Ed. RICHARD McKEON. New York: Random House, 1941. 1487 pp.

——. *On Interpretation (Peri hermēneias)*. Commentary by ST. THOMAS and CAJETAN. Trans. from the Latin and with an introduction by JEAN T. OESTERLE. Milwaukee: Marquette University Press, 1962. 271 pp.

———. *Organon.* Vol. I: *Categories, On Interpretation, Prior Analytics.* Loeb Classical Library, 325; Cambridge: Harvard University Press, 1938. 542 pp.

AST, FRIEDRICH. *Grundlinien der Grammatik, Hermeneutik und Kritik.* Landshut: Thomann, 1808. 227 pp.

———. *Grundriss der Philologie.* Landshut: Krüll, 1808. 591 pp.

AUERBACH, ERICH. *Mimesis: The Representation of Reality in Western Literature.* Princeton: Princeton University Press, 1953. 563 pp.

BACHELARD, GASTON. *La Formation de l'esprit scientifique: contribution à une psychanalyse de la connaissance objective.* Paris: Vrin, 1938. 256 pp.

———. *Le Nouvel esprit scientifique.* 5th ed. Paris: Presses Universitaires de France, 1949. 179 pp.

———. *Poetics of Space.* Trans. MARIA JOLAS. New York: Orion Press, 1964. 241 pp.

———. *La Poétique de la rêverie.* 2d ed. Paris: Presses Universitaires de France, 1961. 183 pp.

———. *Psychoanalysis of Fire.* Trans. A. C. Ross. Boston: Beacon Press, 1964. 115 pp.

BOLLNOW, OTTO FRIEDRICH. *Die Lebensphilosophie.* Berlin: Springer, 1958. 150 pp.

BOSSERMAN, PHILLIP. *Dialectical Sociology: An Analysis of the Sociology of Georges Gurvitch.* Boston: Extending Horizons Books, 1968. 300 pp.

BREKLE, HERBERT E., ed. *Grammatica Universalis.* A series of volumes in linguistics and philosophy of language; selections from the seventeenth century to the present. First volume forthcoming in 1969, Frommann-Holzboog, Stuttgart.

BRILLOUIN, LÉON. *Scientific Uncertainty and Information.* 2d ed. New York: Academic Press, 1962. 164 pp.

BRUNNER, AUGUST. *Geschichtlichkeit.* Bern/Munich: Francke, 1961. 204 pp.

BRUYN, SEVERYN T. *The Human Perspective in Sociology.* Englewood Cliffs, N. J.: Prentice-Hall, 1966. 286 pp.

BURKE, KENNETH. *A Grammar of Motives and A Rhetoric of Motives.* Meridian Books. Cleveland: World, 1962. 868 pp.

———. *The Philosophy of Literary Form.* Rev. ed. New York: Vintage Books, 1957. 330 pp.

CAMPBELL, JOSEPH. *The Masks of God: Primitive Mythology.* New York: Viking, 1959. 504 pp.

CAMPBELL, PAUL N. *The Speaking and the Speakers of Literature.* Belmont, Calif.: Dickenson, 1967. 164 pp.

CASSIRER, ERNST. *An Essay on Man.* New Haven: Yale University Press, 1944. 237 pp.

———. *Philosophy of Symbolic Forms.* 3 vols. New Haven: Yale

University Press, 1953, 1955, 1957. 328 pp., 269 pp., 501 pp.

CASTELLI, ENRICO, ed. *Tecnica e casistica*. Papers from the International Colloquium at Rome, January, 1964 [?]. Padua: A. Milani, n.d.

CHOMSKY, NOAM. *Aspects of the Theory of Syntax*. Cambridge: M.I.T. Press, 1965. 251 pp.

———. *Current Issues in Linguistic Theory*. New York: Humanities Press, 1964. 119 pp.

———. *Topics in the Theory of Generative Grammar*. New York: Humanities Press, 1966. 95 pp.

COLLINGWOOD, R. G. *An Autobiography*. Oxford: Oxford University Press, 1939. 167 pp.

———. *Essays in the Philosophy of History*. Ed. WILLIAM DEBBINS. Austin: University of Texas Press, 1965. 160 pp.

———. *The Idea of History*. Oxford: Clarendon Press, 1946. 339 pp.

CORBIN, HENRY. *Avicenna and the Visionary Recital*. Trans. W. R. TRASK. Princeton: Princeton University Press, 1960. 423 pp.

DAGOGNET, FRANÇOIS. *Gaston Bachelard*. Paris: Presses Universitaires de France, 1965. 116 pp.

DANCE, FRANK E. X., ed. *Human Communication Theory: Original Essays*. New York: Holt, 1967. 332 pp.

DANTO, ARTHUR C. *Analytical Philosophy of History*. Cambridge: Cambridge University Press, 1965. 313 pp.

DIEMER, ALWIN. *Edmund Husserl: Versuch einer systematischen Darstellung seiner Phänomenologie*. Meisenheim am Glan: Hain, 1956. 397 pp.

DUFRENNE, MIKEL. *Jalons*. The Hague: Nijhoff, 1966. 221 pp.

———. *Language and Philosophy*. Bloomington: Indiana University Press, 1963. 106 pp.

———. *The Notion of the A Priori*. Trans. EDWARD S. CASEY. Evanston: Northwestern University Press, 1966. 256 pp.

———. *Phénomenologie de l'expérience esthétique*. Paris: Presses Universitaires de France, 1953. 688 pp.

———. *La Poétique*. Paris: Presses Universitaires de France, 1963. 196 pp.

DURAND, GILBERT. *L'Imagination symbolique*. Paris: Presses Universitaires de France, 1964. 120 pp.

———. *Les Structures anthropologiques de l'imaginaire*. Paris: Presses Universitaires de France, 1960. 513 pp.

EDIE, JAMES M., ed. *An Invitation to Phenomenology: Studies in the Philosophy of Experience*. Chicago: Quadrangle, 1965. 283 pp.

———, ed. *Phenomenology in America: Studies in the Philosophy of Experience*. Chicago: Quadrangle, 1967. 306 pp.

Einsichten: Festschrift für Gerhard Krüger. Ed. KLAUS OEHLER and RICHARD SCHAEFFLER. Frankfurt: Klostermann, 1962. 398 pp.

ELIADE, MIRCEA. *Cosmos and History: The Myth of the Eternal*

Return. New York: Harper Torchbook, 1959. 176 pp.

———. *Le Forêt interdit.* Paris: Gallimard, 1957. 645 pp.

———. *Myth and Reality.* Trans. WILLARD R. TRASK. New York: Harper, 1963. 204 pp.

———. *Myths, Dreams and Mysteries.* New York: Harper Torchbook, 1961. 256 pp.

FALLICO, ARTURO B. *Art & Existentialism.* Spectrum Books. Englewood Cliffs, N. J.: Prentice-Hall, 1962. 175 pp.

FINDLAY, J. N. *Hegel, A Re-examination.* London: George Allen & Unwin, 1964. 372 pp.

FINK, EUGEN. *Sein, Wahrheit, Welt. Vor-Fragen zum Problem des Phänomen-Begriffs.* The Hague: Nijhoff, 1958. 156 pp.

———. *Spiel als Weltsymbol.* Stuttgart: Kohlhammer, 1960. 243 pp.

For Roman Ingarden, Nine Essays in Phenomenology. The Hague: Nijhoff, 1959. 179 pp.

FOUCAULT, MICHEL. *Les Mots et les choses: une archéologie des sciences humaines.* Paris: Gallimard, 1966. 405 pp.

FRANK, ERICH. *Philosophical Understanding and Religious Truth.* New York: Oxford University Press, 1945. 209 pp.

FRYE, NORTHROP. *Anatomy of Criticism.* Princeton: Princeton University Press, 1957. 394 pp.

GARELLI, JACQUES. *La Gravitation poétique.* Paris: Mercure de France, 1966. 217 pp.

GEIGER, DON. *The Sound, Sense, and Performance of Literature.* Chicago: Scott, Foresman, 1963. 115 pp.

GIPPER, HELMUT. *Bausteine zur Sprachinhaltsforschung: Neuere Sprachbetrachtung im Austausch mit Geistes- und Naturwissenschaft.* Sprache und Gemeinschaft series, ed. LEO WEISGERBER, Vol. I. Düsseldorf: Pädagogischer Verlag Schwann, 1963. 544 pp.

GLINZ, HANS. *Ansätze zu einer Sprachtheorie.* Beihefte zum Wirkenden Wort series, Pamphlet No. 2. Düsseldorf: Pädagogischer Verlag Schwann, 1962. 93 pp.

GOGARTEN, FRIEDRICH. "Das abendländische Geschichtsdenken: Bemerkungen zu dem Buch von Erich Auerbach *Mimesis*," *ZThK,* LI (1954), 270–360.

GÜNTERT, HERMANN. *Grundfragen der Sprachwissenschaft.* 2d ed. Ed. DR. ANTON SCHERER. Heidelberg: Quelle & Meyer, 1956. 155 pp.

GÜNTHER, GOTTHARD. *Idee und Grundriss einer nicht-Aristotelischen Logik.* Hamburg: Meiner, 1959. 417 pp. Vol I: *Die Idee und ihre philosophischen Voraussetzungen.*

GURVITCH, GEORGES. *Dialectique et sociologie.* Paris: Flammarion, 1962. 242 pp.

GURWITSCH, ARON. *The Field of Consciousness.* Pittsburgh: Duquesne University Press, 1964. 427 pp.

———. *Studies in Phenomenology and Psychology.* Evanston, Ill.: Northwestern University Press, 1966. 452 pp.

GUSDORF, GEORGES. *Speaking (La Parole)*. Trans. and with an introduction by PAUL T. BROCKELMAN. Evanston, Ill.: Northwestern
University Press, 1965. 132 pp.
GÜTTINGER, FRITZ. *Zielsprache: Theorie und Technik des Ueberset-
zens*. Zürich: Manesse, 1963. 236 pp.
HAERING, THEODOR. *Philosophie des Verstehens. Versuch einer sys-
tematisch-erkenntnistheoretischen Grundlegung alles Erken-
nens*. Tübingen: Niemeyer, 1963. 103 pp.
HART, RAY L. "Imagination and the Scale of Mental Acts," *Con-
tinuum*, III (1965), 3–21.
———. "The Imagination in Plato," *International Philosophical
Quarterly*, V (1965), 436–61.
———. *Unfinished Man and the Imagination*. New York: Herder &
Herder, 1968.
HARTMANN, EDUARD VON. *Ueber die dialektische Methode. Histo-
risch-kritische Untersuchungen*. Darmstadt: Wissenschaftliche
Buchgesellschaft, 1963. 124 pp.
HARTMANN, PETER. *Sprache und Erkenntnis*. Heidelberg: Carl Win-
ter, Universitätsverlag, 1958. 160 pp.
———. *Wesen und Wirkung der Sprache: im Spiegel der Theorie Leo
Weisgerbers*. Heidelberg: Carl Winter, Universitätsverlag, 1958.
168 pp.
HATZFELD, HELMUT A. *Critical Bibliography of the New Stylistics
Applied to the Romance Literatures*, 1900–52. New York: Johnson
Reprint, 1953.
———, with YVES LE HIR. *Essai de bibliographie critique de stylis-
tique française et romane*, 1955–60. Paris: Presses Universitaires
de France, 1961. 313 pp.
HAUSMAN, CARL R. "The Existence of Novelty," *Pacific Philosophy
Forum*, IV (1966), 3–60.
———. "Understanding and the Act of Creation," *RM*, XX (1966),
89–112.
HEEROMA, KLAAS. *Der Mensch in seiner Sprache*. Translated from the
Dutch by ARNOLD RAKERS. Witten: Luther, 1963. 262 pp. Sixteen
collected lectures, including "Text und Auslegung," "Literatur und
Wissenschaft," "Sprache als Wahrheit," "Sprache als Freiheit,"
"Dichtung als Wahrheit," and "Die Sprache der Kirche."
HEGEL, GEORG WILHELM FRIEDRICH. *Phänomenologie des Geistes*.
Hamburg: Meiner, 1952. 598 pp. English translation, with an intro-
duction and notes, by J. B. BAILLIE, *The Phenomenology of Mind*.
2d ed., rev. London: George Allen & Unwin, 1964. 814 pp.
HILGARD, ERNEST R., and GORDON H. BOWER. *Theories of Learning*.
3d ed. New York: Appleton-Century-Crofts, 1966. 661 pp.
HÜLSMANN, HEINZ. *Zur Theorie der Sprache bei Edmund Husserl*.
Munich: Anton Pustet, 1964. 255 pp.

HUSSERL, EDMUND. *Cartesian Meditations: An Introduction to Phenomenology.* Trans. DORION CAIRNS. The Hague: Nijhoff, 1960. 157 pp.

————. *Erfahrung und Urteil.* Ed. and rev. by LUDWIG LANDGREBE. Hamburg: Claassen, 1964. 478 pp.

————. *Ideas: General Introduction to Pure Phenomenology.* Trans. W. R. BOYCE GIBSON. New York: Collier Books, 1962. 444 pp.

————. *Die Krisis der europäischen Wissenschaften und die transzendentale Phänomenologie.* Husserliana, Vol. VI. The Hague: Nijhoff, 1952. 557 pp. A portion (pp. 314-48) of the appendixes, a lecture entitled "Die Krisis des europäischen Menschentums und die Philosophie," appears in *Phenomenology and the Crisis of Philosophy.*

————. *Phenomenology and the Crisis of Philosophy.* Trans. and with an introduction by QUENTIN LAUER. New York: Harper, 1965. 192 pp.

————. *The Phenomenology of Internal Time-Consciousness.* Ed. MARTIN HEIDEGGER, trans. JAMES S. CHURCHILL, with introduction by CALVIN O. SCHRAG. Bloomington: Indiana University Press, 1964. 188 pp.

————. *Philosophie als strenge Wissenschaft.* Ed. WILHELM SZILASI. Quellen der Philosophie series, ed. RUDOLPH BERLINGER. Frankfurt: Klostermann, 1965. 107 pp. English translation included in *Phenomenology and the Crisis of Philosophy.*

HYMAN, STANLEY EDGAR. *The Armed Vision: A Study in the Methods of Modern Literary Criticism.* Rev. ed. New York: Vintage, 1955. 402 pp.

INGALLS, DANIEL H. H. *Materials for the Study of Navya-Nyāya Logic.* Cambridge: Harvard University Press, 1951. 181 pp.

INGARDEN, ROMAN. *Das literarische Kunstwerk.* 2d ed., rev. Tübingen: Niemeyer, 1960. 430 pp. Translation forthcoming from Northwestern University Press.

JOLLES, ANDRÉ. *Einfache Formen: Legende, Sage, Mythe, Rätsel, Spruch, Kasus, Memorabile, Märchen, Witz.* Darmstadt: Wissenschaftliche Buchgesellschaft, 1958. 272 pp. Originally published in 1930.

JÜNGER, FRIEDRICH GEORG. *Sprache und Denken.* Frankfurt: Klostermann, 1962. 232 pp.

KAELIN, EUGENE F. *An Existentialist Aesthetic: The Theories of Sartre and Merleau-Ponty.* Madison: University of Wisconsin Press, 1962. 471 pp.

KAINZ, FRIEDRICH. *Psychologie der Sprache.* 4 vols. Stuttgart: Ferdinand Enke Verlag, 1940-1956. Vol. I: *Grundlagen der allgemeinen Sprachpsychologie,* 1940; 3d ed., unchanged, 1962. 373 pp. Vol. II: *Vergleichend-genetische Sprachpsychologie,* 1943; 2d ed., extensively rev., 1960. 760 pp. Vol. III: *Physiologische Psychologie der Sprachvorgänge*, 1954. 571 pp. Vol. IV: *Spezielle Sprachpsychologie*, 1956. 537 pp.

KAMLAH, WILHELM. *Der Mensch in der Profanität*. Stuttgart: Kohlhammer, 1949. 216 pp.

———. *Wissenschaft, Wahrheit, Existenz*. Stuttgart: Kohlhammer, 1960. 73 pp.

KAUFMANN, FRITZ. *Das Reich des Schönen: Bausteine zu einer Philosophie der Kunst*. Ed. H.-G. GADAMER. Stuttgart: Kohlhammer, 1960. 404 pp.

KITTO, H. D. F. *Form and Meaning in Drama*. New York: Barnes & Noble, 1957. 341 pp.

———. *Poiesis*. Berkeley: University of California Press, 1966. 407 pp.

KOESTLER, ARTHUR. *The Act of Creation*. New York: Macmillan, 1964. 751 pp. Reviewed in Hausman's "Understanding and the Act of Creation," cited above.

KRIEGER, MURRAY. *The New Apologists for Poetry*. Bloomington: Indiana University Press, 1963. 225 pp.

KRÜGER, GERHARD. *Freiheit und Weltverwaltung: Aufsätze zur Philosophie der Geschichte*. Freiburg/Munich: Alber, 1958. 254 pp.

———. *Grundfragen der Philosophie: Geschichte, Wahrheit, Wissenschaft*. Frankfurt: Klostermann, 1958. 288 pp.

KWANT, REMY C. *From Phenomenology to Metaphysics: An Inquiry into the Last Period of Merleau-Ponty's Philosophical Life*. Pittsburgh: Duquesne University Press, 1966. 246 pp.

———. *The Phenomenological Philosophy of Merleau-Ponty*. Pittsburgh: Duquesne University Press, 1963. 257 pp.

———. *Phenomenology of Language*. Pittsburgh: Duquesne University Press, 1965. 270 pp.

LACAN, JACQUES. *Ecrits de Jacques Lacan: le champ freudien*. Paris: Editions du Seuil, 1967. 911 pp.

———. "The Insistence of the Letter in the Unconscious," *YFS*, Nos. 36–37 (1967), 112–47.

LANDMANN, MICHAEL. *Die absolute Dichtung: Essais zur philosophischen Poetik*. Stuttgart: Ernst Klett, 1963. 212 pp.

LEEUW, GERARDUS VAN DER. *Religion in Essence and Manifestation: A Study in Phenomenology*. Trans. J. E. TURNER. London: Allen & Unwin, 1938. 709 pp. Rev. ed., 2 vols., Harper, 1963.

LEVI, ALBERT WILLIAM. *Literature, Philosophy, and the Imagination*. Bloomington: Indiana University Press, 1962. 346 pp.

LIDDELL, HENRY G., and R. SCOTT, eds. *Greek-English Lexicon*. New York: Oxford University Press, 1940.

LIPPS, HANS. *Die Verbindlichkeit der Sprache: Arbeiten zur Sprachphilosophie und Logik*. Ed. EVAMARIA VON BUSSE. 2d ed. Frankfurt: Klostermann, 1958. 240 pp.

LITT, THEODOR. *Die Wiedererweckung des geschichtlichen Bewusstseins*. Heidelberg: Quelle & Meyer, 1956. 243 pp.

LONGFELLOW, HENRY WADSWORTH. *Prose Works.* Vol. II. Boston: Houghton Mifflin, 1886. 486 pp.

LÖWITH, KARL. *Meaning in History.* Chicago: University of Chicago Press, 1957. 257 pp.

————. *Nature, History, and Existentialism, and other Essays in the Philosophy of History.* Ed. and with a critical introduction by ARNOLD LEVISON. Evanston: Northwestern University Press, 1966. 220 pp.

MCKELLAR, PETER. *Imagination and Thinking: A Psychological Analysis.* New York: Basic Books, 1957. 219 pp.

MARROU, HENRI-I. *De la connaissance historique.* 4th ed., rev. Paris: Editions du Seuil, 1959. 301 pp.

MERLEAU-PONTY, MAURICE. "Eye and Mind," trans. CARLETON DALLERY, in *The Primacy of Perception and Other Essays,* ed. JAMES M. EDIE. Evanston: Northwestern University Press, 1964. 228 pp.

————. *Phenomenology of Perception.* Trans. COLIN SMITH. London: Routledge & Kegan Paul, 1962. 466 pp.

————. *Signs.* Trans. and with an introduction by RICHARD C. MCCLEARY. Evanston: Northwestern University Press, 1964. 355 pp.

MILLER, JAMES E., JR., ed. *Myth and Method: Modern Theories of Fiction.* Lincoln: University of Nebraska Press, 1960. 164 pp.

MOHANTY, J. N. *Edmund Husserl's Theory of Meaning.* The Hague: Nijhoff, 1964. 148 pp.

MOLES, ABRAHAM A. *Information Theory and Aesthetic Perception.* Trans. JOEL C. COHEN. Urbana: University of Illinois Press, 1965. 217 pp.

NATANSON, MAURICE. *Literature, Philosophy, and the Social Sciences: Essays in Existentialism and Phenomenology.* The Hague: Nijhoff, 1962. 220 pp.

NEHRING, ALFONS. *Sprachzeichen und Sprechakte.* Heidelberg: Carl Winter, Universitätsverlag, 1963. 227 pp.

NIDA, EUGENE A. *Toward a Science of Translating: With Special Reference to Principles and Procedures Involved in Bible Translating.* Leiden: Brill, 1964. 331 pp.

NISHIDA, KITARŌ. *Intelligibility and the Philosophy of Nothingness.* Trans. R. SCHINZINGER. Honolulu: East-West Center Press, 1966. 251 pp.

OXENHANDLER, NEAL. "Ontological Criticism in America and France," *MLR,* LV (1960), 17–23.

"*La Pensée sauvage* et le structuralisme," *Esprit* (November 1963). A special issue on structuralism.

PEPPER, STEPHEN C. *The Basis of Criticism in the Arts.* Cambridge: Harvard University Press, 1956. 177 pp.

PHILLIPS, LESLIE, and JOSEPH G. SMITH. *Rorschach Interpretation.* New York: Grune & Stratton, 1959. 385 pp.

POLANYI, MICHAEL. *Personal Knowledge: Towards a Post-Critical*

Philosophy. Chicago: University of Chicago Press, 1958. 428 pp.

PORZIG, WALTER. *Das Wunder der Sprache: Probleme, Methoden und Ergebnisse der modernen Sprachwissenschaft.* 2d ed. Bern: Francke, 1957. 423 pp. Originally published in 1950. Chap. 4 deals with "Sprache und Seele" and Chap. 5 with "Die Sprachgemeinschaft."

QUILLET, PIERRE. *Bachelard.* Paris: Seghers, 1964. 220 pp.

RAPAPORT, DAVID, ed. *Organization and Pathology of Thought.* New York: Columbia University Press, 1951. 786 pp.

RICHARD, JEAN-PIERRE. *Onze études sur la poésie moderne.* Paris: Editions du Seuil, 1964. 302 pp.

———. *Paysage de Chateaubriand.* Paris: Editions du Seuil, 1967. 184 pp.

———. *Poésie et profondeur.* Paris: Editions du Seuil, 1955. 248 pp.

———. *L'Univers imaginaire de Mallarmé.* Paris: Editions du Seuil, 1961. 653 pp.

RICHARDS, I. A. *Practical Criticism: A Study of Literary Judgment.* New York: Harcourt, Brace & World, 1966. 362 pp. Originally published in 1929.

RICOEUR, PAUL. *History and Truth.* Trans. C. A. KELBLEY. Evanston: Northwestern University Press, 1965. 333 pp.

———. *Husserl: An Analysis of His Phenomenology.* Trans. EDWARD G. BALLARD and LESTER E. EMBREE. Evanston: Northwestern University Press, 1967. 238 pp.

———. "La Structure, le mot, l'événement," *M&W,* I, 10-30.

———. *The Symbolism of Evil.* Trans. EMERSON BUCHANAN. New York: Harper, 1967. 357 pp.

RUGG, HAROLD. *Imagination.* New York: Harper, 1963. 361 pp.

RUITENBEEK, H. M., ed. *Creative Imagination.* Chicago: Quadrangle, 1965. 350 pp.

RYLE, GILBERT. *Concept of Mind.* New York: Barnes & Noble, 1949. 330 pp.

SCHON, DONALD. *The Displacement of Concepts.* London: Tavistock, 1964. 208 pp.

SCHRAG, CALVIN O. "The Phenomenon of Embodied Speech," *The Philosophy Forum,* VII (1968), 189-213.

SHANNON, CLAUDE E., and WARREN WEAVER. *Mathematical Theory of Communication.* Urbana: University of Illinois Press, 1949. 117 pp.

SNELL, BRUNO. *Der Aufbau der Sprache.* 2d ed. Hamburg: Claasen, 1952. 208 pp.

———. *Die Entdeckung des Geistes: Studien zur Entstehung des europäischen Denkens bei den Griechen.* 3d ed. Hamburg: Claasen, 1955. 448 pp.

SONTAG, SUSAN. *Against Interpretation, and Other Essays.* New York: Farrar, Straus, & Giroux, 1966. 304 pp.

SPIEGELBERG, HERBERT. *The Phenomenological Movement: A Historical Introduction.* 2 vols. 2d ed., rev. The Hague: Nijhoff, 1965. 765 pp.

SPRANGER, EDUARD. *Der Sinn der Voraussetzungslosigkeit in den Geisteswissenschaften.* Darmstadt: Wissenschaftliche Buchgesellschaft, 1963. 31 pp.

STAIGER, EMIL. *Grundbegriffe der Poetik.* Zürich: Atlantis, 1963. 256 pp.

———. *Die Kunst der Interpretation: Studien zur deutschen Literaturgeschichte.* Zürich: Atlantis, 1963. 273 pp.

STEINTHAL, H. *Geschichte der Sprachwissenschaft bei den Griechen und Römern: mit besonderer Rücksicht auf die Logik.* Hildesheim: George Olms, 1961. 742 pp. Originally published in 1863; the present edition is a photomechanical reproduction of the second edition, 1890.

STÖRIG, HANS JOACHIM, ed. *Das Problem des Übersetzens.* Darmstadt: Wissenschaftliche Buchgesellschaft, 1963. 489 pp. An anthology of articles on translation, by Luther, Novalis, Goethe, Schleiermacher, Humboldt, Heidegger, Gadamer, and Oettinger, among others.

STRASSER, STEPHEN. *Phenomenology and the Human Sciences.* Pittsburgh: Duquesne University Press, 1963. 339 pp.

STRAWSON, P. F. *Individuals: An Essay in Descriptive Metaphysics.* London: Methuen, 1959. 247 pp.

"Structuralism," Special Themes of *YFS* (1967), Nos. 36–37 (double issue). 272 pp.

"Structuralismes: idéologie et méthode," *Esprit*, XXXV, No. 360 (1967), 769–976. A special issue devoted to the theme of structuralism.

SUTTON, WALTER. *Modern American Criticism.* Englewood Cliffs, N.J.: Prentice-Hall, 1963. 298 pp.

SUZUKI, D. T. *Zen Buddhism.* Ed. WILLIAM BARRETT. Garden City, N. Y.: Doubleday, 1956. 294 pp.

SZILASI, WILHELM. *Einführung in die Phänomenologie Edmund Husserls.* Tübingen: Niemeyer, 1959. 142 pp.

THÉVENAZ, PIERRE. *What is Phenomenology? and Other Essays.* Ed. and with an introduction by JAMES M. EDIE. Trans. JAMES M. EDIE, CHARLES COURTNEY, PAUL BROCKELMAN. Chicago: Quadrangle, 1962. 191 pp.

TILLICH, PAUL. *Love, Power, and Justice: Ontological Analyses and Ethical Applications.* New York: Oxford University Press, 1954. 127 pp.

TYLOR, EDWARD BURNETT. *Primitive Culture.* 2 vols. New York: Harper, 1958. 416 pp., 539 pp. Originally published in 1871.

ULLMANN, STEPHEN. *Language and Style: Collected Papers.* New York: Barnes & Noble, 1964. 270 pp.

———. *Style in the French Novel.* Cambridge: Cambridge University

Press, 1957. 272 pp.

VERENE, DON. "Kant, Hegel, and Cassirer: The Origins of the Theory of Symbolic Forms," forthcoming, 1969, in *Journal of the History of Ideas*.

———. "Plato's Conception of Philosophy and Poetry," *The Personalist*, XLIV (1963), 528–38.

VICKERY, JOHN B., ed. *Myth and Literature*. Lincoln: University of Nebraska Press, 1966. 391 pp.

VIVAS, ELISEO. *The Artistic Transaction*. Columbus: Ohio State University Press, 1963. 267 pp.

WALEY, ARTHUR. *The Way and Its Power: A Study of the "Tao Tê Ching" and Its Place in Chinese Thought*. New York: Grove, 1958. 262 pp.

WARTENBURG, GRAF PAUL YORCK VON. *Bewusstseinsstellung und Geschichte: Ein Fragment aus dem philosophischen Nachlass*. Ed. IRING FETSCHER. Tübingen: Niemeyer, 1956. 220 pp.

WEIN, HERMANN. *Sprachphilosophie der Gegenwart: Eine Einführung in die europäische und amerikanische Sprachphilosophie des 20. Jahrhunderts*. The Hague: Nijhoff, 1963. 84 pp.

WEINRICH, HARALD. *Linguistik der Lüge: Kann Sprache die Gedanken verbergen?* Heidelberg: Lambert Schneider, 1966. 78 pp.

WEISGERBER, LEO. *Die ganzheitliche Behandlung eines Satzbauplanes: "Er klopfte seinem Freunde auf die Schulter."* Beihefte zum Wirkenden Wort series, No. 1. Düsseldorf: Pädagogischer Verlag Schwann, 1962. 34 pp. A good introduction to Weisgerber.

———. *Das Gesetz der Sprache als Grundlage des Sprachstudiums*. Heidelberg: Quelle & Meyer, 1951. 200 pp. An effort to relate language to society and man in seeing the bases for *Sprachsoziologie*, *Sprachpsychologie*, *Sprachphilosophie*.

———. *Von den Kräften der deutschen Sprache*. 4 vols. 3d ed., rev. Düsseldorf: Pädagogischer Verlag Schwann, 1962. Vol. II: *Die sprachliche Gestaltung der Welt*. 455 pp.

WEIZSÄCKER, CARL FR. *Zum Weltbild der Physik*. 4th ed. Leipzig: Hirzel, 1949. 183 pp.

WELLEK, RENÉ, and AUSTIN WARREN. *Theory of Literature*. Rev. ed. New York: Harcourt, Brace & World, 1962. 305 pp.

WHALLEY, GEORGE. *Poetic Process*. New York: Hillary, 1953. 256 pp.

WHORF, BENJAMIN L. *Language, Thought, and Reality: Selected Writings*. Cambridge, Mass.: Technology Press of M.I.T., 1956. 278 pp.

WIMSATT, WILLIAM K., JR. *The Verbal Icon: Studies in the Meaning of Poetry*. Lexington: University of Kentucky Press, 1954. 299 pp.

WITTGENSTEIN, LUDWIG. *Philosophical Investigations*. Trans. G. E. M. ANSCOMBE. Oxford: Blackwell, 1963. 229 pp.

———. *Philosophische Bemerkungen*. Ed. RUSH RHEES. Oxford: Blackwell, 1964. 347 pp.

Index

kind of objectivity, 212; on historical consciousness, 176-93; on the I-thou relationship, 191-93, 197-98; on linguisticality and the hermeneutical experience, 206-9; on method, 163-65; on the nature of poetic utterance, 210-11; on the noninstrumental character of language, 201-5; on play distinguished from game, 172-73; provides a basis for critique of literary theory, 217, 221; in relation to Betti and Wach, 162-64; on the speculative structure of language, 209-12; on subject-matter, 199, 211; on temporal distance, 184-85; on understanding, 163-64; on the universality of hermeneutics, 164, 212-14; *WM* seen as the first historical account of the rise of phenomenological hermeneutics, 42-43; on the *wirkungsgeschichtliche Bewusstsein*, 191-93, 197

Game and literary interpretation, 248-49. *See also* Gadamer, on "game" and art work

Geist, 102; Ast's hermeneutic of, 76-79; for Hegel and Gadamer, 215

Geisteswissenschaften, 129, 214; defined, 98; and Dilthey's critique of historical reason, 100-101; finding a methodological basis for, 99-103; hermeneutics as methodological foundation for, 98; as including every objectification of life, 112; lived experience as foundational, 108-9. *See also* Dilthey; Scientific understanding

Gurvitch, Georges, 26, 70

Gusdorf, Georges, 70

Hausman, Carl R., 70

Hearing *vs.* seeing, 208. *See also* Scientific understanding

Hegel, G. W. F., 63; Gadamer's affinities with, 215-16

Heidegger, Martin: analysis of understanding, 51; apophantic *vs.* hermeneutical "as," 128, 138-39; concept of "world," 132-34; con-

tribution in *SZ*, 124-39; critique of presentational thinking, 142-47; critique of value philosophies, 145; on derivative character of assertions, 49-50, 137-39; on doing violence to the text, 147; and *Erörterung*, 158-59; explication, 156-59; and *Geschick*, 154-55; the hermeneutical character of his thought, 3, 142; hermeneutics in *SZ*, 41-42; on historicality, 153-55; language speaks, 154-56; on the linguistic character of being, 50; moves beyond Dilthey, 130-32; philosophy as hermeneutical, 13; his relation to Bultmann, 49-50; the "step back," 155; summary of contribution, 161; view of language, 139
—Works cited: "Augustinus und der Neuplatonismus," 143; *BH*, 149, 151-52, 154; "The Doctrine of Judgment in Psychologism," 152; "The Founding of the Modern Image of the World through Metaphysics," 144; *G*, 149, 151; *Ho*, 159-61; *IM*, 149-51, 153-54, 156-57; *KPM*, 147-48; "On the Essence of Poetry," 155-56; *PL*, 142-43; "Die Sprache im Gedicht," 158; *SZ*, 49-50, 124-39, 152-53, 179, 227; *UK*, 159-61; *US*, 148, 152, 158; *VA*, 145, 148, 151

Heisenberg principle, in historical knowledge, 52

Heresy of paraphrase, 18. *See also* New Criticism

Hermēneuein and *hermēneia*: meaning "to explain," 14, 20-26; meaning "to say," 14-20; meaning "to translate," 13, 26-31; three directions of meaning in ancient usage, 12-14

Hermeneutical circle: Ast's conception of, 77-78; Betti's canon of "context of meaning," 57; in Dilthey, 118-21; in oral interpretation, 16; in relation to explanation, 25-26; in Schleiermacher, 87-88, 95

Hermeneutical experience: a dialectic of question and answer, 233; and

Oral interpretation, 16-18
Ortega y Gasset, José, 116-17

Pannenberg, Wolfhart, 54
Phenomenological literary criticism: in France, 69, 246; in Roman Ingarden, 70. *See also* Literary interpretation; Phenomenology
Phenomenology: Heidegger's definition of, 127-30; as hermeneutical, 125, 127-30; and literary interpretation, 3; objected to, 55-56; and the scientific perspective, 6; and the subject-object schema, 246; two types of, 124-30
Philology. *See* Ast; Hermeneutics, as philological methodology; Wolf
Plato, 79, 146, 199; *Ion* cited, 13; *Seventh Letter* cited, 15
Prepredicative meaningfulness, in Heidegger, 134-39
Presentational thinking and literary interpretation, 224-25
Presuppositionless interpretation, denied, 121, 135-36, 182-84
Preunderstanding: according to Bultmann, 51; in relation to Scriptural interpretation, 24-25. *See also* Heidegger; Presuppositionless interpretation; Understanding
Psychoanalysis, a form of hermeneutics, 43
Psychologism, 80, 185; in Schleiermacher, 89-96

Question and answer: in hermeneutical experience, 233; as hermeneutical process, 150; in literary interpretation, 250
Questioning: as dialectical, 201; future-orientation of, 182; Heidegger on, 149-51, 154; and historical knowledge, 51; negativity in, 201; structure of, 198-201

Rambach, J. J., 187
Reconstruction: according to Dilthey, 104; Ast's conception of *Nachbildung*, 79-80; of author's mental

experience, 89-90; basic in Betti's hermeneutics, 57-58; criticized in Dilthey and Schleiermacher, 123; *vs.* integration, 186, 234-37, 245; understanding (Schleiermacher), 86. *See also* Restoration
Restoration, in relation to literary interpretation, 250-51. *See also* Reconstruction
Richardson, W. J., 149
Ricoeur, Paul, 69, 246; *De l'interprétation*, 43-45; psychoanalysis and hermeneutics, 43-44

Schlegel, Friedrich, 101-2
Schleiermacher, 46, 64, 68, 82-83, 104, 106, 130-31, 212; contribution to hermeneutical theory, 84-97; criticisms of, 96-97; on the divinatory character of interpretation, 87-90; as father of science of linguistic understanding, 40; on grammatical and psychological interpretation, 88-90; his growing psychologism, 89-96; on the hermeneutical circle, 87-88; on hermeneutics oriented to dialogue, 85-86; relation to Ast and Wolf, 75; on style, 90, 94; on *subtilitas intelligendi*, 187; transition from a language-centered hermeneutics, 91-94
Scientific perspective: *vs.* humanistic in Dilthey, 100-106; in literary interpretation, 6-7
Scientific understanding: *vs.* historical, 10, 19; *vs.* humanistic (Dilthey), 115, 121-22; kinship with Husserl, 126; and lifeworld, 179-80; as oriented to analysis, 7; temporal and prestructured, 182
Scriptures, kerygmatic character of, 19
Semler, J. S., 39
Shakespeare: *King Lear* discussed, 119; *Macbeth* and demythologizing, 190
Significance *vs.* verbal meaning. *See* Hirsch

discussion of his three-level herme-
neutics, 82
Word event. *See* Language event
Wordsworth, William, 31

Work, contrasted with object, 7, 226
World, in Heidegger, 132-34. *See also*
Prepredicative meaningfulness;
Tradition